THE IMPERIAL POST

THE MEYERS, THE GRAHAMS
AND THE PAPER
THAT RULES WASHINGTON

by Tom Kelly

WILLIAM MORROW AND COMPANY, INC.

New York, 1983

Library of Congress Cataloging in Publication Data

Kelly, Tom, 1923 Aug. 2–
The imperial Post.

Includes index.
1. Washington post.   2. Journalists—Washington (D.C.)
—Biography.   I. Title.
PN4899.W31W34   1983   071'.53   83-5404
ISBN   0-688-01919-6

Printed in the United States of America

First Edition

1 2 3 4 5 6 7 8 9 10

BOOK DESIGN BY ELLEN LO GIUDICE

To Marguerite,
the best of wives,
and all the gang at Stanton Grill

ACKNOWLEDGMENTS

I am indebted to many people (some of whom shall be nameless): the late Wes Barthelmes, who gave me insight as well as information; Clare Crawford-Mason, generous as always; the late Ed Folliard, who gave me a copy of his unpublished history of the *Post;* Jack Limpert of the *Washingtonian;* and Elizabeth Frost Knappman, my editor at William Morrow, who was and continues to be the very model of an ideal editor.

CHAPTER

1

On a Saturday afternoon in August, 1963, Philip Graham, the publisher of *The Washington Post,* loaded a shotgun with bird shot and walked into the first-floor bathroom of his estate in Middleburg, Virginia. He braced the butt of the gun against the floor and wall, sat on the edge of the tub and put the barrel end to his right temple. He was a tall man with a long reach and able to push the trigger. The explosion blew him backward into the tub.

Two servants found him seconds later. His wife, Katharine, was upstairs taking a nap; Donald his son, eighteen, a Harvard freshman, was in Washington working at his summer job with the New York Times bureau. His daughter, Lally, twenty, was in the Mediterranean with her maternal grandmother, Agnes Meyer, cruising from Athens to Istanbul. William, fifteen, and Stephen, eleven, were at camps, one in Vermont, one in Colorado.

The next day the *Post* was edged in black. Graham was buried quietly on Monday, and for the rest of the week the *Post* carried eulogies and reactions. Senator George Smathers, Graham's old college roommate, said that in his opinion no other "private citizen of contemporary America was more respected by people of influence."

On Wednesday official Washington, including President Kennedy, the members of the Supreme Court and Cabinet and Alice Roosevelt Longworth, the daughter of Teddy, attended the memorial service conducted at the Washington Cathedral by retired bishop Angus Dun.

Twenty-three years earlier Graham, a boy from a prosperous

Florida farm, polished by Harvard Law School and high society, had married Eugene Meyer's daughter. A few years later his father-in-law had given him the *Post,* a poor, earnest paper that tried hard but lost money. Graham tried harder. He made gargantuan efforts in pursuit of power and moral glory, manipulated politicians, picked and fostered candidates and sought, with some success, to shape the nation's political and social policies. He made the *Post* rich, arrogant and powerful. In his latter years he swung between weeks of frenzied activity and months of despair.

The Washington Star, the still great but fading voice of the old Washington establishment, noted at the time of his death, with a measure of awe, that "the nature and ultimate scope of Mr. Graham's ambitions were, of course, unknown to us."

Perhaps they were not clear to him either and in the end he threw them all away but he left an enduring memorial behind. The *Post* would continue to grow greatly in wealth and power and quality. Today, some twenty years after his death and ten after it unraveled Watergate and drove President Nixon from office, the *Post* has an effective monopoly on the daily printing of news and opinion in Washington. It is still manipulative and it is still arrogant. It is, in terms of breadth and quality of coverage and prestige, the second-ranking newspaper in the country. The *Post* may be more powerful but *The New York Times* is less partial, more disciplined, more reliable and more devoted to the reporting of difficult essentials.

Four people made the *Post* what it is: Eugene and Agnes Meyer, who bought it bankrupt, kept it alive during the Depression and World War II and gave it its basic personality; Graham, who gave it the foundation for great influence; and Katharine, his widow, who made it a paper of high if erratic quality. This is the story of the Meyers and the Grahams and the *Post.* It begins with two births.

CHAPTER

2

Eugene Meyer was born in October, 1875, on Halloween, in Los Angeles, a raw town with whorehouses and gingerbread mansions, hills, flowers, ocean sands, pigtailed coolies, railroad barons and mining kings. He was the fourth child and first son of rich French-Jewish parents, living sedate and circumspect lives in a bulky Victorian house, surrounded by spiky California bushes and slim, barbered trees, behind a high iron fence, remote from their neighbors.

His mother, Harriet Newman Meyer, was an invalid suffering from dyspepsia and the strains of repeated childbirths. Eugene would soon be followed by two more sisters and two brothers. His father, Marc Eugene, was half owner of a department store, The City of Paris, and a part-time banker. The parents can be seen carefully posed in old photographs, she still young and pretty, standing straight in an elaborate, sculptured dress, her figure a tidy hourglass, her face in profile, gazing into the distance; he erect, plump, pale, with a Louis Napoleon moustache and goatee, his long torso encased in a black double-breasted broadcloth coat with an inch of white cuff showing at his wrists. His feet, heel to heel, form a neat right angle and he is holding a pair of gloves. Neither is smiling. When Marc Eugene Meyer was informed of his son's birth, he said:

"Tell me, is he intelligent-looking?"

He was told that he was.

The Washington Post was born two years later in a red-light district at the foot of Capitol Hill called Hooker's Division (in memory of a licentious Civil War general whose name would become synonymous with prostitute). The first issue, dated December 6, 1877, offered four pages for three cents and it did not seem particularly bright. Its principal front-page story began, "The Capitol was rather a dull place yesterday," and its one-column grab bag of foreign news, headed "Over the Waters," reported that the Pope was breathing his last and that the Turks had beaten the Russians at the battle of Elena.

It announced its own birth on page three. "When a newspaper is born there is always a reasonable excuse. In the case of The Post it need only be said that Washington City is too large and too important to be denied the benign influence of a Democratic Journal." It would refer to the Republican President, Rutherford B. Hayes, as "His Fraudulency" for the rest of his administration.

The Meyers, California Republicans, were unaware of the partisan, Democratic *Post.* Father was becoming a full-time banker, and when Eugene was five they moved to an excellent neighborhood in San Francisco but they were Jews amid rich Protestants who considered all Jews gross materialists, and they would not be part of the highest society. When Eugene went briefly to public school his classmates called him "sheeny." When he was knocked down by a swinging bat while playing with the neighborhood boys, his father, suspecting that it was not accidental, decided that he would play no more team games.

He and Eugene would instead go horseback riding every afternoon, down the shady suburban streets, an imposing solemn man and a small boy slight in the saddle, sitting above the heads of other small boys.

Eugene would never be an athlete. Mr. Meyer enrolled him in fencing and boxing classes at the Olympic Athletic Club under the renowned instructor James J. Corbett but "Gentleman Jim" arranged a publicity picture showing Eugene and another pupil sparring, with himself in the background, and Mr. Meyer pulled his son out of class. Still Eugene would drop Gentleman Jim's glamorous name for the rest of his life.

He remained an isolated youngster, under wraps. His mother spent her days in her darkened room, and Eugene's oldest sister, Rosalie, ran the house. His father treated him like a valuable investment, training him to be a man of business. Eugene read the financial journals of New York, London, Berlin, Frankfurt and Vienna, and when U. S. Senator Stephen White, the family's lawyer, called, he was allowed to sit up late and listen to the Senator's pronouncements.

He rebelled against the soft solemnity of the household and became a bully, sassing the servants and pulling the hair of his younger sisters. Rosalie bought a cat-o'-nine-tails but first tried a gentler scheme. She offered Eugene a contract: his behavior would improve immediately or she would ask his father to cancel his horseback riding in the afternoons. Eugene, who knew contracts were sacred, signed and kept his pledge.

Eugene was in awe of his father who watched him always, but from a distance. When he won a medal for standing third in his class, Mr. Meyer said harshly, "The world is full of people who stand third, they don't amount to much."

When Eugene was eleven his mother and Rosalie went to Europe to visit the health resorts. When they headed home Mr. Meyer decided abruptly that he and Eugene would meet them in Nevada. Eugene was out playing at the moment of decision and when he returned at four o'clock a white-faced father was waiting in the entrance hall.

"Where were you?" he shouted, slapping Eugene's face.

Eugene sulked through the long night's journey. In the morning the train stopped for water and the father and son got off to stretch their legs. They found themselves surrounded by families of Apache Indians, hostile and in rags, who had been driven from their homes by cavalry troops. Eugene, badly frightened, clutched his father's hand and begged for forgiveness. The father solemnly gave it but Eugene would never forget the slap or his own openly expressed fear.

The Meyers came home and life went on. Rosalie married Sigmund Stern, the nephew and heir of Levi Strauss, the man who gave cowboys unrippable jeans; and Elise, the second-oldest daughter, married his brother.

The father focused on Eugene's formal education and hired Professor Henry Senger of the University of California to tutor him in Greek, Latin and math. Eugene would idealize the Professor and remain near the top of his class, but never quite at it. When it was time to go to college he clashed with his father, who wanted him to go to school in France. He won and enrolled in the University of California.

In college he rebelled again, this time discreetly. Safe on campus, he spent his evening hours playing poker and drinking beer and hardly studying at all. A picture commemorates one rowdy outing: the freshmen have posted their class numerals on a hillside and a few sophomores who tried to tear them down have been captured and tied up for the camera. Eugene is in the background with a satisfied smirk on his face.

As a cautious playboy he had a certain success. He won at poker much more frequently than he lost, and when a loser sent his money in an envelope addressed to Eugene Meyer, neglecting to add "Jr.," his father opened it and was baffled. He spoke to Eugene about it and Eugene said he was baffled too.

His first year in college served a purpose—he sowed his mild, wild oats and emerged an independent young man who would soon be a model of industry. Destiny was taking him to Yale and Wall Street.

In Washington the *Post* had had its difficulties too. It had moved to a respectable neighborhood, downtown near the Patent Office, but in 1885 the building burned down. The *Evening Star* loaned the *Post* its presses, and the *Post* survived and in 1888 began publishing an evening paper in competition with the *Star*. It soon died, and the morning paper was sold to Frank Hatton and Beriah Wilkins, the latter an ex-Congressman from Ohio. One day the new owners met John Philip Sousa, the celebrated leader of the Marine Band, on the street and Wilkins asked him, casually, if he would compose a tune to be played at a children's outing the paper was sponsoring on the grounds of the Smithsonian Institution. Sousa obliged with "The Washington Post March."

CHAPTER

3

It was 1892. Eugene's father was fifty—a new partner in the New York branch of Lazard Frères. The Meyers moved by train across the country, the mother in seclusion and Eugene and his sister Elise in charge of the younger children. They took a week's rest in Chicago and continued to Manhattan, where they stopped at the Savoy Hotel, which, as Eugene wrote Rosalie, had "a luxury of furnishings and magnificence of interior unsurpassed anywhere" but which was on a "noisy, dirty square with a few trees and no grass to relieve the eye."

That summer Mr. Meyer arranged a minor job on Wall Street for Eugene, who spent as much time as he could looking down from the visitors' gallery on the tumult of the Stock Exchange below. In September he went to Yale to share a room in a boardinghouse with the son of another Lazard partner. His heart was on his sleeve. Yale, he wrote Rosalie, had "quiet simplicity and lack of pretension combined with immutable evidence of civilization." Yale did not respond. Young Jews were tolerated, not sought after, and he soon felt the New England chill. He took twenty-one credit hours instead of the usual fifteen and divided his days precisely: an hour for exercise, the minimum time necessary for meals and the rest for work.

"I often feel so lonely," he wrote Rosalie, "and so often want to talk to you about things going on in my mind, that if I wrote to you everything, all the forests would be denuded to provide the paper."

That summer, 1894, he studied logic, ethics, psychology, Spanish and the history of English literature, and then, with permission from his faculty adviser, William Lyon Phelps, he skipped the third year.

That fall he fell under the spell of William Graham Sumner, a professor of economics, who taught that labor unions that tried to tinker with the economy were grievously wrong. Eugene could only agree.

"Work," he wrote, "is the key to success."

He graduated in 1895, a Phi Beta Kappa, at nineteen.

The next spring he went to Europe to visit relatives and work as an apprentice in a variety of banks and found anti-Semitism in a more frightening form. His aunt Ernestine and his uncle Zadoc Kahn, the Grand Rabbi of France, were deeply concerned with the case of Captain Alfred Dreyfus, the Jewish army officer charged with treason. As he sat chatting with the Kahns in their apartment in Paris an anti-Dreyfus mob screamed "Down with the Jews" in the streets below.

He worked in banks in Frankfurt and Berlin to improve his German, took a course of economics, worked in the Lazard branch in London and on the Stock Exchange and returned to Paris in the spring, where he received an offer of marriage. Alexandre Weill, a friend of the Meyers in San Francisco and a Lazard in-law, promised that if Eugene would marry a Lazard daughter he would be made head of the firm's London branch. Eugene, who preferred to make his own plans, declined.

He came home to humbler duties at the New York branch, invested in Northern Pacific Railroad stock, studied law and found it boring, and saw his salary rise from $12 to $50 a week. He arranged a stock sale that netted the firm $100,000 and was given a $2,000 bonus.

That summer he and young Max Lazard, carrying a letter from the French Ambassador in Washington to the Archbishop of Montreal, and accompanied by four guides, took a canoe trip through the Quebec wilderness, eating poorly and sleeping in tents during the bitterly cold nights. Eugene returned to New York with typhoid, double pneumonia and pleurisy. He lost sixty pounds and spent a year in convalescence. Lying in bed, he read *The Map of Life* by William Edward Hartpole Lecky. Lecky said a young man should plan his life precisely and Eugene was persuaded. He would, he decided, marry at twenty-eight and work until he was forty, establishing a "competence." He would retire from business at fifty and devote his remaining vigorous years to public service. He would then embrace a life of contemplation and grow old gracefully.

When he regained his health he set about following the plan.

His father had given him $600 for not smoking until he was twenty-one. He had invested it in Northern Pacific stock and the stock was now worth $5,000. It was 1900 and William Jennings Bryan, the Democratic champion of silver-backed money, was trying to get William McKinley, the Republican, out of the White House. McKinley had beaten Bryan badly four years before and there was ample reason to believe he would do it again, but the stock market, by tradition, always held its breath during an election year. Eugene did not hold his. He cashed his stock and bought gold bonds as a hedge against the outside chance that Bryan would win. He took options on the best railroad stocks with the rest. When McKinley triumphed, Eugene cashed his gold bonds and bought more options. In January, 1901, he sold the options for $50,000, a 900 percent profit, and bought a seat on the New York Stock Exchange.

In Washington the *Post,* as Eugene did, had reason to approve of the way the world was being run. It was making money, had ads galore, and its typography was crisp and clear. When the Supreme Court decided that an income tax was unconstitutional it had a front-page cartoon showing a dog, labeled income tax, yelping out of the Court with a can tied to its tail. The *Post* was housed in a new building, a Gothic-Romanesque gray-stone pile off Pennsylvania Avenue, was averaging twelve pages daily and had a close relationship with its advertisers and the business community.

Its readers could get a free sample of Swamp Root kidney remedy just by asking for it by mail.

Eugene had grown up, a sobersided, shortish, plumpish, conservatively dressed young man. He had a seat on the Stock Exchange; he had ambition and potential customers, rich friends and relatives. But he had no working capital, so he allied himself with an established brokerage house. Unfortunately the one he picked turned out to be a house of ill repute, a bucket shop pushing dubious stocks at inflated prices. He quit when he found out. The family rallied around—when an abusive brother-in-law made a heavy joke about it at the dinner table, Eugene's father said sternly, "There is no need to humiliate my son anymore." Rosalie wrote, "We feel as you do, that if the situation faced was intolerable you were wise to break free of it without a second's delay."

Eugene survived and bloomed. He had an essential quality: he would always learn from his mistakes. He was soon back in Wall Street action, watching John Pierpont Morgan and Edward Harriman fight over the Northern Pacific Railroad.

Morgan controlled the Northern Pacific, which controlled the Chicago, Burlington and Quincy. Harriman wanted the Chicago, Burlington and Quincy so he began buying Northern Pacific stock quietly. Morgan found out and began buying too. The price climbed from $100 to $110 a share, and Morgan wound up in control of most of the common stock while Harriman had a large block of common and most of the preferred. Harriman moved to elect a new Northern Pacific board of directors, and thousands of not-very-innocent bystanders who had gone along for the profitable ride assumed that the fight was over and that the stock prices would drop. They sold short, agreeing to deliver shares they didn't have at a future date. Morgan didn't quit. He started buying again and so did Harriman. The price went to over $300 a share and the short sellers were desperate. To get money to buy the stocks they had already sold, they had to sell other securities for whatever they would bring. Eugene, who had watched it all patiently, moved fast. He advised his father to buy the under-priced securities as fast as they were offered, and together they did. In a few hours the panic was over (Morgan and Harriman let the short sellers off the hook for $150 a share) and Eugene and his father had made a great deal of money. In time the father's fortune would increase fourfold under Eugene's guidance.

Eugene was now the boy wonder, clever and confident. He was also abrasive and often rude. He moved on to further triumphs and an occasional comeuppance. Henry Morgenthau, Sr., was his summer neighbor in Elberon, New Jersey. Eugene sold some over-the-counter construction company stock for him, and when the stock was later listed on the Exchange he asked if he could continue to handle it.

"Not so fast, not so fast," Morgenthau said.

"Why not so fast?"

"Because you are still a young fellow and a young fellow should get the crumbs."

"And what should the older fellow get?"

"The cake."

"As a matter of justice or a matter of age?"

"As a matter of power."

"What is power?"

"The ability to say no to you," Morgenthau said, "and make it stick."

Eugene learned another lesson. He would depend on nerve and knowledge and not on the goodwill of summer neighbors.

He specialized in mining stocks and he made Lyman B. Kendall, the former head of the U. S. Geological Survey, a salaried partner, with $20,000 a year and a share of the profits. Kendall knew a lot about the country's natural resources, its transportation facilities, crops and climate, and he had access to the Survey's scientists and statisticians. Eugene also hired reporters from financial papers and sometimes precipitously fired them.

"But, Mr. Meyer, I thought . . ." one young man protested.

"If that's what you do when you think," Meyer said, "stop thinking."

He had a contempt for the incompetent but he prized and kept the best. When the Chicago, Milwaukee and St. Paul paid high dividends and the Southern Pacific none, most brokers assumed that the former was the better buy. Meyer had information the others lacked. The Southern Pacific spent $150 a year in maintenance for each car, the C M & P spent only $40. The Chicago, Milwaukee and St. Paul was highballing toward bankruptcy and the Southern Pacific was building a solid future. Meyer advised his clients to buy Southern Pacific and bought some himself.

Away from the market he was a different man. He collected Dürer and Whistler etchings and cultivated artists. He met Gutzon Borglum, the future sculptor of Mount Rushmore, and became a patron. Borglum was chiseling a monumental head of Lincoln out of a six-ton block of stone. Meyer said he'd like to give it to the nation and offered to buy it for $8,500 so he could. Borglum said there was a law against such gifts. When the head was finished Borglum showed it to President Theodore Roosevelt. Roosevelt put it on display at the White House and suggested that it should reside forever under the Capitol dome. Borglum arranged for Meyer and Roosevelt to meet and Roosevelt arranged for Congress to pass a joint resolution permitting acceptance of the gift. The head came to rest in the Capitol Rotunda, where it still sits with Eugene Meyer's name incised in the base.

He was an oddly balanced young man: aggressive in brokerage houses, at ease with Presidents and at home in art galleries but not very sophisticated with young women. He lived at home, on Seventy-second Street, near Central Park. His parents tried to arrange a proper marriage but he said he would only marry a girl of his own dreams.

He lacked glamour but he was rich, could be generous and had good manners.

He wanted to marry a beautiful girl who lived in the exciting world of the arts.

He first saw Agnes Elizabeth Ernst on Lincoln's Birthday, 1908, at the American Art Galleries on Twenty-third Street. He was browsing with a friend, Edgar Kohler, when Agnes swam into view: golden hair, blue eyes, cleanly chiseled features and a boyish figure. She was talking animatedly and wearing a gray tweed suit and a fur cap trimmed with an eagle feather.

"That's the girl I'm going to marry," Eugene said.

"Are you serious?" asked Kohler.

"Never more so," said Eugene.

"Then you'd better speak to her or you'll never see her again."

"I don't think she would like that," Meyer said. "We'll meet her again somewhere, you or I. If you meet her, you introduce her to me, and if I meet her, I'll introduce her to you."

Kohler met her at a costume ball, introduced himself and arranged a luncheon. He introduced her to Eugene but she was not impressed.

In Washington the *Post* was also active socially. John R. McLean, publisher of the Cincinnati *Enquirer,* bought the paper in 1905. He was married to a former Miss Beale, a member of the highest level of Washington society. Their ne'er-do-well son, Ned, would marry a remarkable young rich woman named Evalyn Walsh and in time their paths would cross the paths of Eugene and Agnes Meyer.

CHAPTER

4

When Agnes was nine, her older brother Bill shot her in the head. They were in their pleasant country home outside New York City on a sunny afternoon, examining a .32 pistol.

"I was about a foot away from the muzzle when he pressed the trigger," Agnes recalled much later. "At the flash I threw my head aside and avoided being hit in the middle of the forehead."

The bullet entered her head and lodged in the back of her brain. Her mother held a towel to her bleeding head and together they waited for the doctor.

"*Muss ich jetzt sterben?*" Agnes asked. ("Do you think I am going to die?")

The mother, faltering, said no. Agnes said firmly, "Well, I don't think so either."

Agnes would always believe herself a child of destiny and she would always exaggerate her abilities—no one can dodge a bullet.

Years later her head would be X-rayed while she was being treated for sinus attacks and she would report that there was "very little bone left on the right side of my skull, the whole brain was sprinkled with what can only be powder and resting behind my right ear is the rest of the bullet."

She was born in Pelham Heights, a community of a half-dozen houses, the child of German immigrants. In her autobiography she seldom mentions her mother and the mother remains dim, but her father, Frederick, the son of the last Lutheran chaplain of the Hanover court, was the most important man in her life, an active ward politician, a casual lawyer, an unsuccessful writer and a man of many shallow enthusiasms. He campaigned for William Jennings Bryan, sang Wagnerian arias in a rich baritone, and woke Agnes in the summer to watch the sun come up. Agnes's grandfather, the chaplain, wrote long lecturing letters on the sacredness of family life, the education of the young and the need to maintain cultural standards in the raw, new world. They were read aloud at the dinner table and Agnes would always keep her grandfather's picture on her worktable.

The family moved to the Bronx so the children could attend New York's excellent public schools. Mr. Ernst neglected his law practice and spent his time writing books and plays which Agnes would later describe as "incredibly amateurish." The one produced, a celebration of the American Revolution, closed almost immediately. When Agnes graduated with high honors from high school her father declined to send her to college. In her phrase he "finally broke the golden cord." She never forgave him.

"He never expressed it in so many words but from my mother I gleaned that he would be freer to pursue his fantastic mode of life if I should begin remunerative work sooner than would be possible if I continued my academic career . . . the father who had inspired in me the love of learning was betraying the very ideals he had taught me to cherish."

She would later look back in less anger. "My father-fixation subjected me to extraordinary emotional extremes," she would write, and indeed she would fall in love with father substitutes, older, successful men, for the rest of her life.

She won a scholarship to Barnard on the basis of her high marks in the entrance exam and enrolled in 1903, majoring in mathematics and physics, but she got a D in her first-year math and lost the scholarship. She blamed the teacher.

She was brash, self-confident, bitter, beautiful and determined. She took two summer jobs. In the mornings she ran a Baptist summer school on West Thirty-sixth Street, in Hell's Kitchen, and she worked in a lending library from 6 to 10 P.M. She returned to Barnard in the fall, prepared to pay her own tuition, and was given another scholarship, but she soon suffered new humiliations. At midyear one of her professors, William Tenny Brewster, gave selected readings from the students' efforts at creative writing. He picked two for special comment. The first, which he praised, contained humorous vignettes of the city's people. The other was written by Agnes. In her own words they were "melancholy, introspective, nostalgic yearnings for the evanescent beauty of childhood, the pathetic revelations of all my hidden grief."

Brewster told the class that the first student was interested in the world, the second only in herself. The other students fell into the habit of asking, "How's your soul today, Ag?" when they met her in the corridors, and at the end of the year her yearbook picture had a mock quotation next to it: "Fortunate is he who acts as the Columbus of his own soul."

Agnes did not surrender. She joined a sorority and acquired a few friends. One was a morose young woman named Juliet Points, the daughter of a policeman. Juliet—in Agnes's opinion—was a "rootless intellectual doomed to an early, tragic end." She became a Socialist, then a Communist, married, broke with the Party and, one day in the thirties, disappeared. Agnes concluded that the Communists had murdered her. She would note with satisfaction that Juliet's presumed fate showed "with comic clarity" what happened to the rootless.

Agnes herself remained a resentful and mediocre student.

"As long as I was in college my mood of rebellion continued because the academic atmosphere made me feel as if I were at a perpetual funeral service without being able to discover who was being buried or where the corpse was concealed."

When she tried to persuade the school authorities that she should graduate a year early they turned her down. She went full term, graduated in 1907, and got a job on the New York *Morning Sun* as a space-rate writer earning five dollars a column.

She was the paper's first woman contributor and she did well; some weeks she made $40. When she found an assignment too difficult she asked for and received help from the men from the other papers. She was assigned to cover private charities but found herself indifferent to the poor people she saw on her rounds.

"My brother Bill was working in Montana and Fred was married with family responsibilities of his own. That left me to cope alone with our household expenses. 'Why worry about the poor?' was my frame of mind. I too was not only poor but always hopelessly in debt, as my father at this time was spending money much faster than he or I could earn it. That there were impoverished millions who were contending with long working hours and low pay, as well as horrible conditions of labor in sweatshops and mining areas, found no trace of sympathy in my egotistical young mind. The devil take them."

The self-portrait is candid but slightly askew. Her family was not poor by the standards of the city and they maintained a shabby gentility without much help from her. She would contribute to their income reluctantly and for only a few months. After that they, once more, would contribute to hers.

She had already found a way out of her dilemma. She had met Eugene in February, 1908, and had immediately been aware of his determined intentions. She had two other beaux, one an "adoring slave, sensitive but physically unattractive" and the other a German aristocratic playboy named Alfred von Heymel. Eugene, rich and patient, was clearly her best bet.

At the end of the year she borrowed $500, quit the *Sun* and went abroad. When she told Eugene she was going alone he was aghast. He promptly gave $500 to a friend of hers named Nancy so they could go together.

Agnes would later explain that she went for the benefit of her family as well as herself:

"I was trying desperately and consciously to escape from my own unruly disposition and father complex. I was sorry to leave my mother alone with her household cares but I knew my father would never again face his own financial responsibilities as long as I was there to foot the bills."

On the boat she met Dr. Harigan, an older man and the director of the Massachusetts Board of Health, who called her "Angel Face" and who told her he had never seen such "shrewd innocence." He was among the first of her father-figure attachments. He had a measure of wealth and renown but his successors would be much richer and better known.

Agnes had a wonderful time in Paris. She was, above everything else, beautiful, a Gibson girl, straight and graceful with delicate, chiseled features and a haughty air.

"Nobody," she would write later, "was more thoroughly spoiled by male adoration than I."

She was also thrifty. Her mother sent her "small sums" and Eugene appeared from time to time and took her and her friends to expensive restaurants. She dazzled Constantin Brancusi, who sculpted an abstract of her head. She became Auguste Rodin's untouched darling and acquired a snobbish frame of artistic reference that she would use the rest of her life.

"Who," she would say in the years to come, "has not seen the Russian ballet between 1909 and 1912 has no concept of what ballet can be."

She loved famous men and despised famous women. She met Gertrude Stein and found that she had always distrusted "masculine women," finding their "self-assertion distasteful." She became one of the great teases of the Edwardian age.

Merlo Pusey, a *Post* editorial writer who wrote the official autobiography of Eugene Meyer, decided, kindly, that Agnes was "passionately in love with the artistic atmosphere but coolly aloof" to the promiscuity that prevailed. In her own unpublished manuscript, *Life as Chance and Destiny,* Agnes said she wrote that she clung to "an ideal of purity and perfection" and described her technique of attachment.

Once, in reply to an ardent telegram, she kept a rendezvous with the aging Rodin in his garden. She found him seated in an armchair, and when he drew her to him she seized his hands and fell to her knees.

"Dear Friend," she would remember saying, "you cannot imagine what you mean to me. You are the greatest artist, the greatest teacher I have ever known. Dear, dear Friend, there are many great men in the world, there is only one Rodin. I don't wish to lose him."

When she finished, she would remember, there were tears on Rodin's face. She concluded that he was enchanted, that "at last he had found a woman who was different, who loved him for his art alone."

She kept all her swains at a safe distance.

Years later Eugene would remember her letters as "very intelligent . . . but there was no love in them."

Still he pursued her as systematically and coolly as he would a stock deal and in time he got what he sought.

Agnes ran out of money and came home. She found life with her father an "exaggerated burning shame" and decided to leave home once more. She met Eugene for lunch one January day.

"I am going back to Paris to straighten out my inner confusion," she said.

"I have decided to get away for a bit myself," he replied. "I'm going to take a trip around the world, starting next month."

There was a long pause.

"I'm going with you," she said in a small voice.

"I know," Eugene replied, "I have your tickets."

Agnes needed to be rich and powerful and she seized the opportunity. She had negotiated shrewdly, if unconsciously, and Eugene, who could arrange complex business deals most successfully, had not.

She would never pretend she had married for love but would insist that she had not been simply calculating.

"It had never occurred to me until I became engaged that it would be impossible for me to marry anyone who was not well-to-do. For the only dowry I had to bring a husband was my father's debts and my own."

They were married on Lincoln's Birthday, February 12, 1910, exactly two years after he first had seen her, by a Lutheran minister at Agnes's home in the Bronx. *The New York Times* devoted half a column to it, *The Washington Post* let it pass unnoticed. Agnes's dream had come true; she was rich and if not yet personally powerful, at least she could mingle with those who were. They began life on a grand, impersonal scale, and Eugene did, indeed, settle her debts and her father's.

CHAPTER

5

The newly married Meyers first spent a week at Seven Springs, Eugene's pleasant farmhouse at Mount Kisco, New York, then they went to Washington and a grand ball at the home of society matron Mrs. Herbert Wadsworth. The invitation had been arranged by Postmaster General Frank Hitchcock, a Republican Party stalwart, who knew Eugene as a generous contributor. Agnes met Cabinet members and Supreme Court Justices and Eugene noticed that he was the only Jew among the guests.

They were at first glance an odd couple, rich and poor, Jew and Lutheran, sober and frivolous, but they shared a resentment and a determination. They were both outsiders on the fringe of high society and determined to belong to America's ruling class, to rise, as it were, above their origins, to erase past humiliations and triumph over old tormentors.

They went west, aboard a private railway car, The Constitution, rolling past the Grand Canyon, stopping in Montana to visit Eugene's mining partner, "Big Bill" Thompson, staying with Eugene's sisters in San Francisco, and then sailing for Honolulu. They spent seven weeks in Japan and met the Japanese nobility in their flower gardens. The Marquis Shigenobu Okuma showed them his art collection and gave them tea.

"The Japanese," Agnes would write in self-congratulation, "are apt to withhold their finest objects from those who have no real appreciation of art but they take all the more delight in sharing their treasures with anyone in whom they discern a genuine love of beauty."

The newlyweds found Korea depressing and skipped India because of the heat. They went to Manchuria and then across Siberia by private car to Moscow.

Along the way they conceived a child and they soon found they were getting on each other's nerves. Agnes had morning sickness and complained frequently. Eugene grew less romantic and one day at lunch he lost his temper and Agnes went sobbing to her compartment. She would conclude bitterly that happiness with Eugene was impossible.

They both, in their different ways, were young, and each was married to a stranger. Agnes was brooding about her pregnancy. She had married an older, protective man who seemed perhaps the perfect father substitute. But when he lost his temper that day, she examined her new, rich, strange life and concluded that "happiness with such a man was impossible." He was a young tycoon with other things on his mind.

In Shanghai, Eugene had learned that the Guggenheim copper interests and their rival, Anaconda, were having a price war. He was a Guggenheim associate as well as an investor in Anaconda's subsidiary, Inspiration Copper, and while Agnes stared out of her compartment window at bleak Siberia, Eugene planned a coup.

In Moscow he learned that John D. Ryan, Anaconda's head, was traveling in Europe. He climbed back aboard his private car, intercepted Ryan in Berlin and offered a formula for mutual gain: the copper giants would limit production and raise their prices. It was a suggestion that was clearly illegal under American law. Ryan tentatively agreed, and Eugene arranged a meeting with the Guggenheims in Paris, where he had similar success.

In Paris, Eugene relaxed and Agnes became reconciled. They bought paintings by Cézanne and Picasso and then came home to a mansion on Fifty-first Street, across from St. Patrick's Cathedral. They had a handsome home, millions of dollars, rooms full of masterpieces and a baby on the way. They lacked only true love, contentment and peace of mind.

Their honeymoon would be a metaphor for their marriage. They would travel through life in the same private car, each in a separate compartment; she dependent, resentful, rebellious and adolescent, he a withdrawn and isolated man of business and of dreams.

They came home in August, 1910, and Eugene found that marriage had changed his circumstances but not the essentials of his life. He had established a family and achieved a great deal more than a competence. He was still a rude loner in business, a careful conformist in behavior and something of a poseur in society. He was also thirty-six, and by definition no longer a boy wonder.

He had converted most of his holdings to cash before he went abroad and he now had the strong urge to play a more important role in the world of industry and finance, to be not merely a shrewd judge of other men's railroads and mines but a man in control of enterprises of his own. His luck, which had been phenomenal, would now become spotty.

Things began well. In Paris the Lazards had introduced him to a new process for refining lead, zinc and copper that would capture 90 percent of the metals and make low-grade mines profitable. He bought an interest and when he came home he set up an American corporation to sell licenses for the process to mine owners. He underwrote a $50,000 demonstration which won the Guggenheims over, and as a result their low-grade mine in Chile would become one of the world's great copper producers. Meyer's corporation would collect tens of millions in royalties in the coming years.

So far, so good, but when the stock market went into a prolonged slump in 1913 he found himself short of cash and badly overextended. Since he never talked about his failures the details remain obscure, but his holdings in Inspiration Copper and other stocks were selling below their value and there was no easy way out. He tried to borrow money from his brother-in-law George Blumenthal (the man who had mocked him at the family dinner table), but Blumenthal, who was in Paris, did not respond immediately and Eugene found himself on the edge of bankruptcy. He was helped by other relatives and he survived and bounced back.

He soon set off on another bumpy ride. He had owned several automobiles and he considered himself an authority on their performance. On the advice of George W. Perkins, a Morgan partner, he invested heavily in the United States Motor Company, the makers of the Maxwell. The company was controlled by James Brady, a utilities tycoon, and his family, and was badly managed. In the scenario put together by Perkins, Eugene was to become the strong member of the company board of directors and reform the management. It didn't work out that way. He became a director but Brady and his cohorts continued to set policy. The company collapsed and was reorganized as Maxwell Motors, with Brady still clearly in control.

Eugene bought more stock but it continued to dwindle in value and he was forced to cut down his personal expenses; he and Agnes sold their Fifth Avenue mansion and moved to an apartment at the St. Regis. People began to talk.

By now he owned 50 percent of the Maxwell common stock but he was still outvoted and outmaneuvered by Brady. In December, 1916, he resigned and sold his holdings with some difficulty but without suffering a great loss. He would eventually make an automobile connection—with the Fisher Body Company—that would make him millions.

Meanwhile his relations with Agnes had been as tumultuous as those with Brady, and again he was fortunate to break even.

Agnes remained egocentric. She had brought two things home from the East: a baby girl, who would be named Florence, and an interest in Oriental art she had picked up in the Marquis Okuma's garden.

Florence had the lesser attraction.

"What a horror," Agnes said when she saw her for the first time, and as soon as she could get out of bed she was back with her old art-crowd friends at Alfred Stieglitz's gallery on Fifth Avenue.

She would serve as her own most damaging witness.

"When my first child was born in 1911," she wrote later, "I insisted on nursing her but I would often forget to go home at the hour of feeding the poor child if I happened to get too deeply involved in one or the other of my extramural activities. Reminded by my overflowing breasts that I was neglecting my infant, I would rush back conscience-stricken, to find the nurse walking the floor to comfort a baby screaming with hunger."

She studied Chinese at Columbia and gave some of Eugene's money to the founding of the New School for Social Research. She began, once more, to collect old, rich and famous men. She met Charles Freer one day at a show of Oriental paintings. He was a financier and an ardent art collector. They would have a long, strange, intimate and unconsummated love affair.

She also fell "a little in love" with James Harvey Robinson and Charles Beard but when she met Thorstein Veblen, the caustic author of *The Theory of the Leisure Class,* she found him a repulsive "black pessimist."

By 1914 she had been married four years, had a second child, Elizabeth, and was finding her duties as wife and mother onerous. The children were left to the care of their nurse, Margaret Powell, called "Powelly," who would raise all of Agnes's children, and Agnes spent her days with the friends of her early youth, as if she were still free and unattached. When other wealthy matrons came to call she threw their cards in the wastebasket.

That spring she ran off to Europe, leaving husband and daughters behind. Eugene let her go. Perhaps he felt she needed one last fling.

She wrote him blithely from Berlin that Von Heymel, her old playboy beau, "took me to his charming apartment for tea."

"Don't be shocked," she added, "it was full of domestics and as proper as any menage."

She lunched with Von Heymel the next day and wrote again.

Von Heymel had confided that he hated all women "with the deepest kind of sex-hatred" but that he might marry, since, he said, "I need someone's arm to go to sleep upon at night."

That was a daring thing to say in 1914 and Eugene was not amused.

He wrote back: "The importance of your going to von Heymel's apartment must have been great to have justified the cost. I am asking myself what I have done to deserve this sort of treatment. I felt so sure after our talks that I could rely on you. Do you want me to feel, as we reach what I take to be a definite understanding about anything, that I must still feel uncertain as to what course you will pursue?"

She replied by cable: "SORRY HEYMEL BUSINESS MISUNDER-STOOD. UNDERSTANDING NOT FORGOTTEN. TRUST ME."

Later she wrote in abject surrender: ". . . I could not stop thinking about myself and last night as I lay in bed I had only one feeling, 'How did I ever get anybody to marry me—most of all you?' I have a big picture of Florence in my room which I swiped from Ruth, it comforts me a lot. At least my babies are sweet, aren't they honey?"

Eugene was not so easily appeased. She had asked him to consider her side of the incident. He asked by letter, "What is your side?"

Had Agnes been born fifty years later, she might have gone her own way, with a divorce and a substantial settlement, leaving her babies behind. Perhaps not. She needed the justification of the babies and she also needed a permanent father figure—even by her reckoning, Eugene was wiser as well as older—and there were times when she could look at herself with a critical, cold eye.

She now wrote Eugene that "only a blind man could have failed to be uneasy about the woman who left you. I do not think you will be uneasy about the woman who returns."

She added: "I have been thinking hard since I left you and I feel easier because part of the answer at least I have found. When I left you I wanted another child because I thought it would keep me occupied, help me feel that I was at least some use in the world—but I want one now not as a soporific but for a very vital reason which I shall tell you about when I come home. Do not let us dodge any more but face each other frankly and our life will develop."

Eugene accepted her peace offering with reservations. "I have had my mind much distressed. . . . You say, 'be happy and know that I shall work for you always in any and every way.' This is a sweet expression and I am sure you would do so—if you happened to think of it. Thinking after all is what counts."

They were badly matched but affinity would keep them together for almost fifty years. He was a wealthy, powerful man who kept his contracts and she was a woman who needed wealth and power. They would pursue power together and they would enjoy each other's triumphs.

Eugene had married foolishly but he was, perhaps, incapable of marrying wisely. Agnes, in terms of commitment, had never married at all.

On the boat coming home she had a bad dream.

"I dreamed that I was watching the sunrise, an experience that I had often in childhood shared with my father. Gradually the sun was eclipsed by the face of my father which looked straight at me with an expression of sadistic triumph. He did not speak. It was unnecessary. The expression said more clearly than any words: 'I've got you. You are just another me. And you are doomed to go the way I did.' I awoke in terror. My agony, guilt and self-contempt were so acute that I can feel them today. I could not help but realize that in escaping from home responsibilities I was repeating the self-centered, irresponsible conduct of my father which had cost his wife, his children, and especially his only daughter, such bitter humiliation. The Bible does not take modern psychiatry or just plain human intelligence into account when it says that the sins of the fathers shall be visited upon the children unto the third and fourth generations."

Agnes would try to change but she would remain essentially the same—egocentric, emotional, partisan, resentful of those who did not accept her as an intellectual and moral leader, a tyrant, an uncommon scold and a fan-club president in puppy love with men of artistic or cultural renown.

Still Eugene's hope had come partly true. Her escape to Europe in that last spring before the Great War would be her last fling of full defiance. She would come home to Eugene, and Eugene, forevermore, would be the one in charge. He was moreover preoccupied with his own ambitions.

When World War I exploded in August, 1914, Eugene was prepared. He closed down his New York office—"I fear new and more acute tensions between Germany and America," he told his staff—and he advised his clients to trade conservatively.

He gave more candid advice to Charles Freer, who had become his business associate as well as Agnes's friend. Invest, he said, in essentials, businesses supplying food, clothing and other necessities.

His own particular interest was in aniline dyes. They had been a German monopoly and Eugene learned that William Gerard Beckers, a former salesman for the cartel, was the one person in the country with a knowledge of their production. Beckers blew himself up while cooking up a batch in his garage in Brooklyn, but by February, 1916, he had recovered, and he and Eugene were organizing the W. Beckers Aniline and Chemical Works. Its dyes were poor but soon improving, and within months there were 250 research men at work in a $2.5 million plant. Eugene soon merged Beckers with two other firms to form the National Aniline and Chemical Company. National Aniline would supply the blue dye for sailors' uniforms and its assets at war's end would total $60 million.

Eugene was anxious to play a more direct role in wartime Washington. Supreme Court Justice Louis D. Brandeis, a friend, wrote Treasury Secretary William Gibbs McAdoo recommending him for a dollar-a-year job but nothing came of that, and Eugene wrote directly to President Wilson.

Washington and public America were run by wellborn WASPs but people in high places believed that proper Jewish bankers and brokers made the best financial advisers. Wilson had already picked his chief wizard, Bernard Baruch, but he gave Eugene an obscure post on the Advisory Commission's Committee on Finished Goods. Eugene took it reluctantly, and spent some months arranging the purchase of cloth for the Navy.

In April President Wilson asked Eugene to serve on the American commission to Alexander Kerensky's new revolutionary Russian government. The commission would be led by an old business enemy, the elderly Elihu Root, but Eugene was delighted anyway. He generated plans for the commission without consulting his fellow members, and did nothing to heal old wounds by suggesting that Root, old and fragile, be accompanied by a physician.

Then Eugene was summoned abruptly to the State Department and Secretary Robert Lansing told him his appointment had been rescinded.

"We have some cables that make us think that you'd better not go," Lansing said, offering no further explanation.

The truth was that the American Ambassador to Russia, David R. Francis, had advised the State Department that some members of the Kerensky government were anti-Semitic and he had asked that Meyer therefore be dropped.

Eugene pointed out that the press had already announced his appointment. Lansing suggested that he say that the published list had been inaccurate.

Eugene bound up his wounds. He quit his job as textile adviser and attached himself to Baruch's Raw Materials Committee, without being asked, commandeering an office and creating his own small empire dealing with the purchase of copper.

Eugene was on the march, and Agnes was now a housewife, though she'd never be a contented one. Katharine was born at Seven Springs in the summer of 1917, and that fall Agnes left her three daughters in New York with their nurse, Margaret Powell. They would remain there for three years while Agnes carved a new career. "I helped my husband by making our home a center for the social gatherings which in Washington are an extension of the working hours but I was so engrossed in translating Chinese texts and in writing a book on the philosophy of Chinese art that it never occurred to me to make an active contribution toward the war efforts."

The war ended and the Meyers stayed in Washington. Eugene had found the place in which to make his greatest dreams come true.

CHAPTER

6

The Washington Post was a powerful force in Washington, and the family who owned it, the McLeans, were among its social leaders.

On Sunday, February 20, 1921, the paper had forty-four full-size pages, plus a tabloid of fiction, a variety of colored comics—"Bringing Up Father," "Mr. Dubb," "Little Jimmy" and "The Katzenjammer Kids." It had a rotogravure section of sepia pictures, including one of a girls' basketball team from Community Service House and another of a couple doing a modern ballroom dance. It had ads offering new red-brick bungalows for $6,000, suits and coats for $29 and a cure for rheumatism that was roundly recommended by a clergyman named Pastor Reed.

On its front page President-elect Warren Harding was reported to be concerned with the settlement of the Japanese Question and a Congressman named McLeod was complaining that "slightly unbalanced" war veterans were housed in the same building at St. Elizabeth's Hospital as nonveterans who were completely insane.

The *Post*'s play of the news was somewhat bizarre. Its eighth column, traditionally the home of the day's most important hard news, carried the third installment of a series on Kaiser Wilhelm, then living in exile in Holland. It was headed "Ex-Kaiser Nervous at Aide's Wedding," was written by Lady Norah Bentinck, and was about a social occasion that had occurred some months earlier.

The *Post* was now owned by Edward B. McLean, who was listed on the masthead as Editor-Publisher. Ned was the unfortunate product of an indulgent mother who had bribed other boys to let him win at Parcheesi and baseball. He grew up with an unwarranted belief in his own abilities. He married Evalyn Walsh, the big-hearted, impulsive daughter of Thomas F. Walsh, a rough-cut multimillionaire with silver mines in the West.

Ned and Evalyn would plumb the more tumultuous pools of the roiling twenties.

"Drink has been an evil influence in my life," Evalyn would say as an old woman, "drink and drugs."

She would survive, Ned would not.

They had begun their married life full speed ahead. On a yearlong European honeymoon, Ned, under the influence of God knows what, drove a rented touring car lickety-split across France with Evalyn beside him on the front seat and the French chauffeur, terror-stricken, in the back. When they finally drew up before their hotel in Paris they discovered that the chauffeur had died of a heart attack somewhere along the way.

Ned's father, John R. McLean, a tyrant described by Evalyn as "both potent and crafty," died in 1916 and Ned inherited the paper and an income that varied between $500,000 and $800,000 a year.

He would devote the rest of his life to golf, whiskey, amateurish political meddling and his own strange brand of journalism. When a Commissioner of the District of Columbia, a member of the local governing board appointed by the President, failed to name Ned's choice as police chief, Ned ordered that the Commissioner's name never be mentioned in the *Post* again. It made for some odd evasions.

Ned was sometimes absurd on a more dangerous level. In 1919 the *Post,* on his orders, reporting on one racial clash, somewhat gratuitously and almost gleefully predicted another, more calamitous one.

The story began:

Aggravation of District citizens and soldiery stationed in Washington at the recent attacks on women by Negroes, led to race riots last night when more than 400 men of mixed civilian and military dress, armed with revolvers and clubs, marched into the Southwest section of the city on an avowed mission of terrorism.

Last evening's development was more significant in its augury than in its enactment. . . . It was learned that a mobilization of every serviceman has been ordered for tomorrow evening near the Knights of Columbus hut on Pennsylvania Avenue between 7th and 8th. The hour of assembly is nine o'clock and the purpose is a "cleanup" that will cause the events of the last two evenings to pale into insignificance.

A good many white men read the story and followed the explicit directions. Black men read it and armed themselves. Thirty-nine persons were killed in the riot that followed.

Ned, who had not anticipated the results, was badly shaken. He withdrew from direct management of the paper, drank more and went into frequent depressions until a handsome, amiable, feckless Senator from Ohio entered his life.

"The one time when I thought that Ned McLean was going to be saved from a disastrous end," Evalyn later wrote, "was when he was going around with Warren Gamaliel Harding."

They were natural-born companions—Harding at fifty-one liked to drink whiskey, play poker and fool around with accommodating young women. He was eager to enjoy his access to a new world of riches.

Ned, who had been more of a drinker than anything else, saw his chance to surround Harding with flashy luxuries and to shape his own destiny.

He invited Harding and his Senatorial cronies, Frederick Hale of Maine, Davis Elkins of West Virginia, and Joe Frelinghuysen of New Jersey, to play at his own nine-hole golf course at Friendship, Ned's estate on the edge of Georgetown, anytime they wished. Harding, who loved the game, showed up a couple of times a week, and Ned hired a professional golfer named Freddie McLeod for $10,000 a year to teach the two of them the finer points of golf.

In time everyone of importance came for one reason or another. William Randolph Hearst and his wife, Millicent, came to dinner frequently. Alice Roosevelt Longworth came to everything. Calvin Coolidge came to play golf in a business suit, and Herbert Hoover, a solemn, chubby man in a hard high collar, came to the more sedate gatherings.

When Harding was nominated for the Presidency Ned threw himself into the campaign. The *Post* was nominally independent politically and the McLeans' older paper, the Cincinnati *Enquirer,* had been Democratic since the Civil War. As Evalyn put it, Ned "made it clear he wanted nothing printed that would interfere even a little with the success of the campaign."

He also seized two opportunities to perform what he considered valuable personal campaign chores. A rumor that the nominee had a Negro great-grandfather had surfaced when Harding had run for the Senate, and it now surfaced again. In 1920 that was a rumor that could cost him the election.

Ned wished to deal with it directly. He suggested to Harry Daugherty, Harding's campaign manager and the future Attorney General, that the Cincinnati *Enquirer* say the charge had been fabricated by the Democrats and that in view of such outrageous behavior it was endorsing Harding.

Daugherty turned down the plan, to Evalyn's relief. Ned retreated for the time being.

He soon found another opportunity. Harding's sister, Mrs. Helen Votaw, a Washington policewoman and a former missionary in Burma, had agreed to address an assembly of black women. Harding was alarmed that anyone in his family should meet with black people in friendly, public circumstances and he asked Ned to stop her. Ned sent her a note.

> Dear Mrs. Votaw,
>
> Sen. Harding has just gotten through talking to me on the telephone and he wishes you to receive a message of imperative importance from Mrs. McLean before you go to your office this morning. My wife had a slight automobile accident yesterday or she would come to see you. We are living at Friendship and will send a machine for you anytime you wish or will send one to show you where the place is. With very best regards, I remain
>
> Yours very truly, Edward McLean
>
> P.S. For reasons which Mr. Brown [who had delivered the note] will explain to you, I am asking him to return this letter to me. . . .

Mrs. Votaw was kept under wraps at Friendship until the scheduled meeting was over and then put on a train to Marion, Ohio, the Harding hometown. As election day came near, Ned, acting on his own, moved to quash the still persistent rumor. The day before, the *Post* carried a story that he probably wrote himself: "The most dastardly conspiracy in the history of American politics was exposed yesterday. In an effort to steal the election, the Democrats have been sending out hundreds of thousands of circulars asserting that Senator Harding has Negro blood in his veins. . . ."

Neither the charge nor the rebuttal had a discernible effect. Harding won in a landslide, and Ned was named chairman of the Inaugural Committee. He promptly announced the most stupendous public ball since the latter days of Rome, but a group of Republican Senators, alarmed at the grotesque possibilities, had it canceled.

Ned rubbed his bruised feelings and carried on. As Inauguration Day approached, the front pages of the *Post* were crowded with triumphant and sometimes frivolous stories.

"Harding's Game of Golf Marked by Determination—Easily Makes 200 Yard Drives and Observes All Etiquette and Every Rule," said one, by-lined Fred McLeod, Ned's own private pro.

On March 4, Inauguration Day, the *Post* carried a large and flattering drawing of Harding's noble head on its front page and the *Post*'s reporter George Rothwell Brown announced in a lead story that "Practical Statesmanship Will Succeed Idealism."

The single editorial inside concluded that the inauguration of the amiable nonentity from Ohio was "the most fortunate event that could occur for the world at this time." It also said with ironic truth that no one could "foresee the end of the forces that begin their operations today."

When Attorney General Daugherty and his bagman, Jesse Smith, came to town, Evalyn loaned them a house at 1509 H Street, N.W. The President-elect was grateful and he wrote Evalyn a note, saying he hoped soon to reward their "valued and devoted friendship."

Evalyn threw a huge, private inaugural dinner party. The guests included the President and Mrs. Harding, the Vice President and Mrs. Coolidge, the Supreme Court Justices, the Cabinet, the Senate, the diplomatic corps and, far down the list, Eugene and Agnes Meyer.

Mrs. Harding soon relied on Evalyn to select her clothes and guide her ways. The President kept two horses at the McLeans' Virginia farm, and when Mrs. Harding, constantly frightened, began brooding about assassins, the Hardings spent Christmas hidden away at Friendship.

In March the Hardings and the McLeans went for a holiday on a houseboat up and down the Florida coast. There were other excursions and many parties.

In the summer of 1923 the President and Mrs. Harding set off for an official trip to Alaska. Evalyn was in shaky health, and she and Ned declined an invitation to go along.

On the way back the President became ill in San Francisco. On August 2 the *Post* had a three-column front-page headline: "President Rests Well After Uneasy Day, Lungs Are Improved."

The subheads went on: "Indigestion from Eggs Cause of Distress in the Daytime; Complications Only Fear of Physicians; Bulletins Indicate a Gradual Trend Toward Absolute Recovery of Health; Sister Is the First Visitor Received; Chief Executive Anxious Over Display of Speech Given Out Yesterday."

In his column "Post Scripts" George Rothwell Brown opened as usual with a quotation: "As cold waters to a thirsty soul, so is good news from a far country." The column began: "The President is much better and sees his first visitor, his sister. What more could one ask in the way of good tidings? After a restless day he is more comfortable at night, with a lower temperature and a slight improvement in the lung condition. Back to normalcy. . . ."

The President died the same day, and the next morning the *Post* wrung its hands in public grief:

"President Harding Is Dead of Apoplexy; End Comes Instantly as Wife Is Reading to Him; Coolidge Takes Oath of Office; No Warning Is Given of Fatal End; Mrs. Harding Sends Call for Doctors Who Arrive to Find Patient Dead; 'I Am Not Going to Break Down' Are First Words of Mrs. Harding . . . Funeral Train Will Start East This Evening."

George Rothwell Brown now had a more mournful quotation, "Ill news is wing'd with fate and flies apace," and his column began, "The President Is Dead, like a lightning bolt from a sunny sky came the dread ill news, winged with fate for the American people at a great crisis in their history. . . ."

The crisis was rhetorical but a real one was brewing, the Teapot Dome scandals that would send one Cabinet member to jail and another into disgrace. Some would say that Harding had learned of the approaching disaster and wished to die. Some would even say that Mrs. Harding poisoned him to save him the embarrassment.

Mrs. Harding called Evalyn to the White House and led her to the East Room, where the President was stretched in his coffin.

"Warren, the trip has not hurt you a bit," Mrs. Harding said to the dead man and then, after a pause, "No one can hurt you now, Warren."

Scandals followed, and Ned would tell a foolish lie to try to save a friend. He would be involved, not as a crook but as a clown.

Senator Thomas J. Walsh, a Democrat from Montana, began cranking up an investigation into Teapot Dome. Teapot Dome was the name of a geological site in the state of Montana with untapped oil fields held in reserve for the Navy. Harding's Secretary of the Interior, Albert Fall, had persuaded Secretary Edwin Denby of the Navy to transfer control of the fields to Interior and had then leased them to an oilman named Edward L. Doheny in return for a $100,000 bribe.

At summer's end Ned received a telegram from Fall, asking him to meet him in Atlantic City. Ned went up in his private car, The Enquirer. Fall asked him to say, if asked, that he had loaned him $100,000 in 1921. Ned said sure.

Ned was soon having a wonderful time; all his life he had wanted to play a central role in great events. He took his two personal employees, John Major and William Duckstein, and President Coolidge's secretary, Bascom Slemp, with him to Palm Beach and set up headquarters. He had a direct telegraph line laid between his Palm Beach house and the *Post* and he sent frequent messages, some in the Justice Department code, to which he'd been made privy when Harding's Attorney General had him appointed a dollar-a-year special FBI agent, and some in a code that he had invented himself. He sent Major back to Washington to watch developments and he conferred daily with Bascom Slemp.

The Senate investigators began uncovering evidence that Secretary Fall had turned over the oil leases to Doheny and they also found that Fall had bought a ranch, paying $100,000 in cash.

Ned heard that he would be subpoenaed by the Senate and on Christmas Day he hired A. Mitchell Palmer, who had been Woodrow Wilson's Attorney General, as his counsel. Then he sent Fall a telegram:

"PLEASE WIRE ME WHERE YOU WILL BE SATURDAY. WE WANT MY SECRETARY TO SEE YOU ON IMPORTANT BUSINESS MATTER THAT DAY. MRS. MCLEAN JOINS ME IN WISHING YOU AND MRS. FALL A MERRY CHRISTMAS. WIRE ANSWER."

He also wired Major to have Palmer tell the Senate committee that he had indeed loaned Fall $100,000 in cash, on his personal note, in 1921. Then he sat down to Christmas dinner.

The next day Fall told the committee that he had gotten the money from Ned, and Palmer backed it up with Ned's telegram. Fall then caught a train for Palm Beach, where he would sit day after day on Ned's porch, looking out to sea.

Senator Walsh's committee called Ned, and Ned had Bascom Slemp's physician say that he, like Slemp, was suffering from a sinus attack and unable to travel. Senator Walsh, an obliging man, went to Palm Beach himself and set up a one-man hearing with Ned as the only witness.

Fall decided it was time to tell the truth, at least to Evalyn. He said that Doheny had indeed given him the $100,000 and that only Ned stood between him and disaster.

Ned suddenly realized that he was in a trap himself, that he was open to criminal charges.

After further consultations, he told Walsh that he had given Fall $100,000 but it had been in checks, not cash, and that Fall had eventually returned them uncashed. He did not, however, even have check stubs to support his story. Walsh said dryly that it was fortunate Fall hadn't tried to cash them since there hadn't been enough money in Ned's accounts to cover them.

The Senate Committee on Public Lands and Surveys began its Washington hearings in February, and Washington was agog. The *Post* was caught in a cleft. It could not ignore the hearings but it did its best to ignore their importance.

On Saturday, February 23, the *Post* devoted most of its front page to a marathon it had sponsored. James Norris, of Philadelphia, led a field of one hundred to the finish line behind the White House, and a two-column picture showed him being congratulated by President Coolidge.

Over in column eight an Associated Press story announced that "Slemp To Be Asked By Oil Inquisitors About Florida Trip."

The headlines and stories on the Senate hearings continued to occupy column eight for the next two weeks, all but one of the stories from the Associated Press. Slemp admitted that he had indeed talked about the oil scandals with Fall and McLean but said he had done so only casually. Bank officials testified that at the time McLean had supposedly given Fall the checks for $100,000 he did indeed have only a few thousand in the banks. Senator Walsh said that "the general belief is that the transaction never did take place."

McLean's telegrams were recovered from the telegraph company and an army cryptographer easily decoded them.

The *Post*'s editorials never mentioned its publisher's predicament nor did they have anything to say about Fall, Doheny or Teapot Dome. Most of them were devoted to unrelated noninflammatory subjects, tax reductions, the tariff and on two occasions the Constitution and the Declaration of Independence.

One editorial, entitled "Prosperity Speaks Louder Than Politics," skirted the scandals, saying that Coolidge would be reelected despite feckless Democratic Party efforts to blacken the Republican record.

Other scandal stories crept onto page one. The head of Harding's Veterans Administration, a Mr. Forbes, was indicted by a grand jury for selling hospital supplies direct from the warehouse, and Senator Burton K. Wheeler, like Walsh a Democrat from Montana, began investigating the behavior of Harding's Attorney General and reputed bagman, Harry Daugherty.

The *Post,* which seldom ran cartoons, ran a couple designed to minimize the scandals: one showed the Mexican eagle wrestling with a snake labeled "The Usual Revolution" while the American eagle sat in relative calm atop a teapot labeled "The Dome." The soothing caption said, "We All Have Our Troubles." The other showed a Senator busy reading a paper headed "Gossip, Rumors" while stacks of papers labeled "Needed Legislation" and "Appropriations" went untouched.

Mr. Doheny was featured in the single staff-produced story on Teapot. It quoted from a letter he had written and it was headed "Muckraking To Affect Election Is Beclouding Oil Issues Says Doheny," and the *Post*'s columnist George Rothwell Brown noted in a paragraph on the other side of the page, "Mr. Doheny takes his pen in hand and dashes off a snappy essay on politics and gelatin backbones." The backbones, clearly, belonged to the Republican Senators who were now criticizing Fall and demanding that Daugherty resign.

Two enigmatic telegrams sent by President Coolidge to Ned in Palm Beach, which might or might not have referred to Fall or Teapot, were read into the record at the Senate hearing, and the *Post* exploded in righteous indignation. It ran a collection of editorials from around the country on the front page, headed "Leading Newspapers of the Nation Denounce Attacks Upon President," but the *Post*'s own lead editorial that day was on a perceived national improvement in industrial relations.

The end of the *Post*'s ordeal came on March 13, when Ned finally took the stand. He sat across from the Senators, his elbows on the table, and spoke softly.

The *Post*'s banner the next day said, "E. B. McLean Answers Clearly and Frankly All Questions of Senate Oil Investigators," but the story, again by Associated Press, showed him in somewhat less favorable light.

It quoted him, clearly, frankly and at length:

"I was trying to go down the line as far as I could for a friend. I have never done a dishonest thing in my life, financially. I have never had anything to do with this damned Teapot Dome thing. This is really the truth. You can decode telegrams, you can look through them for the next year, and you will never find anything dishonest I have done."

Evalyn would note later that Ned escaped punishment "thanks to a child-like manner when responding to questions [and] to a squad of high-priced lawyers."

The ordeal sent Ned further into retirement. He hired as editor Colonel George Harvey, the politician in whose smoke-filled hotel room Harding had been chosen as the Republican Presidential candidate in 1920. Harvey had an impressive editorial background. He had been a reporter on the Springfield *Republican* and the Chicago *Daily News*, managing editor of the New York *World*, president of Harper Brothers, editor of *Harper's Weekly*, and editor and publisher of the *North American Review*. He still had high political connections—he had just finished a stint as Coolidge's Ambassador to the Court of St. James's, he had furnished Coolidge with a campaign slogan, "Coolidge or Chaos" (which the candidate had not used), and he was living in the White House. He was, however, strikingly unqualified to be the editor of a responsible paper. He regarded newspapers as tools to be used in political wars, he had a violent temper, and he was an across-the-board bigot, anti-Catholic, anti-Semitic and anti-Negro.

He dominated Ned, and the *Post* staff found it dangerous to disagree with him.

"To have him work for one," Evalyn would remember later, "was something like having a tiger as a pet—a most flattering arrangement as long as the tiger likes his keeper. Once the hating mechanism of George Harvey got in motion it never seemed to stop."

Ned paid him $75,000 on a one-year contract, and Harvey ran the editorial pages as he saw fit. On one occasion he wrote a poem, intended to be comic, about a mouse eating the Host on a Catholic altar. John Major, afraid to confront him directly, faked a telegram from Ned ordering him to kill it. On December 22, 1924, Harvey ran a Christmas editorial in which he chose to say something on behalf of one he regarded as an underdog.

"As we approach the season of Yuletide, when hearts are warmed by emotions of forebearance for saints and charity for sinners, it would seem fitting that somebody should say a good word for the devil. . . ."

In the twenties most Americans still took the devil seriously, and thousands of readers canceled their *Post* subscriptions.

With one thing or another both the *Post* and Ned were slipping badly. The paper lost money in 1924, for the first time in decades, and the losses would rise. Eugene Meyer and William Randolph Hearst each offered to buy, but Evalyn, who wanted to keep it for her sons, refused to sell.

The most capable staffers, including star reporter George Rothwell Brown and a young man named Ed Folliard, went over to the *Herald.* In 1929 the stock market crashed, the Great Depression began, and the *Post*'s decline acclcerated. Gin and drugs and destiny caught up with Ned and he had a final mental collapse while trying to whoop it up in Montreal. He was shipped home and put in the Sheppard and Enoch Pratt Hospital in Towson, Maryland, outside Baltimore. The American Security and Trust Company, in which the McLeans had heavy holdings, was named the paper's trustee and Ned was removed as publisher.

Evalyn would later sum it up. "Ned lives on," she wrote, "a fancied fugitive in an asylum where he pretends with characteristic slyness that he is someone else who does not know McLean."

CHAPTER

7

The Meyers had been leading less spectacular but more productive lives.

In the twenties Eugene put together the biggest deal of his life, merging his company, National Aniline, with General Chemical, Solvay Process, Semet-Solvay and the Barrett Company. They were the four richest firms in the field.

Before the plan was well under way, the other companies began to spread rumors designed to drive the price of National stock down, to undermine Eugene's position in the deal.

On Labor Day, 1920, Dr. William H. Nichols, of General Chemical, sent his son to Eugene to say National Aniline would not be included as a full partner. Eugene suggested arbitration. Nichols the younger declined.

Eugene sent a message back to the father. "I'll give you twenty-four hours to make up your mind to take our terms or agree to arbitrate."

If he didn't, Eugene said, he would accuse the Nicholses publicly of conspiring to drive his stock down and would take them to court.

The Nicholses and their associates retreated, and National was merged as one of five equals into Allied Chemical. Allied would make $212 million in profits in the next ten years and would pay $134 million out in dividends. It would continue to pay through the years of the Great Depression and would boom in World War II. Eugene, who had never been poor, would now become unassailably rich.

It was now time by his life schedule to move into public service.

He had already made an impressive start. After the Russian fiasco Woodrow Wilson had appointed him to the War Finance Commission, which helped companies recover from wartime dislocations.

Eugene decided the commission had a broader mandate, "to preserve confidence in the whole economy." His boss, Secretary of the Treasury William McAdoo, did not agree.

Eugene arranged a confrontation. The Brooklyn Rapid Transit had been dislocated but not by the war. It had overextended its track system beyond profitable limits. Eugene wanted to bail the company out anyway and he and his business allies put pressure on McAdoo. McAdoo gave in, and the War Finance Commission loaned Brooklyn Rapid Transit $20 million.

McAdoo's successor, David F. Houston, proved a harder man to browbeat.

When Eugene wanted to loan $150 million to a group of export companies that had suffered no war-connected damages, Houston said no adamantly. Eugene, who may have been looking for an opportunity, resigned.

Agnes, who had become the most partisan of Republicans, said she was glad to see him leave the "rotten" Wilson administration.

When Warren G. Harding, whose administration would set new standards for rottenness, was swept into office, both Meyers were overjoyed and Eugene offered his services to the government once more.

Harding revived the War Finance Commission and put Eugene in charge and Eugene continued his permissive loan policy.

When Harding was stricken in San Francisco, his attending physician happened to be an old associate of Eugene's and a member of his national network of information gatherers. He wired Eugene that the President was fatally ill and Eugene was one of the first in Washington to know.

Calvin Coolidge named Meyer chairman of the Farm Loan Board, and *The Washington Star* would credit him with doing a "terrific job" of cleaning up the mess left by Harding's people. When Hoover succeeded Coolidge, Meyer finally got the job he wanted, the governorship of the Federal Reserve Board. It would not, however, prove as satisfying as he had hoped.

Agnes meantime had been seeking her own political destiny and cultivating powerful men. She returned to Westchester County, New

York, and her daughters in 1920, but Nurse Powell remained in charge of the nursery and Agnes saw little of them.

One spring day in 1921 she met William L. Ward, the Republican boss of Westchester, at a Republican ladies' lunch and she would remember it as "one of the curious moments of fate that have played such a decisive role in my life."

Ward was, in her words, a "very tall, broad-shouldered, aristocratic, eagle-eyed gentleman" and not at all what she had imagined a political boss to be.

"Young woman," he had asked, "what are you doing for your country?"

"Nothing," she replied.

"Do you mean to tell me that you can live in this beautiful country and not try to improve its government?"

Agnes said she didn't know where to begin.

"You begin at the front door," he replied. "Your town of North Castle is one of the few townships that have been Democratic. The women are voting now. Why don't you help get out the women's vote and elect a Republican supervisor?"

Agnes was swept off her feet.

She would call Ward "the last of the barons," a title that had a certain touch of reality since he had inherited a great deal of money and lived in a castle he had built himself. She also called him the "fighting crusader," which would seem somewhat less appropriate.

He was a traditional political boss and he told an enchanted Agnes that he had modeled his career on that of Tammany Hall's notorious Richard "Boss" Croker. As a young man he had sought out Croker and asked him what particular quality a political boss most needed.

A somewhat impatient Croker had replied gruffly, "Patience."

Young Ward persisted. "What else?" he asked.

"More patience," Croker replied.

Agnes would never be an effective politician (she would for one thing lack patience) but she would be an industrious one. She did get out the women's vote and she would be appointed a delegate to the Republican convention in 1924. After a bit she decided to run for Congress.

"Girl," Ward said when she told him, "you have to make up your mind whether you want to be an office holder or a boss. You can't be both at the same time."

Agnes decided to be a boss and Ward made her one by creating a five-woman County Recreation Commission with her as chairman. At her suggestion the County Board of Supervisors appropriated one million dollars for a country theatre, and soon the Metropolitan Opera was performing in Westchester County and the *New York Post* was crediting her with making it the center of music in rural New York.

Agnes also spent some active hours in Washington, giving elaborate dinner parties at her Crescent Place home (flowers were sent daily by Railway Express from Mount Kisco), where the guests, the discussions and the cuisine were international in scope.

"These functions were more than mere festivities," she would write immodestly. "Busy officials could talk their problems over after-dinner coffee more quietly than during their busy working day."

She came to some startling conclusions about her significance as a hostess.

Once she gave a party for a new prime minister (she did not say of what country) and she absentmindedly told him that his ambassador was well liked in town. The ambassador was soon replaced and she decided that her casual remark had, in his prime minister's view, ended "his usefulness to his home government." It is difficult to understand why.

She also continued to collect important men, and Eugene would watch with some annoyance although he was careful to learn as little as he could about the specifics of her infatuations.

One was with an Indian diplomat named Shrinvasi Sastri, with whom, she would later write, she journeyed "through leagues of emotions." Once when Sastri was leaving town and they were having a "few, hurried moments of conversation" Florence, her oldest child, came in with a warning, "Daddy wants you to know that he is at home."

She had an intense and enduring crush on the French Ambassador, Paul Claudel, a poet, playwright and philosopher. He would, in her dramatic phrase, put her "soul on the rack and stretch it to the limits of its capacities."

He would spend weeks at the Mount Kisco mansion, "making fun of my social work and urging me to save my soul, not by devoting myself to the welfare of others but by becoming a Catholic."

He was not, however, a man for crowds, and when too many

houseguests arrived "his spirit departed at once and his body followed soon thereafter."

There were many men in Agnes's private emotional life but one was central for years: Charles Freer, the multimillionaire collector of Oriental art whom she had met by chance at a Fifth Avenue gallery in 1913.

He was a polished man of the world and he became a business associate of Eugene's. To Agnes he was an added indication that some destiny was watching over her.

"What," she would ask herself dramatically when describing that first meeting, "is chance?"

There was as customary a disparity in their ages—she was twenty-six when they met, he was fifty-six.

He was her kind of man. Rich, cultured and unlikely to get too fresh.

She was beautiful and he was pathetically susceptible.

Once he and Stanford White, the architect of the original Madison Square Garden and scores of splendid New York homes, had hired young Italian girls to swim nude before them while they dined in a grotto at Capri. White would in time be shot to death by the crazy husband of his former teen-age mistress, but Freer would have a milder life and death. He had congenital syphilis and was doomed to a life of celibacy. This suited Agnes though she may well not have known the cause. She liked relationships that were titillating but not too compromising.

Eugene was as usual annoyed.

"He continued to insist that I invite a friend to accompany me into the dangerous lair of Prince Charming. Out of consideration for Eugene's sense of propriety and Mr. Freer's sense of the aesthetic, I first chose Marion Beckett and next Katherine Rhoades. Mr. Freer called us the Three Graces."

Together Agnes and Freer would sort the contents of hundreds of crates of Oriental art that his agents had shipped from China. Agnes would write a pretentious book, *Chinese Painting As Reflected in the Thought and Art of Li Lung-Mein,* as a result. It was beautifully illustrated and bound, but it read like selections from the *I Ching.*

The nation would get the Freer Gallery of Art in Washington, on the Mall between the Capitol and the Washington Monument, a lovely villa set on the green lawn containing a splendid but miscellaneous collection of painting, tapestries and room furnishings.

Agnes was still a mother.

She now had four children: Florence, Elizabeth, Eugene III (called Bill), and Katharine.

She and Eugene were both casual and demanding parents. Eugene drilled the competitive spirit into them—they were expected to do well in games, in school and in conversations at the dinner table. Competition was the central fact of family life—the parents spent most of their time apart and much of their time together in a perpetual game of dominoes that evolved into a perpetual game of gin rummy with a cumulative score. The children were kept to demanding schedules. In the summers at Seven Springs they made their own beds, attended breakfast, where they reported their school progress to Eugene, studied French and math from 9 A.M. to noon, and were drilled in French history and literature in the afternoon. Those who were nine or older were taken on extended pack trips in the West by Agnes some summers, on cruises with both parents on others. Sometimes they all went to Europe. On weekends the children rode and swam in the morning and played tennis and swam again in the afternoon. They were kept to the schedule, scolded and ignored by Agnes and expected to perform for Eugene.

In 1921, when Florence was eight, Elizabeth seven, Eugene six and Katharine four, Agnes had them recite pieces in French and German at Eugene's birthday party and they each presented him with a present made or bought with their own money. Agnes's own present was a letter that, as she put it, "might have been entitled 'To Any Man Who Is On The Road To Fame.' "

In the words of Eugene's official biographer, Merlo Pusey, "neither parent took time to teach the children the mechanics of living and Father's goading in the direction of success was often undercut by Mother's penchant for criticism and belittlement of what they did." Katharine, the fourth child, would seem clumsy to herself, in mind and body, and would avoid the competition as much as she could.

When Katharine was ten she told her mother that she had much enjoyed reading *The Three Musketeers.* Agnes replied that she could not have enjoyed it as much as she had, since she had read it at an earlier age and in the original French. When Katharine was a few years older she asked permission to have her hair bobbed. Agnes, about to leave for Europe, said positively no. Katharine had it bobbed anyway. When her mother returned, Katharine stepped forward, ready for a confrontation. Agnes didn't even notice.

When Herbert Hoover took office in 1928 the Meyers took a rest.

They were at Red Rock Ranch, the family spread at Jackson Hole, Wyoming, when the stock market crashed. Eugene came back at once to offer his services to the new President. Hoover was receptive—Eugene had contributed $25,000 to his campaign—and was soon telling Agnes that he was "the most valuable man I've got." He decided to make Eugene the governor of the Federal Reserve Board but there were difficulties.

The board was designed to be free of partisan influences. Its members, chosen by region, were appointed to twelve-year terms, and to put Eugene in charge both the member from New York, Edmund Platt, and the governor, Roy Young, had to be persuaded to resign.

Andrew Mellon, Hoover's Secretary of the Treasury, offered Young a job as governor of the Federal Reserve Bank of Boston. It paid $30,000 a year, more than twice the salary of the governor of the board. Young took it.

Platt was harder to budge. He was making $12,000 and he had eight years left in his term. His fellow members considered him "capable and fearless" and he liked the job's security.

Mellon arranged a position with a banking group that would pay $20,000 and called Platt to his office. Platt said he'd take it if the salary was raised to $24,000. Mellon agreed. Platt said he'd like to stay on until the end of September and Mellon said no, he'd have to go at once. Platt was so annoyed that he told friends he was thinking of killing the deal, but after thinking it over, he agreed.

No one on the board knew who the nominee would be, and Charles Sumner Hamlin, a member from Boston and a former governor, listed six possibilities, including Eugene, whom he considered the least likely since "being a Jew would be persona non grata with New York."

Hamlin was surprised but not displeased when Eugene was appointed, sworn in on September 16, and immediately nominated for governor.

Some Congressional Democrats were suspicious of the swift movement of events, and Representative McFadden, chairman of the House Banking and Currency Committee, questioned Platt and

Young, but they did not tell all they knew and the appointment was approved 72 to 11.

Eugene set out at once to remake the Fed staff, bringing in Floyd R. Harrison and Chester Morrill, who had worked for him at the Farm Loan Bank. He also set out to remake policy. The Fed resisted.

Hamlin, a mild man, soon decided that Eugene was "a little bit inclined to be arbitrary." Later he wrote that "Meyer thinks Hoover and he constitute the Federal Reserve Board" and by the end of February he was writing, with bitterness, that Eugene was "an opportunist, something like Lloyd George . . . ready, apparently, to jump on either side of any great question . . . rude and almost insulting."

Eugene in turn felt frustrated by the Fed and he shifted his energies in another direction. Hoover wished to set up an agency to be called the National Credit Corporation which would make loans to banks. Eugene liked the idea but wanted to go further. He suggested that the corporation be created as an interim organization. It was and in the next few months it loaned $155 million to 575 banks, a relatively small amount.

Meanwhile he went ahead with his more ambitious plan, to bring back the old War Finance Commission under a new name, the Reconstruction Finance Corporation, and with greatly expanded powers. He, Harrison and Morrill, acting in the name of the Fed but without the knowledge of its members, drafted a bill to set up the RFC. Hamlin found the situation "grotesque." As drafted, the bill would make Eugene, the Fed governor, a member of the RFC board as well. But he had enemies. Charles E. Coughlin, the radical Michigan priest, castigated him as one of "Four Modern Horsemen of the Apocalypse —Morgan, Mellon, Mills and Meyer"; and Congressman Fiorello La Guardia, the future Mayor of New York, tried to amend the RFC bill to keep him off the board, losing by only eight votes, 131 to 123.

The RFC with Eugene as its first president was much praised by Henry Luce's *Fortune* magazine, but his relations with the other members of the Fed continued to deteriorate, and he was losing much of his influence with Hoover. The President would call him to his unpretentious fishing camp on the Rapidan River in Virginia to ask his advice on how to handle the ex-veterans of the World War who were camped on the edge of Washington demanding a bonus. But he would then ignore it.

In turn Eugene, according to Hamlin, began making "very discourteous remarks about Hoover, and when Hoover made former Vice President Charles Dawes the chairman of the RFC board he considered quitting. He didn't, and Hoover was soon complaining that the RFC was "all Meyer and not enough Dawes."

Hamlin thought that Eugene "seems all at sea as to economic conditions . . . [he] has little or no initiative . . . [he] loves money lending as done by the RFC but has no time and only languid interest in Federal Reserve matters . . . [he] has a total incapacity to work with anyone else."

Agnes disagreed. She wrote:

"I know the whole Washington crowd considers Eugene unbearably dictatorial but I doubt whether a really great intellect ever got anywhere with soft words. What they cannot get away from is that he knows his stuff as nobody else does."

Franklin Delano Roosevelt swept Hoover from office, and Hoover, a bad loser, asked his top appointees to resign en masse on Inauguration Day. Eugene said no. His term on the Federal Reserve Board had seven years to run and he wanted very much to stay.

Agnes wrote: "Eugene is nearly killing himself . . . he has no support anywhere. The President goes ahead without consulting him, the Board is no support whatever and Woodin [the new Secretary of the Treasury] flutters between the White House and the Treasury like a butterfly with a broken wing."

The new Congress solved the dilemma. It passed a law aimed precisely at Eugene: it said no one could hold two top federal jobs at the same time. Eugene, an old poker player, knew it was time to drop out. He resigned from the Federal Reserve on March 24, 1933, the same day Agnes fell in love with Paderewski.

CHAPTER

8

Eugene went to his Seven Springs estate in Mount Kisco, to recover. It was a glamorous retreat on a bluff overlooking a lake. A Palladian mansion had replaced the century-old farmhouse and there were twenty-four servants, indoors and out.

It was time for him to reexamine his life plan.

His opportunities for government service in Democratic Washington were gone so he considered being a big Republican frog in a small Republican pool. Boss Ward, old and ailing, asked him to take over as the boss of Westchester County and, for the moment, he said yes.

Cissy Patterson, the publisher of the Washington *Herald,* came to see him to ask if he intended to buy the bankrupt *Washington Post.* She knew he had tried to buy it in 1925 and again in 1929 but he said no. She was pleased since she intended to buy it herself, but he was not telling the truth.

Cissy, a raddled redhead who had kept her figure but lost her beauty in the course of a wild, impulsive life, would not forgive him and she would be a dangerous rival. She had enormous energy, drank too much, had many flagrant love affairs and did whatever she felt like doing, whenever she felt like doing it.

Eugene told Boss Ward he'd decided to go back to Washington and he hired a lawyer named George E. Hamilton to act as his agent. Hamilton was a friend of Samuel H. Kauffmann, one of the owners of *The Washington Star,* and Eugene believed that the curious would assume that Hamilton was acting for Kauffmann, not for him.

The *Post,* which had been profitable for decades, had been ruined by Ned's bizarre management and was unable to pay its newsprint bill. It was in receivership and was offered for auction on a sunny afternoon in May. A man from the American Security and Trust, the trustee, stood on the steps of the old gray-stone building and asked for bids.

He was surrounded by somber men in dark, vested suits, some wearing Panama straw hats, some in old-fashioned boaters—creditors, worried employees of the *Post* and a half-dozen bidders. Bascom Timmins, a Texas newsman, was looking for a bargain. Cissy and a representative from William Randolph Hearst, the *Herald*'s owner, were there to buy a morning monopoly. Ben McKelway, editor of the *Star,* was there to keep her from getting it, and Evalyn Walsh McLean, who had borrowed bidding money on the Hope diamond, was at an upstairs window looking down on her agent below. She hoped to buy it back for her sons.

The man from the bank opened the bidding. Hamilton raised the first one by $25,000 and kept raising and wishful dreamers like Timmins dropped out. Evalyn ran out of money and the Hearst man quit at $825,000. Cissy asked the auctioneer to call a recess while she phoned Hearst but Hamilton said he'd withdraw if he did and the auctioneer said the *Post* was going, going, gone.

Hamilton refused to name his principal, and to shake off anyone who might follow, he took a cab to the Meridian Hill Hotel, walked in one door and out another and then crossed Sixteenth Street to Eugene's Crescent Place mansion.

The mansion was closed for the summer but Eugene and his aide, Floyd Harrison, were inside among the dust covers. Hamilton reported his success and Eugene was delighted—he'd been prepared to pay two million dollars.

A *Washington Star* delivery truck pulled up in the curved driveway and the driver got out and knocked on the door. Harrison answered. The man asked if Mr. Meyer was in. Harrison, feigning surprise, said no. The truck left and Eugene had Harrison drive him to the airport, where he bought a ticket under an assumed name and flew to New York.

His daughter Katharine, a high school junior, was with a friend taking the college boards when she heard that the *Post* had been sold.

"Nancy and I sat speculating who had bought it. I had no idea. When I was through taking the boards I went up to Mount Kisco and

I heard my mother say something to my father about 'when you take over the *Post.*' I said 'What?' and my mother said, 'Oh, darling, didn't we tell you? Daddy bought the *Post.*' "

Eugene later told friends that he had been afraid that if the Democrats had known what he was up to, they might have tried to block the sale. Evalyn did try. With the help of her lawyer, Charles Evans Hughes, Jr., she asked the court to reopen the bidding but the bankruptcy receiver objected and the court ruled the sale was final.

On June 13 the *Post* carried a discreet announcement on its front page, signed by the publisher:

"It will be my aim and purpose steadily to improve The Post and to make it an even better paper than it has been in the past. It will be conducted as an independent paper devoted to the best interests of the people of Washington and vicinity and hopes to have their interest and support. I think I should, in this connection, make it clear that in purchasing The Post, I acted entirely on my own behalf, without suggestion from or discussion with any person, group or organization."

The *Evening Star* offered its editorial opinion that the *Post* was now "under the direction of . . . a broad-minded, capable and public-spirited man."

Publishers and papers often speak in platitudes and they usually speak of their own intentions with a kind of awed respect. Eugene would later say, more casually, "I bought a newspaper because it's a place of ideas. If you study out ideas and translate them . . . you exercise power." He would also say, "People like to be told what to think."

The paper he had bought was housed in a tall, narrow, grime-streaked, mouse-gray, forty-year-old building on E Street, diagonally off Pennsylvania Avenue. It was a good spot to watch the frequent parades that moved down from the Capitol to the White House.

It was musty upstairs and smelled of printer's ink below. An open-air elevator, just big enough to hold three fat men, jerked and swayed from floor to floor. Copy boys and timid visitors used the narrow, splintered stairs.

The city room was on the first floor, sports and advertising on the second and the women's department on the third.

The presses were held together with wire and accumulated muck and the few unimaginative pictures used looked as if they'd been engraved on stale bread.

The paper that emerged was poorly written, poorly edited, without coherent direction and read by a relative handful of people. The circulation had been 75,000 in happier days but it had dropped to less than 50,000. The competition was brutal. The *Star* was dominant. It ran the Board of Trade, picked the District Commissioners, and had a headlock on local advertising. Even its newsboys had a superior air, freshly scrubbed and neatly dressed, pulling fine sturdy wagons stacked with neat piles of papers. The paper, like the boys, was both proper and dependable.

William Randolph Hearst had two papers, one, the *Herald,* run by Cissy Patterson, and the *Evening Times,* run by a series of men including George Preston Marshall, the future owner of the Redskins. Both papers were harum-scarum, irreverent, unreliable and readable. The *Daily News,* founded in 1925 as a Washington showcase for Scripps-Howard, was a sassy tabloid run on a shoestring by a capable man named Lowell Mellet.

The *Times* and the *Herald* had the sensation lovers. The *News* depended on street sales and was the noontime reading of government workers. The *Star* had some of each and everybody else.

Cissy's *Herald* was the *Post*'s direct competition. Cissy had a huge private fortune and little respect for tradition, discretion or high-mindedness. Her paper was a mirror of her tastes, enthusiasms and biases. She wrote highly personal, often eccentric, front-page editorials attacking enemies and whatever friends had recently annoyed her. She fought dirty. She also knew how to run a profit-making paper. When she took over, the *Herald* and the *Times* had a total deficit of $1,363,000. Ten years later, after she had combined them, they made a profit of one million dollars in a single year.

She immediately picked a fight with Eugene.

The *Post*'s most conspicuous editorial assets were its Associated Press franchise and four comic strips, "Andy Gump," "Dick Tracy," "Gasoline Alley" and "Winnie Winkle," which it bought from the Chicago Tribune–New York News Syndicate.

Cissy's brother, Joe, owned the New York *News* and her cousin, Colonel Robert R. "Bertie" McCormick, owned the Chicago *Tribune.* She was herself a major stockholder in the syndicate.

Cissy notified Eugene that she now intended to publish the strips in the *Herald.* Eugene asked his business manager if the comics were worth fighting for and he was assured that they were. His lawyer wrote the syndicate asking the status of the strips, and the syndicate replied that the *Post* had lost its right to them when it had gone into bankruptcy and Ned McLean had been replaced as editor.

Cissy phoned Eugene and asked him, as a gentleman, to let her have the strips. Eugene said no. Cissy replied, in her low, throbbing voice, "You know this means a fight."

Eugene asked Hearst to intervene but he said he couldn't make Cissy behave. Eugene asked Joe Patterson and Bertie McCormick to talk to her and they said they couldn't make her do anything she didn't want to do. For a while the comics appeared in both papers. Eugene sued. Judge Peter Schmuch ruled for the *Post* and Cissy appealed. When the court of appeals ruled against her, Cissy appealed to the Supreme Court. The Supreme Court declined to review the case and that was that.

The *Post* ran a triumphant front-page cartoon showing Andy Gump, Dick Tracy, Skeezix and Winnie Winkle trooping out of the Supreme Court home to the *Post*.

Cissy asked one last favor. The Sunday color comics were already printed and she asked for permission to run them one last time. He said she could if she also ran a front-page box saying that from then on they would be available only in the *Post*. She ran the comics but not the box.

She then sent Eugene a box full of flowers and hidden within the flowers was a pound of raw meat.

Inside was a note saying, "So as not to disappoint you."

Agnes was the first to get the message.

"It must be a pound of flesh [for] a dirty Jewish Shylock."

Eugene was greatly upset.

Cissy would never apologize though she did later say to a friend, "I guess I made a mistake that time."

Several months later a mutual friend arranged for them to meet at lunch and Cissy threw her arms around Eugene and he gave her a hug back but they would never be close friends.

The *Post* relied on the Associated Press to cover Bruno Richard Hauptmann's trial for the kidnapping of the Lindbergh baby while the *Herald* sent a man of its own. When the AP sent a false bulletin on the verdict, the *Post* printed a few hundred front pages with the headline "Hauptmann Guilty But Escapes Electric Chair." The error was caught in time before a single copy left the building but Cissy bought one from a *Post* pressman for $50 and ran a picture of it on her front page with the caption "False Verdict Fools Readers, Wrong Again."

Cissy would be a persistent problem as long as she lived but Eugene had a good many others that were more pressing.

When he bought the paper he rescinded a pay cut imposed by the bank, and a sense of euphoria swept the newsroom. It would not last. Eugene remained remote from the staff and made Floyd Harrison, his old aide, secretary-treasurer and editorial hatchet man. Soon new reporters and editors were being quickly hired and often quickly fired.

Carlisle Bargeon, a writer of sarcastic opinion who had left McLean's *Post* for the *Herald,* was lured back. The *Post* intended to syndicate him but when his heavy, ultraconservative political wit failed to catch on after a year he was sacked. McLean's last editor, Ira Bennett, was kept around for a few months, then replaced by Felix Morley, the public-relations man for the Brookings Institution, and Mark Ethridge took over the editorial page.

Under McLean the *Post* had been blatantly Republican and under the bank it had been neutral and as bland as a one-egg Depression cake. Now it became vehemently anti-Roosevelt. Eugene's strong feelings about the New Deal were apparent not only in the editorials but all over the paper. Small stories appeared under sniping headlines: "NRA Means Ruin Says French Chief"; "Bootblack Faces $10 Fine For NRA Breach"; "Pastor Thinks Religion Lack Handicaps NRA"; "British Woman Calls NRA Primrose Path To Socialism." In one longer wire story labor leaders praised the New Deal for putting 4.5 million people back to work but the headline said, "Labor Reports NRA Failure To Aid Workers." It was supported only by an incidental fact mentioned in the body of the story: while employment had risen, the average wage had remained the same. When the Administration took umbrage, however, the *Post* was inclined to back down. In early 1934 it ran a series entitled "The New Dealers" under a fictitious by-line, Jay Franklin. Each installment was preceded by the announcement that the publication of the series "did not necessarily imply editorial indorsement [sic]."

The anonymous author approved of the Administration's broad aim but was critical of some of its leaders. The installment that ran February 18, 1934, was headed "Farley, Flynn, Walker New Deal's Strong Arm Squad." A subhead said that "Genial Jim [Farley] Decrees Who'll Get the Spoils/Suave Ed [Flynn], Boss of the Bronx, Fastens Grip on Tammany/and Wool-Headed Fran [Walker] Coordinates." The most abusive adjective, "wool-headed," was a misprint; the text made it clear that "cool-headed" was intended. The article said the Squad members were honest, intelligent and efficient. It described other administration figures in unflattering but not vicious terms. Attorney General Homer Cummins was said to be "another politician though not a miraculously smart one. His real flair is for hero worship."

It seemed rather mild, but one of those described critically, General Hugh Johnson, the NRA administrator, responded in a national radio broadcast. He called the *Post* a "dying newspaper" and Eugene an "old Dealer—a cold-blooded reactionary who was one of the principal guides along the road to the disaster of 1922."

The *Post* replied mildly that it had a "high regard for Johnson's ability, energy and devotion to the public interest" but that it did not "admire his self control and temperance in public utterances."

On occasion the *Post* carried Eugene's own opinions on its pages, slightly disguised as news. When Congress restricted the sale of securities, Eugene collected statements from financiers, bankers and business executives denouncing the move and ran a full page of them. Congress felt the pressure and amended the act. In the spring he tried his hand at anonymous reporting with a front-page story by-lined Ernest Lamb. It was based on an interview with Senator Carter Glass of Virginia and it was headed, "The New Deal A Mistake Says Glass, Holding U. S. Will Regret It./Senator In Interview Tells Unvarnished Truth."

It began: "The New Deal, taken all in all, is not only a mistake, it is a disgrace to the nation and the time is not far distant when we shall be ashamed of having wandered so far from the dictates of common sense and common honesty."

Glass was described as a "man who is again seen by many emerging as the banner leader of his party, the most respected, the most feared, the most beloved of them all."

Some of the Senator's opinions were offered in direct quotes—"the suggestion that we may devalue the gold dollar fifty per cent means . . . dishonor . . . it is immoral"—and some were given indirectly— "in his opinion everything which this country has stood for, everything that has made the United States the happiest and freest place in which to live [has been] ruthlessly discarded by a lot of young jackasses called a Brain Trust."

The *Literary Digest* revealed Ernest Lamb's identity and noted that Glass and Eugene did not make strange bedfellows since the former was an "orthodox Virginia Democrat" and the latter an "orthodox Republican" and both were against the "liberal turn of the New Deal."

It was a singularly lopsided and tendentious story and Ernest Lamb never wrote again.

Eugene would say later that he had made every mistake possible while learning the newspaper business and his most notable ones would be in handling people. In the words of one otherwise admiring employee, he had "an unconscious contempt for his fellowman."

He moved Mark Ethridge from the editorial page to the business office, and Ethridge soon left to become the editor of the Richmond *Times-Dispatch*. Eugene made him promise that he'd take no *Post* executives with him, and when Ethridge later hired a *Post* reporter named Sid Olson and made him the *Times-Dispatch*'s city editor Eugene was furious.

He fired another reporter, Leon Dure, who had acted as a go-between and phoned Ethridge and accused him of breaking "a gentlemen's agreement." Ethridge wrote a mild letter back, saying he felt Eugene had been "unnecessarily offensive."

In November Eugene pushed the newsroom too far. He announced that from then on the business manager would pass on all editorial raises and promotions. There was an immediate revolt. Twelve editors, including managing editor William Haggard, presented Eugene with a list of demands, the key one being restoration of editorial autonomy. Eugene refused and the twelve quit, a brave thing to do in a bleak Depression year.

The remaining staffers were resentful and insecure and many joined the new American Newspaper Guild, the union founded by columnist Heywood Broun. They began organizing the *Post* with occasional help from Broun, who would come down from New York on weekends. Eugene decided to calm the militants with a fatherly talk.

He called the staff to the fifth floor and took his place on a platform at the end of the room. He told them the paper was losing money and that sacrifices must be made by all.

So far, so good but he went on talking.

He, personally, he said, had forgone his annual trip to Europe, and had not added to his collection of French Impressionist paintings.

Sam Lubell, a young business columnist, asked how much the *Post* was losing, and Eugene, flustered, said, "Do you want me to tell you before all these people?" Managing editor Alexander "Casey" Jones announced abruptly that the meeting was over.

The Guild militants were now in command and Eugene agreed to negotiate. A modest contract was signed, recognizing basic bargaining rights. Wages and hours continued as before: a $25-a-week minimum for reporters, rewrite men and photographers, rising to $50 after three years.

Raises above scale would be few and hard to get.

Eugene particularly liked the work of the business columnist, Sam Lubell, the young man who'd asked the embarrassing question at the meeting. When Jones offered Lubell a $5 raise, Lubell said he'd been expecting $10. Jones said if he didn't like it he could quit. Lubell did. A short time later he met Eugene walking down the hall and Eugene complimented him on his column that day. When he told him that he'd just quit, and why, Eugene looked uncomfortable and said, "Well, I still liked the column," and walked away.

The future was chancy. The answer to Lubell's question was that the *Post* was losing a million dollars a year, an enormous sum at the time. It was still mediocre and it had few faithful subscribers. Under Joe Meglia, Eugene's first circulation manager, it had achieved a circulation of 100,000 at a cost of $50,000, but one month's subscribers apparently quit as soon as the next month's signed up. It took 100,000 new orders a year to maintain the figure and it cost three times the revenue produced by street and home sales to do it. Even the total was suspect. The *Herald* ran a front-page picture showing *Post* deliverymen dumping stacks of papers in the Potomac, and Harold Fenton, who succeeded Meglia, had a squad of toughs known as "Fenton's Flying Circus" whose job it was to intimidate news dealers.

The *Herald,* with a solid circulation of 120,000, was far, far ahead. Eugene, making the best of bad fortune, told friends and advertisers that he was deliberately limiting circulation. He wrote Samuel E. Blythe, an old associate, that he was concentrating on Chevy Chase and other high-rent districts where the average family income was more than $45 a week.

"I am being very sordid about this," he wrote. "I am not selling the paper to any who haven't got an interest in buying goods."

The fight was not entirely lopsided, however. The *Herald* at that time was also losing money and in the spring of 1936 Hearst was ready to unload. Eugene offered him $600,000 and he initially agreed. Cissy heard of the deal at the last moment and called Hearst at three o'clock in the morning and cried, cursed, pleaded, threatened and finally offered to loan Hearst one million dollars if he would lease both the *Times* and the *Herald* to her with an option to buy. He would and did.

It was a logical time for Eugene to quit. He was losing a fortune —$1,306,036 in 1935 alone—and there was no prospect for profits. Andrew Mellon, an even richer Republican, offered to buy him out, paying all his accumulated losses with one million dollars added. Eugene declined. He had never been finally beaten in any contest and he could not accept his first defeat. In the words of his friend Elizabeth Young, "Mr. Meyer kept the *Post* because of his determination not to be a failure."

CHAPTER

9

Agnes at forty-six had two great interests, romance and politics.

One spring evening Paderewski had performed at her Westchester County Music Festival and afterward came to dinner.

"I do not care that he is one of the greatest living statesmen. I do not care that he is one of the world's greatest living artists. I am captured and held by the greatness of his soul and its indescribable beauty. Is it not significant that on the 24th [of March, 1933] a great meteor fell from the heavens? What a day. A great star falls from the heavens. Eugene resigns from the political firmament and I fall in love with Paderewski."

Agnes believed in the greatness of great men, in the righteousness of the Republican Party and in the superiority of the moneyed class. When the New Deal arrived she was appalled at its egalitarian tendencies. Her mentor, Boss Ward, had set up a restrained county public-works program, administered by himself, in competition with Roosevelt's Works Progress Administration, the WPA, but it was soon overwhelmed.

Agnes, who judged people to some degree by the condition of their heels, conducted her own investigation into the local WPA activities.

Friends "from all over the county" brought her lists of "disreputable people who controlled WPA jobs."

"The office of the WPA," she wrote, "put the worst type of down-at-the-heel ruffians in charge of our local works programs; they handed out the soft jobs to enrolled Democrats and the disagreeable ones to the Republican unemployed. This dishonorable behavior . . . was more than I could stand. I gathered the shameful record together in three articles and published them in *The Washington Post.*"

The WPA prevailed and Agnes did not suffer in silence. Back in Washington she appeared with Eleanor Roosevelt on a radio panel discussing the National Youth Administration. The NYA was run by one of Mrs. Roosevelt's protégés, a young man named Joe Lash. It was intended to provide part-time jobs for needy school kids.

Agnes attacked the program on what she termed "purely moral grounds."

If the government found it necessary to subsidize poor schoolchildren, she said, the money should be given to their parents directly, not to the kids. It was an interesting position for a woman who had split with her impecunious father and put herself through college.

The other members of the panel were clearly antagonistic and the audience responded to Agnes with catcalls, whistles and shouts. She struck back with an irrelevant, mean-minded question.

"Who do you think is the latest missionary sent from Washington to Westchester County to tell us how to bring up our children?"

After a pause she gave the answer.

"[It] is a female real-estate agent. This real-estate agent is going to get six thousand dollars a year. . . . She is Harry Hopkins's sister, Mrs. Aimee."

Harry Hopkins, the administrator of the WPA, was a trained social worker and so was his sister. She had sold real estate on the side.

The appointment was withdrawn but Agnes's outburst embarrassed the *Post* and Eugene. She later defended herself on the grounds that Mrs. Aimee (who was not in politics) and her brother "had laid themselves open to criticism and self-defense is the first law in any political battle."

Agnes would continue to write for the *Post* but at Eugene's insistence her stories became less political and slightly more restrained. Many were paeans of praise for her personal heroes.

One was for John Dewey, the philosopher of Columbia University, whom she'd met as a student. Dewey had investigated Stalin's charges that Leon Trotsky had betrayed the Russian Revolution and concluded that Stalin was wrong. When he came to Washington, Agnes interviewed him and the Sunday *Post* devoted a full page to her highly personalized essay. It was headed, "John Dewey, Great American Liberal, Denounces Russian Dictatorship—We Must Reform Our Own Democratic Method, He Warns."

It began:

"When the name Dewey is mentioned nowadays, the average newspaper reader thinks of the District Attorney-elect of New York County, but here is another Dewey who has been a great force in other phases of American Life for two generations before this brilliant young man appeared on the scene."

The story gave little space to the misadventures of Stalin and Trotsky. It was essentially a lecture by Agnes on political morality.

"When a pronounced liberal of Dr. Dewey's moral and intellectual eminence states, as he does in this interview, that Communism has collapsed and that America's radicals must review their whole position in the light of this fact, his views cannot be dismissed with the usual cry of economically conditioned prejudice. . . ."

Agnes would continue to write and she would write well but always tendentiously.

When she and Eugene went to Kansas in 1936 to meet Governor Alf Landon, an unpretentious farmer and oilman who was being promoted as a Presidential candidate by Roy Roberts, the publisher of the *Kansas City Star,* her story began:

"Two nights on the train from Washington to Topeka and two more to return was not a cheerful prospect but curiosity as to the reasons for the increasing popularity of Alfred Landon made obstacles of minor importance."

Agnes dutifully proclaimed the birth of the new statesman and her articles were reprinted and distributed by the Republican Campaign Committee.

She was always partisan and her judgment would soon be impaired by heavy drinking. According to the family's recollection, it first became a matter of great concern one day in 1936 at the Meyers' Red Rock Ranch in Wyoming. Her horse ran away with her and she was rescued by her youngest daughter, Ruth, and a cowboy, but once in the house she began drinking whiskey to calm her nerves. She became intoxicated and Eugene was furious. He would not speak to her the next day and she left the ranch in a fury and went off to a camp high in the mountains. She would later write of her flight, but not of the cause.

"I remained at our last camp, an idyllic spot at an elevation of 9,000 feet, for the enjoyment of complete solitude, which is essential every now and then to my well-being. In the afternoons I went on long solitary climbing expeditions. Every morning I lay in a shaded spot beneath giant trees next to a meandering trout stream and read, in German, Mann's *The Magic Mountain,* and his then recently published novel, *Joseph in Egypt,* while squirrels, mink and various birds circled around me, curious as to why I lay so still hour after hour. As when I first beheld Chinese painting, I fell in love—passionately in love—with Thomas Mann's style."

The children followed her up the mountain and, after some days, persuaded her to come down.

She had been a remote but demanding mother and she would remain demanding but would be less remote. Katharine, now in her late teens, would assume much of the responsibility for keeping her mother occupied. Agnes would resent it, remain critical but become increasingly dependent.

She had found she had a taste for alcohol but she also had a new passion. She wrote a long critique of Mann's work which ran in *The New York Times* as well as the *Post,* and she began an enduring correspondence with the author.

She would have a drinking problem of sorts for much of the rest of her life, but she would keep writing away. In 1937 she and Eugene went to Europe, she to visit the places in Germany where Mann had lived, he to seek out Hjalmar Schacht, who had arranged the financing of Germany's rearmament before Hitler had kicked him out of his cabinet.

The trip would not bring Agnes and Eugene closer together but it would drive Eugene and his editor, Felix Morley, further apart.

That spring, Spain was wracked by war, Germany was arming, France was in continual strife, England was quibbling and Amelia Earhart was flying toward her death.

Eugene and Morley went abroad to take the pulse of Europe. Agnes would operate alone and do a better job of reporting the essential facts.

Eugene and Morley visited London, Brussels and Paris and interviewed the countries' leaders. Morley went alone to Berlin while Eugene went to Vienna.

The results published were strikingly thin. Eugene's interests had always been primarily financial and Morley's irregular dispatches, from a frenzied Europe stumbling toward the Second World War, would focus on the gold standard, on a potential trade agreement between the United States and Britain and on the possibility that Premier Van Zeeland of Belgium would lead the world to an economic recovery. Morley lacked the craft and the instincts of either reporter or prophet. In Paris he predicted that Premier Léon Blum would earn a major niche in history as the builder of European harmony. A few days later Blum's government fell and the prediction with it.

Morley apparently interviewed no one during his time in Berlin. He described with mild humor his confrontation with two officious German customs officers at the border, and after visiting an exposition of Nazi accomplishments, he wrote that he "understood for the first time why the dictatorship is so popular with the mass of the German people." It was, he said, because the Party gave them a sense of accomplishment and security.

"No unemployment, no starvation and plenty of organized 'enjoyment,' that's what the Nazi government offers workers in exchange for the enforced surrender of their liberties."

It was quite possibly an accurate perception but an extremely limited one.

Eugene would complain, accurately, that Morley could have written half of his dispatches without ever leaving his Washington desk.

He was more concerned, however, with Morley's Quaker devotion to peace. The articles contained scarcely a suggestion that Germany was armed and arming for the purpose of rearranging Europe and that the other nations were all running scared.

Agnes did better. In a full-page Sunday feature she wrote about France's International Exhibition of Arts and Techniques. It began:

"There is scarcely a better place to study the social revolution and the political animosities which are shaking France and the other European nations." She went on to contrast, with great detail, the presentations and behavior of the Germans, the Russians, the Italians and the representatives of the various democracies.

On the boat returning, Eugene said to Morley, "Sometimes you argue to a point of exasperating me."

Morley replied, "If you wanted a yes-man editor you got the wrong person."

Eugene did want a yes-man editor. He wanted to have exclusive control over the paper's policies. Morley resigned in three years to become the president of Haverford College. Eugene assumed he was leaving because the college was offering him slightly more money.

He chided him, "You have the most important editorial job in the country and you are leaving to become the head of a boys' school." But he didn't offer him a raise. Only Eugene could have believed that the editorship of the *Post* was the most important editorial job in the country.

Lord Northcliff, the British press tycoon, had once said that he'd rather own the *Post* than any other American paper since it was on the breakfast tables of Congress every morning. But in the thirties, the Washington *Herald, The New York Times* and the New York *Herald Tribune* were also on the breakfast tables. All were more substantial and the latter two a great deal more influential.

Still the *Post* had gained both force and readers since Eugene bought it.

In 1938 *Time* magazine took notice of the fifth anniversary of the purchase.

"In five years The Post doubled its circulation (now 112,000), more than doubled its advertising lineage. By last year its $1 million annual losses had been reduced to $400,000. But Publisher Meyer was having too good a time with his newspaper to be fazed by such deficits. Last week he celebrated the anniversary of his entry into the Fourth Estate by announcing the acquisition of the foreign news service and fourteen features from The New York Herald Tribune, including Walter Lippmann, Dorothy Thompson, Mark Sullivan, Book Reviewer Lewis Garnett, Drama Critic Richard Watts Jr., sports columnist Richard Vidmer and the impeccable Lucius Beebe."

Time would remain the *Post*'s constant admirer for decades to come.

In 1941 it would describe the *Post* as "the capital's sole big league newspaper . . . a journal of national importance, a reading must on Capitol Hill, an institution of high character and independence in its bailiwick."

There were a number of possible reasons for the devotion. Eugene and Henry Luce, *Time*'s founder and chief, were Mount Kisco neighbors and Republicans of a similar stripe: foes of FDR's domestic New

Deal but strong supporters of his foreign policy. Clare Boothe Luce, the former Mrs. Brokaw, was also an old friend and admirer of Eugene's and before her second marriage she may have had romantic inclinations toward him. Katharine Meyer once told a friend that her happy home had been saved when Clare had gone swimming at the Meyers' pool and Eugene had seen her in a bathing suit.

When *Time* said the *Post* was big league it was exaggerating.

It now had legible type and an unjarring, uninspired, symmetrical makeup. It had a small staff of competent reporters, led by Ed Folliard, who had found Cissy Patterson's *Herald* too chaotic and had returned, and Robert C. Albright, and it had its new *Herald Tribune* features. But it had very little that distinguished it from the pack.

On a random day in April, 1940, its front page, laid out as neatly as a head of gray hair parted in the middle, had six serious stories, led by one headed "Allied Columns Converge on Trondheim." It and four of the others were from the Associated Press. Below the fold it had its compulsory light feature, "Census Supervisor Says Husband Wears Pants."

On page two, Harlan Miller's "Salty Comment on Washington Life" livened things up a bit. This day it was about Mrs. Roosevelt and the White House servants.

"Amid all her activities, Mrs. Roosevelt seems to keep an alert eye for the most capable intelligent servants in Washington to add to the White House staff. Twice recently I have heard Washingtonians lament that they have just lost their domestic jewels to the First Lady."

Mr. Miller added that Mrs. Roosevelt paid the servants $90 a month, considerably more than the going rate.

Eugene hoped to syndicate Miller's column but when he became a regular guest at Eleanor's informal Sunday night suppers he fired him.

The picture page that day offered a static and timeless scenic view of Old Point Comfort, Virginia, and some faraway disasters—a West Virginia flood and two train wrecks from New York. The women's page had "Mary Haworth's Mail," which was the *Post*'s first syndicated triumph. Eugene had developed that idea himself. He first offered a psychiatrist $10,000 a year to write it but when the psychiatrist wanted more, he had picked a serious-minded young woman staffer named Elizabeth Young and made her into Mary. Mrs. Young was a divorced Irish Catholic with two daughters and she took life solemnly. Her column was an instant, sweeping success. Mary consulted psychiatrists and others who were professionally wise but her advice was basically her own, crystal clear and blunt. She chastised philanderers and derided self-indulgence. She told a young wife who was reluctant to have her baby that her attitude filled her with dismay. On this particular day she was busy with a shy maiden who wanted a formula for social success. "The secret of being a good mixer is (I think) the unconscious conviction or assumption that one has an interesting, agreeable or stimulating personality," she wrote. "My advice to you is to concentrate (1) on making yourself as pretty as possible so that (2) you can attract a congenial beau. . . ."

The women's page also had Malvina Lindsay, another local, whose heavy-handed satire has not survived very well.

"Charges that Mrs. Henrietta DeGoofey was not only an 'agitator' and a fanatic but also a 'nobody' were made yesterday by Mrs. Marmaduke Wadd who is opposing Mrs. DeGoofey for the Presidency of the Do Something About It League."

The *Post* had lost Dick Tracy, the Gumps and "Gasoline Alley" to the *Herald* when its contract with the syndicate expired but it had Superman, Joe Palooka, Terry and The Pirates, Mary Worth, Donald Duck and nine other comic characters.

The sports pages had a bright young editor and columnist named Shirley Povich, who seemed to cover half the varied events himself.

The *Post* and Eugene's particular pride was the editorials. Felix Morley won a Pulitzer for a clutch of them denouncing Roosevelt as a "traitor to his party" but the ones on display this spring day were not impressive. Each had a one-column, slightly cryptic headline: "Symbol of Tragedy"; "A. F. of L. and Scalise" and "Mr. Farley's Views." They were neither lively nor persuasive.

Mr. Scalise, a union leader charged with extortion, was also featured in Elderman's uninspired cartoon, showing a short man labeled Scalise and a large AFL standing before a stern judge.

On the opposite page syndicated columnist Mark Sullivan praised young Tom Dewey, the Republican hopeful, for being more of an isolationist than FDR and Walter Lippmann predicted, erroneously, that Hitler was about to invade Sweden. Westbrook Pegler, in his syndicated column, gave newspapers in general hell for using syndicated columns instead of developing some of their own.

On the same day the other Washington papers were bigger and better. The *Star* had a cartoon by its superior cartoonist Clifford

President Harding and Ned McLean. Ned's dashing wife, Evalyn, had briefly hoped that their close friendship would save her husband from a life of drink and drugs.

Photo courtesy the Library of Congress

Florence ("the Duchess") Harding and Evalyn Walsh McLean on the houseboat their families leased together. The President's wife relied greatly on Evalyn for social guidance.

Photo courtesy the Library of Congress

Ned and his lawyers on their way to testify before the Senate's Teapot Dome Committee. Ned had earlier lied to Senator Thomas J. Walsh in an attempt to save Interior Secretary Albert Fall from prison.

Photo courtesy the Library of Congress

Ned in Atlantic City shortly before being confined in a mental institution. In his last days he would deny that he was—or had even heard of—Ned McLean.

Agnes's beauty was a type of the popular Gibson Girl look.
Photo courtesy the Library of Congress

Agnes put herself through Barnard College with an assortment of jobs. She is the blond young woman standing on the far right by a class of East Side children she taught one summer.

Photo courtesy the Library of Congress

The Seven Springs farmhouse. Eugene bought this century-old farmhouse at Mount Kisco, New York, before his marriage to Agnes. Years later they tore it down to build a Palladian mansion.

Photo courtesy the Library of Congress

Eugene and Florence, his oldest child.

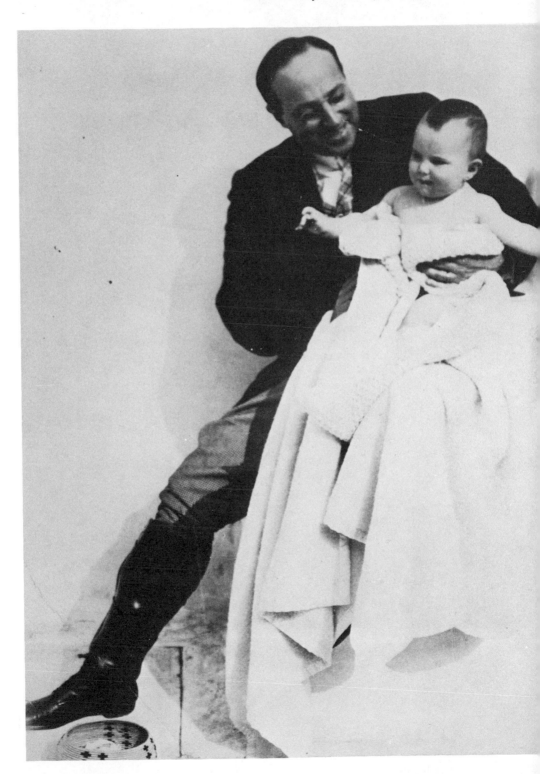

Agnes and Florence. Despite the madonnalike pose, Agnes was, by her own admission, an indifferent mother.

Photo courtesy the Library of Congress

Berryman on the front page (a gang of tough kids with the faces of FDR, Robert Taft, James A. Farley, Senator Arthur Vandenberg and the Republican "Boss" Pew picking on a kid in fancy pants with the face of Tom Dewey).

The *Star* had stories from Europe's new war, written by special correspondents as well as by the wire services, and it had a reporter named John C. Henry at Warm Springs, Georgia, with FDR and Prime Minister Mackenzie King of Canada. It had dozens of local stories written by local reporters and dozens of local pictures all through the paper. It had editorials on local subjects (the tax increase) as well as national (Scalise and the WPA) and international ones (stalemate in Norway). Since it was Shakespeare's birthday it had a poem by one Norman Stackey that began: "Immortal Mind! Your Alchemy has taught/Men to endure life's stings . . ."

It had columnists David Lawrence, Joseph Alsop, Robert Kintner, G. Gould Lincoln and Constantine Brown. It had its own sports reporters at a track meet in New York and a baseball game in Boston and it had Grantland Rice and John Lardner as special correspondents. It had Dorothy Dix and Mutt and Jeff, Moon Mullins and Little Orphan Annie.

The *Post*'s morning rival was now the *Times-Herald*. Cissy Patterson had merged the *Times* and *Herald* into one twenty-four-hour paper the year before. It was at least as impressive as the *Star*. It had squads of talented reporters headed by John O'Donnell, Frank Smith and Thomas Stevens at home and Sigrid Schultz and Donald Day abroad. It had the Chicago Tribune News Service and a first-rate cartoonist named Orr. On the editorial page it had a very long examination of the Scalise case with a picture of Scalise and it also had a very short editorial headed "Stop Dewey Movement," which said, in its entirety, "The Republican Old Guard and the Democratic New Deal have agreed on one thing at least, that the Republicans should on no account nominate Thomas E. Dewey for President." It had squads of sports writers, Vincent X. Flaherty, Charles Barbour, Maury Fitzgerald, Dick O'Brien, Frank "Buck" O'Neill and a sharp woman writer named Rhoda Christmas.

It had Ted Cook's "Cook-Coos" on the comic page as well as "Dick Tracy," "The Gumps," "Bringing Up Father," "The Lone Ranger," "Smilin' Jack," "Gasoline Alley," "Popeye," "Blondie," "Barney Google and Snuffy Smith," and "Believe It or Not."

CHAPTER

10

The *Post* did have some things going for it as the forties began, and one was a new staffer named Katharine Meyer.

She had graduated from the University of Chicago in 1938 and worked for seven and a half months as a reporter on the San Francisco *Examiner.* She spent her days on the waterfront covering the adventures of Harry Bridges, the radical union organizer, and her nights in glamorous gowns at balls and elegant dinners. She loved it but her father summoned her home.

Time, the faithful family chronicler, said: "To Washington, D. C., came comely 21-year-old Kay Meyer, daughter of Publisher Eugene Meyer, to handle for $25 a week The Letters To The Editor department. Said Father Meyer, 'If it doesn't work, we'll get rid of her.' "

Since she didn't want to be conspicuous as the publisher's daughter, she went to work on the editorial-page staff instead of out in the city room. She worked hard and discreetly, writing crisp and clear editorials, most of them on small subjects.

She also fell in love with a tall, gangly young lawyer named Philip Graham. He had been born in a South Dakota mining town and had moved with his family to Florida while still a child. He had gone to public schools and the University of Florida and Harvard Law, where he'd been president of the *Law Review* and had been tenth in his graduating class. He'd been a favorite student of Supreme Court Justice Felix Frankfurter and had served on graduation as law clerk to both Frankfurter and Justice Stanley Reed.

Kay fell in love the night they met. When she brought him home to dinner, her father showed him an Elderman cartoon showing Justice Hugo Black in the white hood of the Ku Klux Klan. Graham said the cartoon was unfair, that Black's recently discovered brief membership in the Klan had been nothing more than the indiscretion of a young Southerner. Eugene was impressed with his resolute young guest.

When rather ordinary ice cream was served, Philip gave Katharine an ironic compliment on the "rich Semitic dessert" and she was delighted at his impudence. When a college friend came to Washington she proudly introduced her to Phil. The friend's shoes squeaked and Phil said, "I see you have new shoes," and Katharine was delighted again. She was twenty-three and he was twenty-five.

They had three dates in rapid succession and on the third he told her that they were going to be married and added, "I hope you don't mind having two dresses because I'm not going to take a lot of money from your family." She was delighted once more.

Phil delighted many people.

"I went to a party at which Kay was a guest," a friend of hers remembered, "and I saw this tall man, slightly disheveled, and my first thought was that he looked like a young Lincoln and my second was that he must be Kay's young man. He was very like Lincoln; he was beautiful with anguish."

Eugene received Phil as a beloved son—he seemed genuinely interested in everything Eugene had to say. Agnes was also enraptured. Phil, she made it clear, was without a flaw.

He and Katharine were married on June 4, 1940, on the lawn at Mount Kisco. As Agnes watched she said to columnist Malvina Lindsay, "There's no doubt who'll wear the pants." Agnes was drinking more, particularly when she had nothing to keep her busy. Phil was given the difficult job of keeping her occupied and he did it well. "It was tough on Phil," Katharine would say later, "but it saved my father."

Eugene was enjoying himself. He locked up the liquor supply and since Agnes was still too proud to buy a secret supply, her sobriety was encouraged if not assured, and in October, 1941, he went to London by himself and had a private conversation with Winston Churchill. Churchill said, "I don't want to fail to impress on you that anything you can do to hasten your entry into the war, which is coming sooner or later, will be helpful."

Eugene, according to his official biographer, merely agreed that the United States would get in, sooner or later.

It would be sooner.

On a December Sunday afternoon the Meyers and forty guests were at their cabin above the Potomac, sitting around open fires, when the phone rang. It was the city editor, and Eugene turned and said, "Pearl Harbor has been bombed by the Japanese." There was a long silence and then Supreme Court Justices, Cabinet members, Senators and lesser men rushed to their cars without saying good-bye.

Agnes became involved in the war that summer. She and Eugene were in constant conflict.

Both Phil and Bill, the Meyers' only son, were about to go into the service. Agnes had been spending her time in her den, which she called her "Chinese Room," writing a book interpreting Tolstoy, Dostoyevsky and Thomas Mann.

She met her son and son-in-law in the library by appointment.

"I know how important your book is, Mother," Bill said, "but to us there is just one thing that is more important today than anything else. That's beating Hitler. While Phil and I are away we'd like to feel that you are doing your special kind of job here at home."

Phil took over.

"You know your way around Washington and you know the grass roots. It will take a lot of doing to keep the federal government in touch with local problems. Many of them are bound to be a headache. Bill and I think that's where you come in and where you can be most useful."

It was an artful presentation. Agnes was proud of her career as a Republican Party worker and recreation commissioner in Westchester County. She considered herself a vigorous defender of the rights of local governments. She did not, however, take their advice. A far more exciting opportunity soon appeared.

Craig McGeachy, a minister at the British Embassy, suggested that she fly abroad and write about the way the British government was handling war production and social adjustments.

On September 2, 1942, she and a friend named Elizabeth Taylor flew across the Atlantic in an army transport. Her tour, organized by

Britain's National Council of Social Service, took her to Edinburgh, Glasgow, Clydeside, Newcastle, Tyneside, Bristol, Cardiff and a mining town in Wales. Prearranged appointments filled all available hours. She returned and wrote six articles for the *Post* which were distributed by the Associated Press and later collected in a book.

McGeachy assured her that they were the "best description of Britain's social militarization that has yet been printed in the United States." Edward R. Murrow sent a note merely saying that she had done a "better job than most of the visiting firemen."

The articles were pure propaganda but they had a certain force. Agnes was a good, crisp, clean writer, a great deal more skilled, for example, than Editor Morley or Publisher Meyer, but she could not keep herself out of the story.

She began her British series with an announcement.

"With food rationing growing tighter in the United States and with the draft of 18-year-olds just around the corner, the war is being brought home to us as never before. Having foreseen this development in our country, I decided to fly to Great Britain to find out what effect similar measures had had upon a democracy in many ways akin to our own. . . .

"Priority on the Clipper was granted me so promptly by our government officials that I arrived in London before my letters of introduction had reached the various ministries. . . ."

Had Agnes covered the second coming she might have begun, "Who, I asked myself as the dark young man with the glowing eyes and the long hair approached me with his arms extended, is this?"

The six articles were mostly about heroines of all classes, including Agnes herself—"I ate in workers' canteens and British restaurants . . . I slept in factory hostels." There were the standard anecdotes about resolute members of the lower classes who seemed to speak in slogans, but the articles did contain clear and instructive information on how Britain had managed the evacuation of children and the drafting of young women to work in the factories with astonishingly little turmoil. Agnes was a New Journalist, twenty years before new journalism arrived.

The forties were eventful years for young Mrs. Graham. She saw Phil as infinitely superior to herself and she quit the *Post* to give him her full attention. Agnes was her rival.

One day at Seven Springs, Phil and Agnes were having a chat when Katharine walked up with her children.

"Pardon us, dear, we're having an intellectual discussion," Agnes said, and sent her on her way.

When Phil went into the Army Air Corps in 1943 Katharine went with him, first to Sioux Falls, South Dakota, then to Air Corps intelligence school in Harrisburg, Pennsylvania. When he went to the southwest Pacific she came home and wrote a weekly column for the *Post* called "Magazine Rack." She was frequently pregnant—she lost the first baby, then had Elizabeth, who was called Lally, and Donald. She was content.

"Phil Graham was so glamorous that I was perfectly happy just to clean up after him. I did all the scut work, paid the bills, ran the house."

They lived at first in a $75-a-month house in middle-class Burleith, on the edge of a Georgetown that was just beginning to be fashionable.

They soon moved on. Phil had once warned Katharine that she would have to make do with a dress or two, but in truth they lived unostentatiously but well. A young friend who had also married a rich wife told Phil to relax and let his wife spend her own money since he was obviously destined to make a great deal of his own. He did.

"I spend a great deal of money in a quiet way," Katharine once told Elizabeth Young.

Eugene was content as well. He had not lost a daughter but gained a son and, as always, he had other things on his mind. He now had solid, significant influence in wartime Washington. His arch rival, Cissy Patterson, of the *Times-Herald,* and her brother, Captain Joe Patterson of the New York *Daily News,* had been among the first and most ardent supporters of Roosevelt's domestic program but they had broken with him when he showed increasing support for Great Britain and had reminded him often and angrily of his promise to keep America out of war.

When bombs fell on Pearl Harbor, Patterson had gone to the White House and offered Roosevelt his full support but he had not been graciously received. FDR had given him a harsh lecture on past sins and that had been enough for Joe and Cissy.

Eugene's record was more to the President's liking. He ran the *Post* in his spare time and went to the White House for weekly conferences with Roosevelt. He hoped for an exalted appointment and was disappointed when the President named him to the Labor Mediation Board, but he did his best to settle management and union arguments in war industries and he kept on promoting the Presidential line.

FDR cited the *Post* editorials as examples of clear and positive thinking, though some of them were more loyal than logical.

After the fall of Luzon in the Philippines, in April, 1942, the *Post* gave a drubbing all around: "The tragic fact is that the heroes of Bataan were finally blasted out of their foxholes because we as a Nation have been painfully slow in disciplining ourselves for sacrifices that are insignificant compared to theirs."

It did not say how, within five months after Pearl Harbor, the Nation possibly could have gone to the rescue of General Wainwright and his outnumbered troops, sick and surrounded, thousands of hostile miles from home.

Eugene now had the title of Editor himself. Herbert Elliston, an Englishman who'd worked on *The Wall Street Journal,* was the associate editor and nominally in charge of the *Post*'s editorial pages but he was not a forceful man. Casey Jones, the managing editor, who ran the newsroom, intruded on his turf with impunity, writing his own frequent, fire-eating front-page editorials whenever he felt the urge. Both deferred to Eugene; his was the last word and on one occasion it led to his being manhandled. Elliston had written an editorial entitled "Mr. Jones' Excuses." It concerned Secretary of Commerce Jesse H. Jones and what Eugene considered his failure to provide an adequate supply of raw rubber. Eugene saw it in proof and added a sentence: "The chief reason for his [Jones's] failure is a boundless ambition for power that has led to his taking on more than he can successfully manage."

That evening Eugene and Jones met at the annual Alfalfa Club dinner at the Willard Hotel. Jones, a very large man, took Eugene, a rather small one, by the lapels and shook him severely. Eugene's pince-nez glasses fell to the floor and, according to his own account, he swung twice at Jones's jaw, missing both times.

The Administration, if not Mr. Jones, was pleased with the *Post* which gained, illogically, a latter-day reputation as an early and ardent supporter of the New Deal, the liberal conscience and civil rights.

It was not. On one occasion it offered a short-tempered response to a letter writer who said the South's poll tax discriminated against Negroes.

"Our critics make the flat statement that there is no denying that the poll tax discriminated against the Negro more than against the white . . . to say a tax which applies to everyone discriminates against one race is to play fast and loose with the intrinsic meaning of that word. . . ."

Eugene was having an eventful war and so was Agnes.

After touring Britain's war plants, she toured America's. In Britain she had found heroines, in America she found villains. Agnes lacked sympathy for ordinary members of the working class. As a young woman she had worked briefly on the New York *Sun,* had quit and gone to Europe on borrowed money and had never worked at a regular job again. Now she displayed a low tolerance for the ways of the young who had grown up in a grinding depression and were working in defense plants in what were often the first full-time, paying jobs of their lives. She patronized them when they behaved and tongue-lashed them when they took time off. In one article she offered some unlikely quotations to illustrate their casual ways.

"What did the workers have to say about this game of peek-a-boo they were playing with the authorities? Most of them laughed.

" 'We just take a couple of weeks off and get a release or we go into non-essential industry for a while and then go to any defense plant and get a new job. You can't blame us for shopping around for the highest pay.' "

Agnes could and did. She berated them at length for "joy riding from plant to plant and city to city." Many, she said, were merely "irresponsible" but others were "spending all they earned in order to be eligible for relief again when the boom days were over."

In Seattle she was outraged by the wilder side of the wartime boom.

"The invisible, nameless, but no less powerful underworld forces, the leeches, panderers and racketeers as firmly entrenched here as in many of our big cities . . . never fight in the open, but work relentlessly to keep their hold on the rich graft to be derived from the prostitution racket."

Agnes also had her adversaries at home. Managing Editor Jones was one. The *Post* had cut its news space to make room for ads, leaving on the average about five pages a day for news and features. Much of it was needed to report the war. Agnes toured the Southwest and wrote long, long articles about the miserable conditions of migrant workers. Jones refused to run them. She persisted.

"As the Publisher's wife I could not remonstrate with the paper's management," she wrote later. "The Managing Editor finally relented sufficiently to try them out on the Washington public. The Post readers responded with so many enthusiastic letters and phone calls that the paper thereafter printed the New Mexico series and all the subsequent stories from Texas." What Agnes wanted, Agnes usually got.

CHAPTER

11

The war affected all the *Post*'s people. Most of the young men went off to war, a dozen as correspondents with the Marines. They were replaced at first by other young men and then more often by young women. Elsie Carper, the daughter of a northeast Washington grocer, had come to the *Post* fresh from college as an assistant librarian. When the librarian went into the Army she got his job. When the picture editor left she got his. Then she was made assistant city editor.

"I was twenty-three and I was assigning reporters to cover stories and sending out photographers, reading copy, and it was marvelous, the things I was allowed to do."

Young people came and went and often had a wonderful time. There were bookies in the composing room and the sports writers kept their bottles on the fire escape, which they called the "brink of destruction."

Sometimes a kind of reckless gaiety took over. Once in 1942 a young man named Howard Dutkin and another named Tom McBride slipped a bogus news release into the city desk mail. It was datelined London and appeared to have been issued by the Royal Ornithological Society. It read: "Frightened by gunfire on the continent, millions of European birds are winging their way across the Atlantic and are expected to darken the skies over Washington, D. C., on or about [a certain date] on their way to breeding grounds in the south. . . ."

Joe Cloud, the day city editor, a hard drinker of uncertain temper, was intrigued. He put the bird item on the news budget and waited for developments. Dutkin had several days off and he spent them calling the *Post,* posing as the Royal Society's Washington spokesman, and giving progress reports. Cloud assigned a copy girl to sit by the window and watch the skies and sent reporters out to scout the countrysides. He put the bird story in the news budget each morning and waited hopefully all day. Managing Editor Jones became impatient and started asking Cloud when the skies were going to be darkened. McBride became alarmed and when Dutkin returned he told him the time had come to confess. Dutkin, fortunately a racetrack companion of Cloud's, went up to the city desk and said softly, "Joe, there are no birds." He was not fired, since there was a chronic shortage of experienced people, but he was moved to the copy desk.

The youthful exuberance did not make up for a shortage of experienced people. The *Post* had five top reporters. Ed Folliard, the senior and the star, covered the White House and the young men copied his relaxed air and wide red suspenders. Bob Albright covered the Senate, and Christine Sadler and Mary Spargo covered the House and most of the burgeoning wartime federal bureaucracy.

Ben Gilbert, who'd been rejected in the draft because of a sinus condition, arrived and covered the Office of Price Administration and the other new agencies. It was a job that required stamina rather than finesse. The government news was delivered daily in neat packages at a huge press room in what would eventually be the Department of Health, Education and Welfare building. Gilbert gathered it all in— information about production controls, gas rationing, labor relations —and on many days he'd have two or three front-page stories.

"We had a joke," a copy editor remembers, "Gilbert's stuff came in not by the page but by the pound."

The wartime *Post* was a strange package. The editorials varied in quality of logic and presentation but they were unquestionably the paper's most distinguished ingredient. They were wrapped in a few pages of news, mostly from the wires, a few features, sports, comics, syndicated columns and an occasional long essay from Agnes. Nevertheless by 1943 the paper was finally making a small profit. That year it had a circulation of 150,000 (nothing sells papers like a war) and 12 million lines of ads (nothing sells ads like a shortage of newsprint).

On a random day that year, eleven of its thirteen stories on the front page were wire stories about the war and half of its twenty-four pages were devoted to ads.

It was however slowly improving and in 1945 hit a modest peak. Eugene belatedly sent two reporters overseas to cover the war, Ed Folliard to Europe and Sports Editor Povich to the Pacific, and he decided to hire a cartoonist. He sent his aide Wayne Coy around the country looking for the best and Coy found Herbert Block. Eugene met Block at the Yale Club in New York, gave him a copy of the *Post,* said "I hire good people," and offered him the job. Herblock took it and for years he would make the *Post* look better than it was.

In September, Eugene took a special team—Elliston, Albright and Ben Gilbert—to San Francisco in a special train to cover the founding of the United Nations. He was now almost seventy years old and ready to retire. He was respected in the profession if not beloved. He was chatty with four newsroom favorites—Elizabeth Young, Ed Folliard, Shirley Povich and Bill Gold, a sentimental columnist who devoted much space to finding homes for surplus cats. Two were Irish Catholics and two were Jews. Eugene believed that the Irish and Jews had "a heritage of intuition" that made them good reporters. They were chatty, too, but they knew, intuitively, that they should not be familiar. They always called him Mr. Meyer. "He was very shy," Katharine would say later.

In October he had his birthday and in December he turned the *Post* over to his son-in-law Phil Graham.

The birthday was celebrated at a luncheon at the Statler with four Supreme Court Justices, six Cabinet members and eight ambassadors among the guests. President Truman sent a message: "You simply haven't time to grow old." It was a time to look back.

His marriage had survived. He and Agnes would now and then play a continuing game of gin rummy before the fireplace but his patience had grown thin. He had often said that she might be a headache but never a bore. Now one day when a bundle of her copy came to his desk, he said to Elizabeth Young, who was sitting across it, "You know, she's beginning to be a bore."

The children had grown up in an atmosphere of rivalry.

A family friend would describe the usual lunchtime atmosphere. "There was a tone of banter; everything had a tinge of irony. You would be mistaken for a boob if you refused to spend all your vital energies in irony."

Katharine, the least competitive, felt at a constant disadvantage.

"It was a family of strivers. I'd sort of given up. We were all fired up, the success syndrome was pretty strong. I regarded myself as not very articulate. I think I was adopting a good formula for survival."

Florence, the oldest, had tried to elope at sixteen and had been stopped by the family chauffeur. She had gone to Bryn Mawr and had had a succession of romances which her mother had broken up. She became a dancer and appeared briefly on Broadway in Max Reinhardt's *The Eternal Road.* When she was twenty she wrote her father, "I wish we'd had more time to talk before we both went in opposite directions." They hadn't and they never would. She married a Hollywood actor, Oscar Homolka, in 1939 and divorced him in 1946.

Elizabeth, the second child, had rebelled constantly. She had gone to Vassar, to the University of Munich, to Barnard, to Columbia. She had studied the violin, had worked as a scriptwriter in Hollywood and had married Pare Lorentz, the producer of the celebrated Depression documentary *The Plow That Broke the Plains.*

Bill had gone to Yale and the London School of Economics. He had visited Russia and had concluded to his father's distress that the Russians were building "a really constructive society" and had considered going to Spain to fight against Franco.

He had decided that he did not wish to inherit the *Post* and had gone to Johns Hopkins medical school. He had served as a doctor in the war, had returned to study psychiatry and had married a proper Boston girl named Mary Bradley.

Ruth, the youngest, had simply graduated from Sarah Lawrence, become a wartime nurse and married Dr. William A. Epstein, an obstetrician.

The children could show a public closeness on great occasions such as Eugene's birthday party, when Elizabeth read a rhyming skit, but beneath the jocularity family tensions still ran high.

CHAPTER

12

Katharine had been her father's favorite from the start. Once, while he was riding in Rock Creek Park with Alice Longworth, he had said, "Watch my Kay, she's the one."

She was, as he had noted, the child most like himself.

She was loyal to father, husband and children. She had an analytical mind behind an emotional nature. She was determined and she learned from her mistakes. As a teen-ager she had stayed with her father in Washington and worked as a copy kid at the *Post* while her mother and the other children were spending the summer at Mount Kisco. She had shared the Crescent Place home with her father, two shy people alone at dinner served by silent servants. She had gone to Madeira School, slipping out pale-faced in the winter mornings and putting on the lipstick her mother forbade while the chauffeur drove her to school.

It may be that Eugene would have preferred Katharine as his successor rather than Phil, but if he did he couldn't admit it to her or, perhaps, to himself. In the 1940s, proper young women did not aspire to be publishers.

Katharine was proper, a tall, shy, diffident young matron. She acquired a proper accent at Vassar and a patrician's sense of democracy at the more rough-and-tumble and demanding University of Chicago, where she'd hung out at Hanley's, the poor students' bar, and embraced the mild radicalism of the New Deal. When she graduated in 1938 her father and mother were too busy to come to the commencement. As a reporter in San Francisco, she fought her shyness by forcing herself to ask people what she considered awful questions. She had enjoyed herself along the way but had not taken herself very seriously.

"I was brought up in the old school. It never occurred to me that I could do anything. It was part of our upbringing that we would work because my mother was fixed on the idea that we not be just rich children. She used to tell us all the time that we wouldn't just sit and clip coupons. So I could picture myself as working but not in any high-up position. I think it was typical, no women thought they could do anything."

When the family was all gathered at Eugene's birthday party he made his announcement. Phil Graham would be his successor. Eugene had told friends, "I've got to know what will happen when I'm no longer around." He was founding a dynasty.

When he made his offer, Phil hesitated.

"Phil was playing Hamlet that afternoon," Joe Rauh, a Harvard classmate and an old friend, would remember. "I didn't understand why. All I could see was that Meyer had offered him a hell of a job, a great opportunity."

Phil took it. On January 1, 1946, he became the *Post*'s associate publisher and the obvious heir.

"It never entered either of our heads that we would go into the paper," Katharine would say later. "Phil loved politics and he was thinking of going back to Florida and starting a law practice and getting into politics. His inclination was to stay away from the family. He didn't want to be a rich man's son-in-law."

The job was an opportunity, not a sinecure.

"My father said, 'Look, this is no bed of roses I'm offering you, it's just a shot at it.' I guess he didn't know how rough and tough it was going to be. We would have to fight every day to survive. Phil used to get so exhausted he'd think he was ill."

Six months later President Truman appointed Eugene the first president of the World Bank and on January 1, 1947, Phil became the *Post*'s publisher. He was thirty-one. Katharine was twenty-nine.

"We led a very odd life, very young, the life that publishers lead. Phil didn't like it very much and used to avoid a lot of it. It was interesting in theory but a lot of the realities were not, they were just grinding. The work was so hard, so tough and so depressing at times but he did it terribly well and one reason, I think, was that everybody had to do their own thing and Phil was, by nature, an involved person. First of all he was fascinated by power."

Wes Barthelmes, a reporter and for several years the leader of the *Post*'s Guild unit, would see a good deal of Phil and remember clearly the first time they met.

"He came across as a driver, purposeful. He wanted to do a great deal with the *Post* and he wanted to do it in terms of Phil Graham, not as somebody's son-in-law. Talking to him was like talking to someone in the barracks, one of the boys. How much of that was contrived, I don't know."

Phil and Eugene were very different men. Eugene was usually courteous, sometimes ruthless, often angry, always distant. Phil was a charmer.

Eugene had wanted acceptance; to advise Presidents and suggest national policies; to be an important man in the great world. Phil wanted more: a direct role in the shaping of the nation's destiny. He would manipulate people and believe, sincerely, he was doing it for their and the nation's good. He was a benevolent elitist. He thought big and spent freely and he used the *Post* as a means to a variety of ends.

"Phil took the old man's millions and threw them around," a *Post* veteran who worked under both remembered. "Meyer was cautious. When he built the building on L Street in 1951 it was too small before they moved in. Kay said her father told her he didn't build it any bigger because he didn't want to wind up in the real-estate business."

Under Phil the *Post* would wind up in a good many businesses including real estate.

When he took over, Herbert Elliston was running the editorial page and Casey Jones the newsroom. Ben Gilbert was city editor. Jones was made an associate editor, a title that would come to be associated at the *Post* with imminent departure. He left soon to be editor of the Syracuse *Herald Journal* and was replaced by Russell Wiggins, who had been an editor in St. Paul, Minnesota, and Phil's friend and fellow Air Corps intelligence officer during the war. More recently, as a special assistant to the publisher of *The New York Times,* he had read the *Times* cover to cover each day and reported on its contents.

Alfred Friendly, who had left the *Post* to join Air Corps intelligence, returned to be the man below Wiggins. He was a graceful writer, born rich, who would pursue status, for himself and the paper, in the salons of Georgetown.

Gilbert, a less prepossessing but more dedicated man, was the team's essential member.

He would remember the first palace revolution with pride.

"Casey Jones didn't care for what he called 'bleeding heart journalism.' When Phil Graham came on the scene he benched him and put Russ Wiggins into the job. Russ was a newspaperman of conscience and he encouraged this type of reporting."

Each of Phil's loyal lieutenants helped change the *Post*.

Wiggins made it stuffy and gave it a righteous tone. The *Post* had not been quite respectable. He made it solemn, serious and moralistic. When he arrived he called the staff together to warn them against the "Jehovah Complex," the illusion that they were the final judges of what the public was entitled to know. It was a sound sermon from an odd man. During Wiggins's long tenure the *Post* would play Jehovah every day.

He was more consistent in pursuing lesser goals. The town's sports reporters had traditionally traveled to out-of-town games as guests of the ball clubs but the *Post*'s would do so no longer. Reporters on the other papers would continue to take all-expense junkets to New York, Hollywood and even, rarely, Europe, but the *Post*'s would stay home. No *Post* staffer was supposed to accept free tickets to movies, plays or horse races. *Post* baseball columnists could no longer serve as the paid official scorers ($20 a game) at Griffith Stadium. Reporters were told they could no longer take Christmas gifts from the people and organizations they wrote about and the drinking of coffee was outlawed in the city room.

Al Friendly was assistant managing editor. He found it difficult to win Washington's old society to the *Post* but he tried. The three regal families who owned the *Star* were on the high ground. Betty Beale, their society columnist, was the town's social arbiter and the confidante of Mrs. Merriweather Post, the breakfast food heiress, who supported the National Symphony. On one occasion a young woman from the *Post* found herself covering the symphony's annual ball and fund raiser from the back of the Willard ballroom while Betty sat at the head table gathering quotes. Friendly, a guest, was so alarmed at the arrangement that he took over, scurrying around until he had enough information to phone in a front-page box.

Ben Gilbert's impact was less frivolous. He hired, fired and herded the city staff. Hiring grew increasingly elaborate—he went yearly to Columbia's graduate school of journalism to find right-thinking recruits, and Elsie Carper, the wartime assistant city editor, was installed by Phil as chief of editorial personnel and she conducted preliminary interviews and administered elaborate examinations. The emphasis was on academic achievement. One reporter who worked at the *Post* in the early fifties described the process.

"I went through this unbelievable personnel rigmarole. There were aptitude tests and this test and that. I said to Elsie that I felt like I was being hired for assistant vice-president or something and she said archly, 'Well, maybe you are.' It turned out I wasn't. They took great pains to get people who could speak nine languages or had just graduated from the Institute of Lower Slobovian Studies or something and then put them covering police in lower Fairfax County forevermore. They broke their spirits. It was a kind of institutional conspiracy."

CHAPTER

13

Gilbert drove the staff relentlessly, in the direction that Phil wanted it to go.

"You came to work feeling apprehensive," one reporter recalled. "Apprehensive and unhappy from the moment you walked in. You never knew when the boom would fall. If one of the rules of good management is that you make people feel good, that you encourage them to do their best, that you compliment them, then Gilbert was the world's worst manager. He made you feel worthless. The older hands would wait when they were making out the weekly work schedule to see what days Ben was working so they could arrange to have those days off."

Gilbert was Phil's front-line commander and together they would do more to change Washington than anyone had since "Boss" Shepherd, the city's governor in the 1870s, planted trees and paved hundreds of miles of untenanted streets.

They saw the *Post,* in Gilbert's phrase, as "a vehicle for positive change," and conducted endless crusades which seemed designed to change the lives of the city's ordinary people, black and white, poor and lower-middle-class, without consulting them.

The first was directed specifically at Robert Barrett, the city's chief of detectives. The police superintendent, a mild man named Callahan, was ill and ready for retirement. Barrett was his heir apparent. Barrett's uncle, Edward J. Kelly, had been superintendent and his nephew had the solid support of the *Star,* the *Times-Herald,* the District

Commissioners and the members of the District Committee in Congress. The *Post* was opposed. It set out, first, to prevent his appointment, second, to remake the department.

The police were not an easy target. Most white Washingtonians thought they were doing a pretty good job. Crime rates were low, and gambling and prostitution were confined to obscure streets behind unlighted doors. There was no bawdy night life. The few stripteasers around Franklin Square finished their acts wearing bras and panties less revealing than the one-piece dressmaker bathing suits on display at the Glen Echo swimming pool.

The force was, however, unselfconsciously racist and sometimes brutal. Burglaries in white neighborhoods received more attention than homicides in black ones. Prisoners were often held illegally and sometimes beaten. Those most likely to be mistreated were the young black men who were rounded up every time there was a rape or an armed robbery.

Barrett was a man of parts, both the department's most decorated and most frequently censured cop. Ben Gilbert saw him as a "crook and a brute."

The *Post* soon had an opportunity to launch its attack. Barrett had been cooking the crime statistics to make his division look good, not recording many burglaries and other crimes against middle-class property owners. A department rival swiped hundreds of suppressed crime reports from Barrett's desk and brought them to the *Post.* Phil himself carried them up to the fifth floor to be photographed, one by one, and the next day Gilbert splashed the story all over page one. It was a good story but not good enough to keep Barrett from being named superintendent. The *Post* dug in for a campaign that would last four and a half years and violate many standards of fair reporting. Reporters were assigned to produce at least one antipolice story a day. Most of those produced were interviews with persons who shared the *Post*'s views, or quasi-editorials.

At one point Phil asked President Truman to have Barrett removed but Truman replied, "Mr. Graham, if I am any judge of character, Major Barrett is a fine police officer."

Barrett was eventually brought down but not by the newspaper.

In 1951 Phil arranged for the Senate subcommittee on crime in Washington to lend a hand.

The Senate investigators sent twenty-eight-page financial questionnaires to the top cops, asking detailed and personal questions about their finances. Some answered and others declined. The *Post* finally had a pair of triumphant headlines: "Barrett Overspent Income $17,400 in 33 Months" and "Beach Suspended After Failure to Explain $5000 in Cash." Captain Beverly Beach, a Methodist elder, was found guilty by a police trial board of taking a $300 donation from a Georgetown matron for a precinct Christmas party that had, apparently, cost considerably less. It was a crime of relatively small proportions but Beach was forced to resign. He later shot himself.

Barrett's leave-taking was less dramatic. He took his pension. As Merlo Pusey put it in his official biography of Eugene Meyer, "the Chief was forced to retire under charges that remained nebulous because he invoked the Fifth Amendment."

On other occasions, when witnesses invoked the Fifth at Congressional hearings, the *Post* had defended their right to remain silent. It did not do so this time.

Barrett left a few scars behind. He discovered that Gilbert had once been a member of the Young Communist League and spread the news. Gilbert, who had seemed destined for the heights, remained city editor for twenty years. It was generally assumed that Barrett's revelation had kept him from rising.

The crusades went on. Friendly and Gilbert developed a type of nonobjective reporting they called "stream of news" coverage. It consisted of developing stories that supported a *Post* cause and suppressing ones that did not. The paper's greatest commitment was to the swift, painless racial integration of public facilities. The same general goal was supported by the *Star* and the *News* but with less involvement. In 1949 Ben Bradlee, the *Post*'s future editor, who was then a young reporter working for the city desk, was sent to cover a racial clash at a public swimming pool in southwest Washington.

"A guy named Jack London and I were covering the East Potomac Park riots. The Progressive Party was trying to integrate the pools and these crazy Wobblies were taking these little black kids into the pool and there were riots, dreadful race riots. One day two hundred whites and two hundred blacks fought a pitched battle all day. Sixteen or seventeen people went to the hospital and it was just luck that nobody was killed. London and I were there all day and we covered it like Dunkirk. We talked to the cops, we talked to the little black kids, we talked to the Commies, we talked to the rednecks. We finally went back to the paper about nine-thirty at night and found that the story had been put back on page seven in the B section. The riot was described as an 'incident.' We had dictated with missiles flying over our heads, and the word incident had not crossed our lips—it was a riot.

"I was tired and very emotional and I had a fight with Gilbert. I said, 'Jesus Christ, it's all true what they say about you.' And I said, 'This great fucking liberal newspaper can't even say what happened.' An awful lot of mouth for a young kid, right? I suddenly felt this little touch on my shoulder and I turned around and there was Graham in a tuxedo. He said, 'All right, buster, come on up with me.' I went upstairs and there in Phil's office, also in tuxedoes, were Clark Clifford, Julius 'Cap' Krug, the Secretary of the Interior, Oscar Chapman, who was Undersecretary, and Phil making an unbelievable big deal. The *Post* would keep it on page B-seven and call it an incident, if they would agree to close the pools the next day—all the pools, not just the one the blacks were trying to get in—and if the pools would be opened the next year on an integrated basis.

"Probably pretty wise. Probably a good deal. But unthinkable to me. I don't think you can pay too great a price for telling the truth. The point was that if we'd put this on page one and called it what it was, you might have had the 1968 riot in 1949. It might have been better if we had. I can't make the judgment but I'm sure no one else can either."

The *Post*'s concern with integration was often more visible in public than in private. It hired Simon Booker, its first black general reporter, in 1952, well before the other Washington papers, but it made no effort to make him feel comfortable. He was allowed to use only one designated washroom and he was given carefully chosen assignments. He quit after two years because "it was a real tense situation and had me neurotic."

When Representative John Davis, of Georgia, created a subcommittee to investigate discipline and violence in the integrated schools of the District, Gilbert assigned a three-reporter team to write instant rebuttals, which he ran next to the testimony. It was an unabashed display of journalistic advocacy.

Later one of the team, Grace Bassett, went to Friendly with a troubled conscience.

"I told him I believed in the same goals as the *Post* but I didn't think it was right for us to print only stories that supported our point of view and suppress others. He just glared at me."

Ms. Bassett resigned a short time later.

It would be a long time before black reporters felt comfortable at the *Post* but the *Post* would continue to offer itself as an unremitting foe of racism and it would continue to suppress stories of racial strife.

In 1962, when thirty-two persons were injured after a football game between St. John's, an almost all-white school, and Eastern High, an all-black one, the *Post* treated the outbreak as a display of high school spirits. Columnist Bob Ade pointed out that punches had been thrown even at games between Ivy League colleges. The next day Booker, the black reporter who had left eight years earlier, wrote a letter to the paper pointing out how deliberately misleading the *Post*'s coverage had been. The outbreak had been one-sided, he said, and had not been started by students from either school but by "gangs of toughs" who started "beating whites in an explosion of hate."

The *Post* had other crusades it pursued with equal fervor. In the fifties it set out to remake southwest Washington in the name of urban renewal. The Southwest at the time was 75 percent black. A *Post* reporter who was involved remembers it as a poor but pleasant place.

"There were small houses and they had dogs and yards and local bars—a neighborhood—and it was wiped out."

Wes Barthelmes covered the Redevelopment Land Agency, the government office in charge of the project, for the *Post*.

"The *Post* and the RLA worked hand in glove. The RLA threw out fifteen to twenty thousand people and then issued phony figures on how many tenants had been relocated in what was called 'decent, safe and sanitary housing.' The figures were patently false. They were made up. The *Post* ran them. We were supposed to ignore instances of duplicity on the part of the RLA. The *Post* had made up its mind that urban renewal was going to bring a shining new Washington and everyone had better get out of the way. The stories were very party-line. It was always full speed ahead. The executive director of the RLA used to call to complain if a story wasn't sufficiently upbeat."

Most of the displaced people moved into old houses in other old neighborhoods, often crowding two or three families into homes designed for one.

The renewal would be only a limited success. The Southwest

would in time have many handsome federal office buildings and streets of pleasant town houses and high-rise apartments. It would have Washington's outstanding repertory theatre, the Arena Stage, but its large, handsome movie theatre went out of business soon after it opened. It would have blocks of slummy public housing and a high after-dark crime rate. The second floor of its principal shopping center would remain without tenants, year after year.

The *Post*'s owners had one other involvement with urban renewal of a strikingly different kind. In 1947 Agnes Meyer bought a derelict mansion, locally called Henderson Castle, and its surrounding six acres, across from the Meyer home on Crescent Place, as an investment for her twelve grandchildren. The National Capital Planning Commission tried to include it in the city's second urban-renewal project but Agnes's lawyers fought the commission to a standstill and the project was dropped. The property was sold in the sixties to a private developer for $2.5 million.

The *Post* also crusaded for law and order but did it selectively. It would come down hard on some lawbreakers but be almost admiring of others.

Alan Barth, who had joined the editorial page in 1943, was an earnest champion of what he thought of as underdogs (Eugene Meyer once asked him, "Do you ever stop to think that the underdog might be a cur?") and he seemed to have a basic distrust of cops.

When the Royal Canadian Mounted Police broke up a Russian spy ring in Ottawa in 1946, arresting twenty-two persons, he made an earnest effort to ridicule the whole thing.

"One cannot but wonder . . . [he wrote] what the Russians were really after. Were they hoping, by any chance, to steal the whole Columbia River [atomic power] plant and ship it, brick by brick, to the Ural Mountains?"

When the RCMP later issued a detailed report on the arrests, the *Post* complained that unless the information stolen was of great value, "the whole thing seems to have been a great waste of energy and expense." It added, in what would become a familiar *Post* editorial equation, that the "practice of suspending civil rights on the pretext of national security is quite as disturbing as the spy plot itself."

In 1948 the *Post* ran a series of editorials denouncing the behavior of the House UnAmerican Activities Committee, suggesting, among other things, that witnesses should be allowed to cross-examine other witnesses, a prescription that would, if nothing else, have produced some notable shouting matches.

When Whittaker Chambers, a *Time* magazine editor who had been a Communist agent before he became a fervent anti-Communist, told the Committee that his old friend Alger Hiss had been an active Communist Party member while serving high in the State Department, the *Post* took almost personal umbrage. Hiss had gone to Powder Point Academy, an acceptable prep school, to Johns Hopkins, an excellent university, and to Harvard's splendid law school. He had set up and coordinated the Yalta Conference and was the newly appointed president of the Carnegie Foundation. He flatly denied Chambers's charges and said, under oath, that he had never even known him.

The *Post* would wonder publicly "why the testimony of turncoats should be preferred to that of men whose reputations are otherwise unsullied."

As *Time* magazine would point out, the *Post* "doggedly sympathized" with Alger, and would take an enduring dislike to an intense young freshman Congressman from California named Richard Nixon, who would pursue Hiss in fits and starts.

When Hiss dared Chambers to make his accusations "outside the protected halls of Congress," Chambers spelled it out on a network radio program, saying that "Hiss was a Communist and may be one now."

Hiss made no reply for three weeks until, nudged by a *Post* editorial, which said it was time for him to "put up or shut up," he sued Chambers for libel. It proved to be his fatal mistake.

Chambers produced copies of stolen government papers that had been typed years before on Hiss's typewriter. Hiss lost the libel case and was indicted for perjury. His first trial resulted in a hung jury. He was convicted in the second. There was overwhelming evidence that Hiss had not only lied but that he had committed espionage, though his hard core of supporters would continue to offer fanciful explanations for decades to come.

Barth responded to the conviction with an odd editorial:

"Alger Hiss had the misfortune of being tempted to betray his country in an era of widespread illusions about communism and of being tried for perjury in connection with his offense in a period of cold war when the pendulum of public sentiment has swung far in the other direction. That does not excuse him or minimize the enormity of the crime of which he has been convicted."

Barth did not say "which he committed" and the *Post* would continue to leave loopholes in its editorials. Twenty-five years later, after writer Allen Weinstein, who had begun as a Hiss sympathizer, had examined the evidence compiled by both the prosecution and defense and had demonstrated beyond question in his book *Perjury* that Hiss was properly convicted, the *Post* would run an interview with Hiss in which Hiss would insist on his innocence but decline to discuss the evidence in the case. The *Post* article would describe him nevertheless as a "man whose case nags at the American conscience."

The *Post*'s editorials in the fifties exposed it to great criticism, some of it exaggerated. Representative George A. Donero called it "the Washington edition of *The Daily Worker*" and the rival *Times-Herald* echoed the label over and over.

The accusation was unsound. Eugene Meyer was a devoted champion of capitalistic free enterprise. The *Post*'s senior editorial writer, Merlo Pusey, was staunchly opposed to Stalin and all his works. Phil Graham had known Alger slightly and had been friendly with his brother, Donald, who also had been accused of being a party member, and he believed in the probable rectitude of people with old school ties, but he recognized solid evidence when he saw it and the evidence against Hiss was solid.

He would also grow wary of Barth. In April, 1950, Earl Browder, the head of the American Communist Party, appeared before Senator Joseph McCarthy's government operations Subcommittee and refused to answer selected questions. Phil, an elitist by assimilation, despised McCarthy, a vulgarian and an opportunist, but he was not about to embrace Browder. Barth wrote an editorial without Phil's knowledge.

"In refusing to identify and stigmatize certain persons whose names were presented to him, Mr. Browder was patently in contempt of the Committee's authority. But this contempt was pretty well earned by the drift and character of [the] questions. . . . Mr. Browder was as responsive as anyone could have wished to those questions relating directly to the McCarthy charges. . . . [Other Senators] saved the subcommittee from engaging in a kind of persecution that might have resulted in its punishing Mr. Browder for adherence to fundamental American decencies. Not everyone in America tests a man's loyalty to his country by his willingness to betray his former friends. The apotheosis of the informer is not altogether accomplished in the United States."

Phil read the editorial while on the train to New York. He was furious and decided to fire Barth, but his old mentor, Felix Frankfurter, talked him out of it. Instead the *Post* ran an explanation composed by Phil that dodged some essential points.

"The purpose of the editorial, which we regret did not seem to come through, was to show what a sorry mess we have come to when a communist can be put in the public position of upholding political freedom and opposing the doctrine of guilt by association. . . . The real question is the value of the testimony of communists, former communists and temporary exiled communists, where that testimony of dubious credibility may do permanent injury to persons of good character."

Later, after the Korean War, Phil objected to an editorial calling for a unilateral effort to end the cold war with Russia. He sent a memo to Robert Estabrook, then chief of the editorial page.

"A year or so ago it was clear to all of us that the Soviet system was one of total evil. . . . Co-existence, I submit, is every ounce a bastard idea, sired by wish and mothered by cold war weariness. . . ."

Phil was speaking out not only as a man with his own political philosophy, but also as the publisher of a paper in chronic financial trouble. The *Post* had no need for new enemies.

He wrote a long editorial, "The Road Back to America," in which he acknowledged the cold war and with some hyperbole spoke of the need for national unity: ". . . real reasons for concern exist . . . our country faces, and will continue to face, dangers greater than we have ever known. [We must] . . . meet them with a constructive program rather than hysterical fright. . . ." The editorial called attention to "the fanatical devotion of fifth columnists in every country abroad, including our own," and said it would be "reckless to ignore the circumstances" that permitted McCarthy to "paralyze American diplomacy and to thrust fears and doubts into the minds of our people."

The *Post* also had problems closer to home.

Phil's mother-in-law was a persistent one. In 1941 she came close to precipitating a boycott of the paper. Agnes had a long-standing crush on Paul Claudel, the profoundly French and Catholic poet, but she found domestic Catholics and their institutions less appealing. She was determinedly against parochial schools. To many a parish priest and to thousands of Irish and Italian families who sent their children to them, she seemed simply to despise their religion. Her daughter Katharine would conclude that she did not.

"My mother went to Buffalo one day and made a speech and she wasn't a bigot but she sounded like one. She was for federal aid to education and a lot of things the Catholic Church was then opposing and so she became very anti-Catholic, not because she was really bigoted but because she didn't like being thwarted. She made statements that sound awful—she made a speech saying no American mother would want her daughter to grow up to be a nun. It came over the wire and Phil sent her a telegram saying, 'I just want you to know I've put out a statement saying you have nothing to do with the paper.' We were already being boycotted by the Catholic Church but that would have brought the roof down."

Phil patched things up. Eugene and Agnes had one close high-ranking Catholic ally, Bishop Bernard J. Sheil, the head of the Catholic Youth Organization. At Eugene's suggestion, Sheil's "Message to America," an appeal to feed the hungry millions in postwar Europe, had been written for the *Post,* and at his further suggestion it was reprinted in the *Reader's Digest.* After the Buffalo speech, Phil ran many pictures of Bishop Sheil and Bishop Sheil said many kind things about *The Washington Post.*

The *Post* was also suffering from continuing financial difficulties. It advertised that 1948 was its greatest year in history, with new highs in advertising linage and circulation, but it was a hollow boast. The *Star* was far, far ahead in ads and it made a lot of money. The *Daily News* made a little. The *Post*'s chief rival, the *Times-Herald,* was having its difficulties too but it was far ahead in circulation, and its prospects, though confused, were bright. Cissy Patterson died that July and left the paper to her seven top employees, who would be known thereafter as the Seven Dwarfs. The arrangement was unwieldy. The Seven found it difficult to agree on management decisions and they were burdened by the need to pay estate taxes. They were ready to sell and Phil made them a secret offer of $4.5 million. He and Katharine were suddenly full of hope. He wanted the paper desperately and whatever he wanted, she wanted too. Then Eugene made the move that probably killed the deal. To make the transfer simpler for the heirs, he offered to buy Cissy's share of the Patterson-McCormick family trust. The trust controlled the Chicago *Tribune* and the New York *News.* Colonel Bertie McCormick, the *Trib*'s publisher, believed that Eugene was trying to get a foothold at the *Trib* and he made a counter offer. The heirs were glad to have the chance to keep the paper in Cissy's family and they took it.

The Grahams were devastated. Katharine wept for days.

"Colonel McCormick just took it and there was no way we could fight back. We were faced with the Tribune Company with about ten million dollars a year in revenue. It was appalling. Families feel so personally about papers when they're involved in them."

Phil slowly pulled himself out of a depression and returned to the war.

CHAPTER

14

Phil Graham played high, hard politics with apparent success.

His role was to be an *éminence grise* and the *Post* was his tool of power. One day when Wes Barthelmes, the Guild unit chairman, was visiting him, he plucked two books from his library shelf and handed them to Barthelmes.

"That's the kind of paper I want the *Post* to be," he said. Barthelmes looked at the covers, expecting to see books about some liberal, independent-minded paper like the *Manchester Guardian.* They were instead a two-volume history of *The Times* of London.

"I read all of one and most of the other, and the significant thing I got out of them was how close the alliance of *The Times* and the British Foreign Office had been all through the height of imperial power. *The Times* was always covering up stories. I think Phil wanted me to understand that he wanted the *Post* to be accepted, established, like *The Times.* "

He did. He wanted the *Post* to be, like *The Times,* the thundering voice of the ruling class, and he cultivated powerful people. He was particularly close to two—Lyndon B. Johnson, the Senate's majority leader, and Frank Wisner, the architect and administrator of the CIA's covert operations. The first connection was the more obvious. Katharine would think "Phil was very like Lyndon Johnson in a way and that's why they had a fascination for each other."

The Wisners, Frank and Polly, and the Grahams, Phil and Katharine, dined together each week. Wisner would refer to the CIA's worldwide undercover apparatus as his "mighty Wurlitzer." He also played the press. When Wisner wanted something from the *Post,* Phil was always glad to oblige. Joseph Alsop, *Post* columnist and a close friend of the Grahams (he would be the godfather of Lally's baby), boasted of his attachment to the CIA's founding fathers, his "close personal friends," and he went on CIA missions to the Philippines and Laos. There would be other *Post* columnists and staffers who had served as actual agents. It is impossible for an outsider (or for most insiders) to measure the significance of the various connections accurately but they would continue through the years. It may be that there was less to them than now meets the eye. The basic truth may be simply that many of the people who ran the CIA and many of those who ran the *Post* had grown up together, had gone to the same northeastern schools and universities, and married women from the same background.

Most of Phil's links were out in the open. He cultivated Senators and used their committee staffs to do the digging the *Post* couldn't do for itself. When the *Post* decided to wage a war against interstate criminals it sent Ed Folliard to New York to interview three prominent "tygoons," Frank Costello, Joe Adonis and Frank Erickson. It then arranged a Senate investigation to follow up.

Graham was also busy selecting Presidents.

In 1951 he decided that Harry Truman would have to have a proper Republican successor. He was, however, also opposed to the probable one, Robert Taft.

That July he wrote to a friend: "I think the most important thing ahead of us now is the election next fall. If we are going to blunder through four more years with leadership on either the Taft or Truman level, then I am nothing but a pessimist. As a result of this thinking I am becoming an Ike man."

Eugene and Wiggins visited General Dwight D. Eisenhower in Paris to sound him out, and in March the paper began running excerpts from his campaign biography, *The Man from Abilene.* In the same month, to the consternation of cartoonist Herblock, Alan Barth and other senior staffers, it announced that "We stand for Eisenhower."

The editorial said in part: ". . . the very air in the nation's capital is poisoned with scandal and corruption . . . twenty years of enjoyment of office has left the Administration blind. . . . This newspaper feels that

Eisenhower would be the dynamic force to rejuvenate our politics. . . ."

Phil's support of Eisenhower was apparently based on his belief that the General would do something dramatic to silence the opportunistic and reckless Senator from Wisconsin.

There was opposition to the stand but Phil stood fast. When Herblock drew a cartoon showing a bland-faced Ike saying "Naughty, naughty" to smeary urchins with the faces of Nixon and McCarthy, Graham refused to let it run in the *Post* and Herblock remained out of the paper for the rest of the campaign.

When the Democrats nominated Adlai Stevenson, a Meyer family friend, and when Eisenhower deleted a laudatory reference to his old mentor, General George Marshall, in deference to McCarthy, Katharine demurred but Phil and the *Post* remained in Ike's camp.

Phil would be disappointed. When Ike was swept into the White House, Phil wrote him a note suggesting he issue a statement saying, "I feel impelled to make clear that the tactics of Senator McCarthy are in direct opposition to my fundamental beliefs." The President declined.

Phil found the early 1950s a rather discouraging time.

Colonel McCormick was pouring money into the *Times-Herald*. It was far ahead of the *Post* in circulation, and gaining ground. It had enterprising reporters who produced well-written if sometimes slanted stories. Its sports coverage and comic strips were the best in town. Its bizarre politics were the Colonel's own (it was the only Washington paper to offer Senator McCarthy consistent and unequivocal support) and it was required to run the Chicago *Tribune*'s daily color cartoon on its front page and the Colonel's eccentric memoirs (including several installments on how he invented the machine gun) on the op-ed. The liberals regarded it with horror but the overwhelming majority of Washington's newspaper readers didn't seem to mind. It had 250,000 subscribers, 50,000 more than the *Post,* and seemed destined to drive the *Post* from the streets. Then suddenly Phil's dream came true.

In late January, 1954, Eugene got a note from Kent Cooper, the former general manager of the Associated Press, and a friend and Florida neighbor of Colonel McCormick's. It said:

Dear Eugene,
    I am wondering whether you expect to be in Palm Beach soon for

I would like very much to talk to you about a business matter of importance to you. Please let me know.

Eugene called Cooper and asked if the matter concerned the newspaper business in Washington and Cooper said yes. Eugene, Phil and the *Post*'s business manager, John W. Sweeterman, met Cooper in Palm Beach and were told that the Colonel would sell the *Times-Herald* for $8,500,000, the same amount he'd put into it.

Eugene agreed at once. The Colonel remained silent for six weeks, then got in touch. The details were worked out. The price went up to $10,300,000 to include $1,800,000 in severance pay for the *Times-Herald* employees.

The Colonel waited until the last moment to break the news to his niece, Ruth McCormick Miller "Bazy" Tankersley, a friend and steadfast supporter of Senator McCarthy's who was married to a former *Times-Herald* editor. Bazy protested vehemently. The Colonel gave her forty-five hours to raise a matching sum but insisted that she not tell possible backers why she needed it. She failed by some six million dollars.

The sale was announced on March 17 by the *Daily News* and it came as a shock to the *Times-Herald*'s staff. It was Saint Patrick's Day and their paper had devoted a page to Irish family coats of arms and mottoes. The motto listed for the McCormicks was "Death Rather Than Desert The Faith." They had assumed that the Colonel would never sell.

For the Grahams it was a sweet triumph but one that came barely in time.

"If you really fought for survival, as I did, indirectly, for twenty years, from 1933 to 1954," Katharine would say later, "you never forget it."

Walter Lippmann saw it in simpler terms and sent a telegram: "Hooray for the canary that swallowed the cat."

The next morning the canary appeared on the city's doorsteps, bulging, with thirty-five comics—more than any other paper in the world—with UP, AP, INS, Reuters and the New York Daily News Service. The *Times-Herald*'s massive sports section had been added in toto to the *Post*'s.

There remained the small mystery of why the Colonel, who had called the *Times-Herald* "Fort Necessity," had surrendered.

The answer was probably simple. The Colonel didn't really believe that Eugene and Phil were dangerous leftists and he knew they'd be willing to pay his price. To out-of-town publishers, the *Times-Herald* would have been a dubious investment. The foolish owners of the *Evening Star* hadn't been interested. Besides, the Colonel and Eugene had both gone to Yale.

Phil seized the opportunity. He used the combined presses and delivery trucks of both papers to get the new big paper out on time. He picked up the *Times-Herald*'s right-wing columnists to keep its right-wing readers and he put the words *Times-Herald* up on the masthead in type as large as *The Post.*

The owners of the *Evening Star,* which had dominated the city for decades, seemed almost amused. Company president Samuel H. Kauffmann bet his colleagues that the *Post* would not keep more than 5,000 of the *Times-Herald*'s 253,000 subscribers. He was grievously wrong. The *Post* kept 180,000 and the *Daily News,* which hired several of the *Times-Herald* people, picked up 30,000. The *Star* got only 8,000.

The advertisers followed the readers. In 1955 the *Star*'s linage rose 3,258,000 lines, the *Post*'s 12,467,000. The future was arriving in installments and the *Post* would get much bigger and much richer.

In 1956 Phil Graham was on the cover of *Time* magazine. *Time* readers were told that "one of the world's most influential journalists . . . Phil Graham, 40, is an energetic charmer whose facial furrows and tall, angular frame, give him a Lincolnesque look. . . . In his gray-curtained office, puffing a Parliament (40 a day) with his long legs stretched over the desk, Graham keeps communications lively between top-layer Washington and The Post on two softly ding-donging telephones. Often he has a Senator, an Ambassador, or a Cabinet officer to his luncheon anteroom. . . ."

Time reported with no apparent dismay Phil's endless manipulating of high public office holders. "He conceived a Congressional investigation [of organized crime] and began scanning the U. S. Senate to cast a likely Senator in the top role."

It noted that, on the advice of friends, he eventually picked Estes Kefauver, a virtually unknown junior Senator from Tennessee. Kefauver was reluctant. As *Time* reported, "Graham gave him a long pep talk [and] finally exploded: 'Damn it, Estes, don't you want to be Vice President?' "

The choice launched Kefauver into the deeper waters of U. S. politics. Phil, *Time* added, "who shudders at the thought of Kefauver for President, had begun feeling like a Frankenstein."

The article was surprisingly candid about the shortcomings of the paper it had called, in earlier, leaner days, Washington's "sole big league newspaper."

"Its local staff is still undermanned and stretched thin; its seven-man National Bureau (one-third the size of the New York Times Bureau) does a spotty job; it has never had its own foreign correspondents."

Phil was delighted with the story nevertheless and in time he made its author, James Truitt, a *Post* company vice-president.

He did not make any great effort to upgrade the quality of the paper. *Time* had described Russell Wiggins, who had been made the *Post*'s executive editor in 1955, as a man with "the cold, neat passion of a spinster picking cat hairs off the chesterfield" and had mocked his preoccupation with color-coded assignment slips—green for simple ones, red for those with photos assigned, pink for those requiring photos from the files. Managing editor Alfred Friendly, a graceful writer, had been promoted beyond his interests. Phil had picked these men and they had served him faithfully. He would turn on them in time but it would have been embarrassing to dump them too soon, and besides, he was more interested in other things.

At the *Post*'s annual Christmas party Phil called 1954 "the year of years."

He and his father-in-law had bought prosperity and laid the foundation of an empire. Its old enemies were vanquished or at least out of breath. Senator McCarthy of Wisconsin had been rendered harmless by the televising of the Army-McCarthy hearings and had then been censured by the Senate, 67 to 22.

Its friends were rising to power; Eisenhower was still in the White House, ignoring much of the *Post*'s good advice, but Lyndon B. Johnson was the second most powerful man in the country with his gaze fixed firmly on the peak ahead.

Money was rolling in and the new prosperity was to be dramatically shared. In 1955 Eugene and Agnes turned over some $500,000 worth of nonvoting *Post* stock to 711 employees, all those with at least five years' service. The juniors got four shares, worth $211.84; the seniors got twenty, worth $1,059.20.

In March, 1956, the *Post* and the Washington Newspaper Guild signed an unprecedented five-year contract. The length was in flagrant violation of Guild guidelines but a majority of the *Post* people wanted it for understandable reasons. In the course of five years most of the newsroom's journeymen would be making at least $160 a week, the highest newspaper wage in the country.

On the face of it, the *Post*'s employees should have been jubilant. They were not. Under Graham, the *Post* had become the most demanding of employers. City editor Ben Gilbert pushed the reporters daily beyond the limits of exasperation. He and the other managers resisted every contract demand and fought every grievance.

Phil stayed aloof. Most *Post* staffers persuaded themselves that Phil was basically on their side. On one occasion after the *Post* negotiators had dismissed some Guild requests with apparent contempt, a reporter suggested at a Guild meeting that things would be much easier if only Phil Graham knew what was going on. Milton Viorst, then a young reporter, replied that obviously he did know, that he was the one who made all the significant decisions. Viorst's candor did not serve him well at the *Post* and he soon left.

Phil had his favorites. Chalmers Roberts, who was one, wrote in his authorized *Post* biography that many of those who worked most closely with him would say "I love that guy." Phil asked young women reporters whom he met in the elevator about their jobs and their social lives and he said pleasant things about their hair or clothes. They would remember what he said, with pleasure, for years. He spoke to the young men with barracks room familiarity. Once in a while he would even seem to share their gripes. "How's Gilbert's hamburger factory?" he once asked Wes Barthelmes jocularly. It was a remark that set Barthelmes to thinking.

Phil was a fascinating, complex man. He loved to manipulate people and he sometimes despised himself as a manipulator. He was in the words of his wife "almost like a candle and a flame."

He was also increasingly out of control. He would move with happy intensity, sweeping all obstacles before him, and then he would sink into frozen despair. As a freshman at the University of Florida he had pursued life and pleasure so recklessly that he had collapsed and his father brought him home for a quiet year on the farm to calm him down. In 1945 he had written home from the Philippines: "Yesterday I was saturated with gloom and had been for some days and could see nothing bright at all, presently or for some time to come, in the world. Today for no good reason I feel quite jubilant, life seems better and easier and all in all I feel that it is my oyster."

The school desegregation crisis that came in that landmark year of 1954 would trigger a sustained burst of furious activity. Joe Rauh, a civil rights lawyer and an old friend, called him in panic one day to say the situation was desperate in Little Rock, Arkansas. Phil called back at 3 A.M. to get the unlisted number of Thurgood Marshall, then the chief counsel of the National Association for the Advancement of Colored People. He had been up all night phoning. He would spend sixteen hours a day on the phone, day after day, for weeks. He was, in his own phrase, a "self-appointed, quite unwarranted needler of the White House and Justice Department."

The White House's reaction would be restrained. When Phil suggested that he and Eisenhower go to Little Rock and together lead a black child into the embattled school the President did not respond. When Phil persisted he did come home from a golfing vacation in Newport, Rhode Island, and he did send federal troops to Little Rock. He would explain briefly on television that he had acted because "mob rule cannot be allowed to override the decisions of the courts."

The difficult integration of the Little Rock schools sent Phil into a prolonged depression. He stayed in semi-seclusion at Glen Welby, the family's estate near Middleburg, Virginia, for most of the next three years. His brother William would later tell the Miami *Herald* that Phil's "disillusionment" with Arkansas "was the first step toward the manic depressive."

In his absence the *Post* was run by Sweeterman and Wiggins. They referred to his condition discreetly, as "Problem A."

He still had occasional bursts of furious activity. In 1956 he wrote a long memo to Lyndon Johnson sketching a program for vast, swift social changes. It would serve as a preliminary plan for Johnson's Great Society and War on Poverty.

When the depression lifted for a bit he would call acquaintances on the phone and talk for hours. Wes Barthelmes was one he phoned.

"He would call at bizarre times and after a while the conversation would sort of trail off and he would go on and it would become a word salad, as if he'd picked up *Ulysses* and was reading it."

Katharine remained the inconspicuous and supportive wife.

"Phil became ill, starting in with really terrible depressions in 1957. After that I was almost totally involved in taking care of him and concealing from the public that he was ill."

He and Katharine took a recuperative trip to Europe in the spring of 1959. When he was away, Wiggins and Friendly ran the editorial side. Things went smoothly if blandly and that year the *Post* passed the *Star* in advertising as well as circulation. Eugene Meyer was dying at eighty-three of cancer and confused in his mind, increasingly suspicious of Agnes but still trusting Phil. Agnes had written Katharine that "the only people who can help me therefore are you and let's admit it, especially Phil, who can say anything because he is the one person who can do no wrong."

Phil and Katharine returned from Europe, and Phil sat by the old man's bedside and talked about the joys and agonies of publishing a newspaper. Eugene died in July.

Phil resumed command of the *Post* in 1960, the election year. He was once more strategically placed. He was Johnson's friend, adviser and speech writer and he had been on friendly, easy terms with Kennedy since 1957. He was now furious with Eisenhower, who he said had given the country "eight years of the dreariest and phoniest mediocrity I ever hope to live through."

In February he sent a note to Wiggins: "As for Ike, if he's sore at us, who can be surprised. All Presidents are sore as they near the end of office and unfortunately we've had to be critical and he's almost as thin-skinned as Lyndon. . . . I am so infuriated at his incompetence that I am frequently awful about him verbally in front of our staff; so I am particularly sensitive to the need for the newspaper not to reflect this kind of intemperance."

Phil led a large *Post* delegation to the Democratic convention in Los Angeles—Alfred Friendly, Robert Estabrook (the chief of the editorial page), Ed Folliard, Bob Albright, Chalmers Roberts, Elsie Carper, Dick Lyon, Ben Gilbert, Maxine Cheshire, Molly Thayer and others. He himself went not as a publisher but as a maker of kings. He had begun as a firm Johnson supporter—"Johnson played Phil like a harmonica," Joe Rauh once said—and he had suggested earlier to John Kennedy that he be patient and let Lyndon go first.

By convention time his loyalties had switched. Kennedy was looking increasingly like a winner and Johnson was not.

Phil and Joe Alsop conceived a plan for what they considered an invincible Democratic ticket, Kennedy in the top spot, Johnson (who could carry Texas and perhaps the rest of the South) in the second. Phil arranged a five-minute audience with Kennedy and made the suggestion. To his mild surprise Kennedy promptly agreed. Phil then had lunch with Johnson, who did not yet consider himself out of the big race.

His reaction was somewhere between negative and neutral.

He was planning a speech attacking Joe Kennedy, the candidate's conservative father. Phil wrote him a new speech and Johnson delivered it but added a few anti-Joe remarks of his own. The *Post,* under Phil's direction, ran a story the next day saying Kennedy would invite Johnson to run with him. Johnson succumbed. The ticket did carry Texas and Kennedy defeated Richard Nixon by the narrowest of margins. For better or worse Phil and Joe Alsop had shaped the future.

After the convention Phil collapsed once more into depression. From now on the cycle would shorten and the ups and downs grow more severe. He grew angrily critical of his late father-in-law, telling friends Eugene's patronage had deprived him of his own career, and he often damned him as a wily Jew.

Ben Bradlee, who had left the *Post* in 1949, was working in *Newsweek*'s Washington bureau in 1961. *Newsweek* had never been profitable and it was up for sale.

"I was stewing about it one night," Bradlee would say later, "it seemed incredible that mature people couldn't have some control over their own future. I didn't know many people with big dough and I was terrified by reports that Norton Simon or Sam Newhouse was going to buy us. One night about ten o'clock I was sitting at home and the thought occurred to me—Why not go over and see Phil Graham? There was a remote chance he might be interested in *Newsweek.*"

Bradlee phoned Phil and Phil said come over. They talked for three hours and Phil seemed only mildly interested. He sent Bradlee home with instructions to write down everything he knew about the *Newsweek* staff. Bradlee wrote fifty pages before he went to bed and the next morning he delivered them to Phil. Phil read them through and said he'd buy the magazine. He went to New York to arrange financing. Friendly had been Averell Harriman's speech writer when

Harriman was the Marshall Plan administrator, and Harriman owned 40,000 shares of *Newsweek* stock. Phil sent Friendly to Rome to persuade Harriman to sell.

"What the hell are you doing here?" Harriman asked when Friendly arrived.

"I'm here to offer you two million dollars," Friendly replied.

Bradlee and *Newsweek* managing editor Osborn Elliott were sent to call on Mrs. Vincent Astor. The Astor Foundation controlled most of the stock. Mrs. Astor was pleased with the delegation and agreed to sell for $15 million. For the money the *Post* acquired 120,000 of *Newsweek*'s 179,700 shares and 45 percent of KOGO-TV and two radio stations in San Diego. *Newsweek* had $3 million in cash on hand and after the *Post* sold the San Diego stations, the net cost was down to $9 million. Phil had borrowed most of it and had to pay only $750,000 in cash. It was a great bargain.

That same year he set up the Los Angeles Times–Washington Post News Service, an immediate and enormous success, and his moods continued to rise and fall.

When he was up he was overwhelming. Chalmers Roberts quotes a description by a British journalist who met him in 1961:

"The fastest talker I have yet heard in this fast-talking country. He has the same power of pitter-patter as a master solo comic. His speech is designed to amuse, to tease and sometimes to outrage. He cannot keep still. He cannot keep silent. With this wild and restless brilliance he must play Pied Piper to every man and woman that comes into his ken."

He was either in constant, articulate motion or frozen in despair. Some of his moves were great successes. Some were not. He bought 49 percent of the Bowater Mersey Paper Company, the paper's main supplier of newsprint, a sound move at a time when paper costs were going up, but he also bought *ARTnews,* which eventually would be sold at a loss.

He took aging Walter Lippmann away from the Herald Tribune Syndicate by offering him $100,000 a year. Lippmann would write for *Newsweek* on the side. He tried to hire Stewart Alsop from *The Saturday Evening Post,* Mary McGrory from the *Star* and Philip L. Geyelin from *The Wall Street Journal* but they all turned him down.

He became the enthusiastic supporter of a plan to build a national aquarium in Washington, a scheme that attracted few other supporters. Herblock made fun of it in cartoons. He bought and leased airplanes and flew all over the country making speeches, sometimes several in a day. He intervened, uninvited, in the New York Printing Pressmen's strike, allying himself with the strikers, infuriating the publishers. He ordered Friendly to write an article extolling the Pressmen's leader, Bertram A. Powers, and when Friendly did so reluctantly he found the essay insufficiently enthusiastic and threw it out. He wrote one himself which Wiggins refused to run. He then tried to make Friendly editor but Friendly refused to take the job.

Phil sometimes seemed to be following the behavior patterns of his least illustrious predecessor, Ned McLean, who had brought his mistress to *Post* editorial conferences. He left the family home in 1963 and acquired a girl friend named Robin Webb, an Australian who had worked as a *Newsweek* secretary in Paris. They traveled together around Europe and checked in and out of Washington. He would bring "the Popsie," as she was known, to inappropriate places including the *Post*'s newsroom. He told people that he intended to divorce Katharine and marry Robin. He told his friend and lawyer, Edward Bennett Williams, to work out a divorce and to draft a new will. Williams stalled. He later told a reporter that he "told him not to make a will and urged him to make no changes until things settled down. I thought it was in his interest that I do everything I could during his period of aberration to influence him to go back to his family."

One February day Phil came to the law offices and directed Harold Ungar, a Williams partner, to draw up a new will. On February 18, Williams reluctantly drew up a will for Phil that left two-thirds of his estate in trust for his children and the other third to Robin.

Williams also put a memorandum in his files noting that he had grave doubts about Phil's competency and that he had drawn up the will only to retain his confidence as a friend so he could continue to try to influence his conduct.

A month later Phil tore up that will and had the lawyers draw up another, this one cutting the children to a third and leaving Robin two-thirds.

He saw himself as a man deprived of his rightful role in life. He would call Joe Rauh, who is Jewish, and ramble for hours, making anti-Semitic remarks.

He had the furniture moved out of the office of one *Newsweek* executive who had irked him and had a new name stenciled on the door. In the middle of an amiable conversation with a writer who was leaving the magazine, he shouted in sudden fury, "All you little pricks are alike. You are in it for what you can get out of us."

Once when talking to President Kennedy over the phone he demanded, "Do you know who you are talking to?"

High-level Washington watched in fascination. When Phil came down from the manic heights he was appalled at his own behavior. He would ask for forgiveness with tears in his eyes and twice he committed himself to Chestnut Lodge, a private psychiatric institution in Rockville, Maryland.

In June, 1963, he was in Phoenix, Arizona, drinking heavily. One afternoon he called the late Tom Donnelly, a columnist for the Washington *Daily News.*

"I'm calling from a cabana," he said, and he rambled on, telling Donnelly, whom he'd never met, how much he admired his writing.

"When I get back to Washington we'll have to walk along the C and O Canal together," he said, "and talk about life."

Donnelly sat stunned and silent.

"You should come work for me," Graham said, "but of course you can't; you're not a whore."

The next day in an unscheduled speech at a publishers' banquet, he attacked the assembled editors and publishers as toadies and sycophants.

Phil's closest friend, Emmett Hughes, flew out and brought him home aboard a private plane. He was committed once more to Chestnut Lodge.

The last months had been a frightful ordeal for Katharine. She had sat with him for hours and endured his manic denunciations. Now he seemed calmer. The attending doctors classified him as a manic depressive but that was obvious—sometimes he was frenzied and sometimes immobile, in despair. It was more a description than a diagnosis. He was also clever and, the psychiatrists learned, able to control his behavior and fool them. He seemed to respond to treatment and after several weeks Katharine and they found him "quite noticeably much better."

Joe Rauh called him one Friday in August and said he'd like to come see him but Phil replied in his soft and pleasant way that he'd have to postpone the visit for a few days because he was, with his doctor's permission, spending the weekend at Glen Welby. The next day, shortly after 1 P.M., while Katharine was upstairs, he killed himself with a light sportsman's shotgun.

His death brought broad public response, much of it rhetorical, some self-serving—his power lived on and he was courted even in death. Ben Bradlee would later describe one attribute in precise detail.

"When he was well," Bradlee would write, "he was one of the most naturally attractive, witty and brilliant men I've ever known."

Arthur Schlesinger, Jr., wrote that Phil "was fascinated by power and by other men who were fascinated by power."

Both were right.

He himself had once told Joseph Pulitzer, Jr.: "Remember that it is possible to be a good publisher and a happy publisher at the same time."

In the last analysis, Philip Leslie Graham was neither. He would be succeeded by a better one, but it would take her a while to get started.

CHAPTER

15

Katharine was forty-six. She had grown up with Picassos on the walls, gardeners in the greenhouse, an egocentric mother, a distant, demanding father, three sisters and a brother. She was always a little overwhelmed.

Her mother made her wear ribbed stockings when no one else did and looked with a cold, demanding eye on her mind, her face and her physique as well as her clothes.

The older sisters, Florence and Elizabeth, were by maternal decree the family beauties, and Ruth, the youngest, was the creative one.

"I thought I was the peasant walking around brilliant people," Katharine would remember.

Her father loved her and respected her and felt she was the only one of his children who took after him but he did not express his more tender feelings.

"She's got a hard mind," he told a friend as she grew older, "she'd make a great businessman."

She married Phil Graham and moved from her father's shadow to his.

She had children.

"I was the kind of wife that women liberationists talk about. I was a second-class citizen and my role was to keep Phil happy, peaceful, calm and functioning and the children the same. I guess because I'd been brought up by nurses and governesses and never saw my parents, I compensated by spending as much time as I could with my children.

I always got up and had breakfast with them and tried to be at home in the afternoon. I liked it. I really liked it."

She was, like father, mother and husband, essentially a serious person.

"I did the welfare boards and things like that for fifteen years. And I did it, I think, more and better than the totally equivalent housewife of those days. I didn't really like the social boards and didn't do many of them. I did get involved in the Department of Welfare and I organized a couple of committees in Junior Village. I was tremendously interested. I mean I wasn't just sitting there."

She was plump, a little dowdy and shy at parties, tongue-tied when she found herself sitting next to a famous stranger. She was not taken seriously but when her husband plunged into deep depressions she rose to the challenge and took care of him, sitting with him for hours, talking through the night to bring him out of his gloom.

"In 1961 I got TB and went to bed and gave up all the committees. By that time he was very ill. It was a matter of enduring from then on and in a way it taught me a lot."

When Phil died she took over the family business. The *Star* wanted to buy the *Post* and so did other papers and other people. Katharine called them "vultures."

On the eve of the funeral she went before the board of the Post Company and announced, at the suggestion of Frederick "Fritz" Beebe, the chairman, that it would not be sold.

"I had lived through the creation of it, through those hard, bad years when you didn't know whether you'd be there tomorrow. Selling what I had seen my father and husband create with such agony and devotion was unthinkable."

She left town, spent a month sailing the Aegean with her mother, Lally, Chief Justice and Mrs. Earl Warren, and Mr. and Mrs. Drew Pearson, came home and moved into her husband's old office.

"I was thrown in cold—not even knowing what administration was. I didn't have enough sense to panic. The company was much smaller then and I'd seen Phil and my father run it in various ways. I sort of perceived that the men wanted me to work. I wanted to. I thought of myself as sort of a family representative who would sit there and learn and the men who were the heads of the divisions would go on running things and making the business decisions."

She went to *Post* business meetings and listened to Editor Wiggins, Managing Editor Friendly, Business Manager Sweeterman and, particularly, Chairman of the Board Beebe. She spent two days each week at *Newsweek,* where her silent presence at editorial meetings was resented by many. Every Monday morning she went over to WTOP-TV. She was used to owning things but not to running them, and no one, including herself, took her very seriously. She told a reporter for *Women's Wear Daily* that she really thought that any man could do a better job.

When WTOP vice-president John Hayes joined a secret CIA task force which considered the practicality of broadcasting propaganda into China, no one mentioned it to Katharine Graham, though his action committed the *Post* to support of the project. If she had known that she had been ignored she would not have complained.

"I didn't feel discriminated against," she told a reporter. "How can someone at the top of the company be discriminated against?"

She paid attention to her mentors, for a while. Lyndon B. Johnson was the most exalted one. He phoned her often and in April, 1964, she, Beebe and other *Post* executives, editors, reporters and editorial writers had lunch with him in the family dining room at the White House. In August she went to the Democratic convention at Atlantic City that nominated him for a second term, and after it was over, while she was waiting at the airport, exhausted, her hair dirty and bedraggled under a bandana, he scooped her up and carried her down to Texas in *Air Force One.* When she returned from the ranch she wrote a thank-you note:

"I feel exactly as though I were the heroine of one's childhood fairy tales, put on a magic carpet and carried in three swift jet hours into Never Never Land."

She was not, however, totally under his spell. She told him, somewhat indiscreetly, that though she and the *Post* were for him 100 percent, it would not endorse him formally. It was considerably less than he expected.

During the campaign she traveled with a group of foreign reporters and made (as she often would) a mixed impression.

Some of her companions found her shy, aloof, unsure of herself and sometimes rude. She did not mingle with the workaday press and when an ordered limousine failed to meet her at an airport she sharply reprimanded the State Department escort. Still a British interviewer found her "tremendous fun to talk to."

A few days after his landslide victory Johnson invited her to the White House. She was in his eyes a nice little widow woman who needed stern guidance.

"He was being friendly. It was an anniversary dinner—I think it was their thirty-fourth wedding anniversary—and after dinner he was very preoccupied, and about eleven or twelve o'clock, he left and went to bed, which meant that everyone could leave. I was saying good night to Mrs. Johnson. His bedroom was next to the Oval Room and he opened the door and said, 'Come here,' and I thought he was talking to someone behind me and I said, 'Who, me?' and he said, 'Yes, you.' Abe Fortas was standing on the other side of the room and he said to him, 'You too.'

"He got us both in the bedroom and the *Post* was lying on the bed. It had a big headline about Commissioner Tobriner appointing a new police chief for Washington. The President had told Tobriner to tell him before he appointed anyone because he wanted to appoint some kind of superchief like Pat Murphy to clean up crime. For some reason Tobriner, incredibly, had failed to tell him. He was furious. We had supported Tobriner's appointment, so somehow it was my fault.

"He just started dressing us down in the famous Johnson way, yelling at me and saying it was our idea to appoint this man who had done such a stupid thing. As he was doing that I suddenly realized he'd started taking off his coat and shirt and tie, throwing them on the bed and talking all the time.

"I was pretty new at this sort of thing, and I could not believe that I was there in the bedroom, being dressed down by the President as he was getting undressed. I thought, When is he going to stop? He suddenly got down to the nitty-gritty and said, 'Turn around.' So I turned around and he went right on.

"When he had his pajamas on he got in bed and finished telling me off. Finally he said good night and Abe and I left."

Katharine would soon rely much less on most of her mentors.

In 1965 she went around the world and she returned with a new independence. First she invited Ben Bradlee, the head of *Newsweek*'s Washington bureau, to lunch.

He was glad to be invited.

A couple of years earlier, on the afternoon of Phil Graham's memorial service, he had sat in his Georgetown garden and told Osborn Elliott, the *Newsweek* editor, that he was ready for a change, that specifically he wanted to be editor of *The Washington Post.*

Katharine was not particularly fond of Ben—when Georgetown had been divided into Phil people and Katharine people, he had been with Phil—but he had the kind of positive, take-charge personality she respected.

At lunch she asked him if he was interested in being managing editor of the *Post* and he replied inelegantly that he'd give his "left one" for the job.

She asked two wise old friends—Walter Lippmann and James Reston of the *Times*—for their opinions of Ben and they said he was just the man to give the *Post* a push in a needed new direction.

The next weekend she summoned Wiggins and Friendly to her Virginia estate and told them she'd picked the next editor of the *Post,* Benjamin Crowninshield Bradlee. She had them all to dinner in town the next day and announced the new order. It was intended that the changeover would not be too abrupt.

Bradlee would begin as deputy managing editor for foreign and national news. Ben Gilbert, who had long been considered the man in line after Friendly, would be deputy managing editor for local news. Gilbert was being told clearly that he'd lost his place in line.

Friendly would remain as managing editor for a couple of years so he could serve a term as president of the American Society of Newspaper Editors. Wiggins would remain as editor until his retirement at sixty-five. That was the scenario but Ben Bradlee would rewrite it.

Katharine picked Ben because he seemed a man who could get things done, and Ben then picked a few people of his own.

The first was Howard Simons, the *Post*'s science writer, a gentle, sardonic man. They met over coffee in the *Post* cafeteria and Ben asked him to be his lieutenant.

Simons saw change as opportunity. He was not, by his own reckoning, a favorite of the old regime.

"I was known to Friendly and Russ Wiggins as an always carping complaining son-of-a-bitch."

He was just what Ben wanted. "I picked him because he was

brighter than hell, he had smarts in an unorthodox way. He's very good politically, in decoding power struggles."

Simons' background was quite different from his own. Ben had been one of the poorer kids at St. Mark's, but Simons, the child of Russian immigrants, had grown up in genuine poverty.

When the Depression wiped out their small store in Albany, his mother had supported the family by working in someone else's shop.

Simons had worked his way through Union College and Columbia's graduate school of journalism and had found a job in Washington with Science Service. He went to Harvard as a Nieman fellow and then returned to Washington as a free-lance science writer. He was soon making $18,000 a year, an impressive income in the sixties. Al Friendly had persuaded him to come to the *Post*.

He and Ben began the revolution in August.

Katharine gave him his head.

"I don't play girl editor," she would tell *Time* magazine. "I don't tell people what to do all the time. I'm interested in finding people, developing them, giving them leeway and backing them up."

Ben made an immediate impression. He arrived early each day and stayed until the next morning. He swaggered across the newsroom, a slim, middle-aged dude with a shoe-leather complexion, cocky grin, jutting chin, button-down collars and cold black eyes. Some editors are eagles, some moles. Bradlee was a quick brown fox.

"I want to have impact on this town," he told everyone. "I want to know they're reading us."

He also set about shuffling the hierarchy. His first target was Friendly, a rich man with a supercilious air who had never much enjoyed the routines of managing a newspaper.

Phil Graham had given Friendly an extra month's vacation each year as a time for reflection and he had continued to take it after Phil's death. This year he took it in October, at his second home in Turkey. When he returned, Walter Lippmann invited him to lunch at the Metropolitan Club and asked him if he had thought "about returning to writing." Friendly knew the question was not casual. He went directly from the club to Katharine Graham's office and asked her, "Is that what you want?" She said yes. "I'd rather have heard it from you," he said.

A small, misleading news story announced the new order. It said Friendly had "asked to be relieved of executive duties to resume an earlier career of reporting and writing on national and international affairs."

He was given the title of Associate Editor and in January, 1967, he went off to London as a free-roving correspondent and, like clockwork, he won a Pulitzer Prize for his coverage of the Arab-Israeli Six Day War. He then retired.

Ben Gilbert, the deputy managing editor for local news, would be the next to be bumped. For years he had supervised the manipulation as well as the gathering of local news and now he would try to manipulate one story too many.

He had been grooming a compliant civil servant named Walter Washington to be the city's first black Commissioner. President Johnson had agreed to name Washington to that post in April, and Gilbert was afraid that any premature announcement might cause Johnson to change his mind. Gilbert decided to keep it out of the paper. Ben Bradlee decided otherwise. He assigned Elsie Carper to dig around. She did and heard about the planned appointment from other sources. She wrote the story and Bradlee ran it, slipping it into the Sunday paper one Saturday night after Gilbert had gone home. He and city editor Steve Isaacs then went to a party at Gilbert's house, ready to intercept any phone calls from the *Post.*

Gilbert was furious in the morning. He said Bradlee had displayed a "lack of confidence" in him, which indeed he had. He, like Friendly, was given a new title, Associate Editor, and a new job, editorial writer on District affairs. He left the *Post* three years later to be Commissioner Washington's confidential assistant.

Two down; one to go.

Russell Wiggins was still editor and in charge of the editorial page, but Ben Bradlee now controlled the news.

CHAPTER

16

Ben had come a long erratic way.

He would often say that he had never had a long-range plan in his life; when he got bored he simply stopped doing whatever he was doing and tried something else. He was probably telling the simple truth.

He had nevertheless been moving steadily forward since he left the Navy at the end of World War II and he always seemed to aim a little higher than his peers.

"Let me try to convince you that I am not wildly ambitious," he would say later. "The move to the *Post* turned out to be a move up but that was by no means a sure thing. I had no contract. I think it was boredom that pushed me. I felt stopped, not from promotions but from being challenged."

His family was of the old New England gentry; his father, Frederick "Beebo" Bradlee, a witty, amiable man, had been an All-American halfback at Harvard, and had gone broke in the Depression. When Ben was sixteen the family was living rent-free on a twenty-acre estate borrowed from friends, overlooking the Atlantic, in Beverly, Massachusetts.

"That summer my old man told me I had to have a job. He wasn't going to just fork over dough all the time. He went down with me to the Beverly *Evening Times* and I got a job. I did this thing called city locals, which was wandering down the fucking street and going into every store and saying, 'Anything happen?' 'Yeh, my aunt's sick.' You filled a column with that and you got five bucks. To put it gently, most of my crowd wasn't working when they were sixteen."

He went to St. Mark's and Harvard but he had the memory of being down and out in Beverly at sixteen and the other boys in the quadrangle did not. He had polio as a youth but had recovered completely and at Harvard he majored in Greek and English and tried hard to be the athlete his father had been.

A classmate, trying to recall him after he became famous, would finally remember him as the kid who had spent all his spare time on the baseball field, hitting fungoes and chasing flies.

He graduated, joined the Navy, married a young woman named Jean Saltonstall, and in 1942 went off as an ensign to the South Pacific. The Navy taught him to act tough and to use the word "fucking" as an all-purpose adjective.

He got out in 1945 and tried and failed to get a job as a reporter on *The New York Times*. He tried *The Boston Globe*, where a cousin who didn't like him was the editor, and was turned down again. He and a few friends, some with money, started a Sunday paper in Manchester, New Hampshire. It was the state's only Sunday paper and the only competition to the Manchester *Union Leader*, a powerful, wildly one-sided daily run by an ultraconservative man named William Loeb. The new paper won prizes but lost money and after two years Loeb bought it and fired most of the staff, including Ben.

He ran an ad in *Editor & Publisher*, got a few answers and, with a couple of letters of introduction from family friends, went south, job hunting. One letter was to an editor on the Baltimore *Sun*. It was raining when the train pulled into Baltimore and Ben looked out on the dreary scene and decided to hell with it and stayed on board to Washington. At the *Post* he presented a letter from Christian Herter, a future Secretary of State, and was hired at $80 a week.

"The accidents in my life," he sometimes says, "have been just incredible."

On the advice of Walter Lippmann, another family friend, he changed his by-line from Ben Bradlee to Benjamin C. Bradlee and he began wearing a racetrack plaid suit handed down to him by his father-in-law.

"I think I was pretty good, a pretty good writer, and I had a lot of energy. I didn't really get along with Ben Gilbert but that wasn't why I quit. I quit because there were a half-dozen people ahead of me on the national beats and they were going to be there for years and because the *Post* was the third paper in town and losing a million bucks a year. I'd gotten up to a hundred and two dollars a week. Who would want to cover Municipal Court on Saturday and play bridge with the guy from the *News* for the rest of his life? Shit."

In 1951 Ben asked Phil to send him overseas as a correspondent and Phil said no. He asked him to recommend him for a Nieman fellowship and Phil said, "You've already been to Harvard."

So Ben got a job as press attaché at the American Embassy in Paris. It would soon lead to more exciting things.

Embassy press jobs were considered glamorous in the fifties—many assumed they were occupied by CIA agents—but Ben found his a bore, "a lot of cautious guys beating off." After months of job hunting, *Newsweek* hired him to cover Europe and the tumultuous Mideast.

Newsweek did have a CIA connection. One CIA agent who worked in Paris during that period recalls that agents were told quietly that purposeful stories, true or false, could always be planted in the "Periscope" column.

Ben nevertheless was restless. He would remain restless, seeking and finding new adventures, new people. He divorced Jean Saltonstall and married Antoinette Pinchot, a beautiful, talented member of an old and wealthy Pennsylvania family.

Again the CIA flickers in the background. Antoinette's sister Mary, also beautiful, was married to Cord Meyer, the head of the CIA's covert operations in Europe. Mary would have an affair with President Kennedy years later and would be murdered in George-town. The killer would never be found (though a man arrested in the vicinity was tried and acquitted), and James Angleton, the CIA's chief of counterintelligence, was later said to have acquired and destroyed her diary.

The casual linkage would continue after Ben joined the *Post*. In the midsixties the *Post* would, at Ben's urging, publish the Penkovsky papers, a CIA concoction which had been offered through a legitimate publisher as the authentic revelations of a Soviet double agent.

Ben denies emphatically that he knew the papers were phony and that he had ever been an agent of any kind or that the CIA had ever even tried to recruit him. He would admit readily that he knew a lot of the top agency people—"you can't have anything to do with people

in this town without getting to know them"—but he says his relationship with them has been more often hostile than not.

"Cord Meyer can't stand my guts. Angleton, whom I used to know
quite well, won't talk to me and hasn't talked to me for years. He
thinks I'm a traitor."

Ben has letters from a variety of CIA directors that say he has
never been an agent, though he says that doesn't prove much since
"those fuckers would lie."

In this case it seems probable that they're telling the truth.

Paris was fun while it lasted but Ben was transferred to *Newsweek*'s Washington bureau after the French government grew disen-
chanted with his behavior as a reporter in Algeria.

He came home unhappy.

"I was assistant to Sam Shaffer, for Christ's sake"; he was a fierce
competitor and a good, accurate reporter and he was soon doing very
well.

He went to the diplomatic beat, to Congress, then to politics and
general assignments. Sometimes as the single *Newsweek* reporter on
a story he would outmaneuver a small crowd from *Time*. When the
Senate investigated Eisenhower's top White House aide, Sherman
Adams, a former governor of New Hampshire, Ben turned up a
Waldorf-Astoria hotel bill signed by Adams and paid by Bernard
Goldfine, a textile manufacturer for whom Adams had done a few
favors.

He also had flair. He quoted Goldfine in broken English and
persuaded his bosses to suspend the ban on dialect and run it as
written, arguing that it was more than fair, since Goldfine was basing
his defense on an immigrant's ignorance of proper American political
behavior. Ben moved up to assistant bureau chief and engendered a
productive friendship with Senator John F. Kennedy, a neighbor on
his Georgetown street. Kennedy pumped Ben on what *Newsweek* was
working on and gave him occasional tidbits in return. After Kennedy
was elected President, Ben was a frequent informal guest at the White
House.

Ben used Kennedy and Kennedy used Ben. He behaved as most,
if not all, of the competing members of the press corps would have
behaved if they had had the opportunity. Kennedy had many obliging
friends. Ben differed mainly from the others in only one respect. When

Kennedy died many journalistic careers died with him, but Ben had already moved onward and up.

Russell Wiggins (like Eugene Meyer and Phil Graham) saw the *Post* as a means to well-defined political and ideological ends.

Ben, by contrast, seemed untouched by ideology, by nature neither a natural philosopher nor a long-range thinker.

Ben Bagdikian, who would work for him in the seventies and find it a bruising experience, concluded that he was "irritated and bored with serious ideas but quick and contemporaneous in his tastes."

Ben would more or less agree.

He had no interest in either writing or reading editorials.

"When people used to ask me, 'What's your philosophy of editing?' I used to be terribly worried.

"I had a very good education in the classics and the philosophers. I can discuss ideas but I'm not an egghead. I've tried very hard not to become one.

"Energy and principle and commitment and brains. That's what I like. I'll tell you I'm very strong on energy."

The great issue of the late sixties was the United States' ever increasing involvement in Vietnam, but the *Post*'s front-line news coverage had been scant. Friendly was preoccupied with Europe, and when he had money enough to send reporters overseas, that's where he sent them. Editor Wiggins's editorial pages were committed to support of Johnson's Vietnam policies.

The policies were made in Washington and interpreted each Sunday in the "Outlook" section. By 1965 there was a clear international conflict—the *Post* editorial pages took one view, the interpretive reporters another. That December, Murrey Marder came out in direct opposition to the White House policy and coined the phrase "credibility gap" in the process:

"Creeping signs of doubt and cynicism about Administration pronouncements, especially in its foreign policy, are privately troubling some of the government's usually stalwart supporters. The problem could be called a credibility gap. It represents a perceptibly growing disquiet, misgiving or skepticism about the candor or validity of official declarations."

Wiggins stood fast on the editorial pages but he now stood alone.

By amiable custom no *Post* editorial writer was required to write in favor of something he was against, and one by one the others—Alan Barth, Selig Harrison, Merlo Pusey and Stephen Rosenfeld—had decided that the war in Vietnam was a great mistake. They tried to persuade Wiggins but failed and he was soon writing all the *Post*'s Vietnam editorials himself.

Ben, meanwhile, was concerned if not with foreign policy at least with foreign coverage. With Friendly disposed of, he began sending a mixed variety of reporters to the Vietnam scene but if he had an opinion on the war he kept it to himself. His concern was with impact. If a story was read and talked about, he didn't care which side it fell on. Reporters were allowed to report their feelings as well as the facts. Most tilted away from the White House. Larry Stern, the sometime national editor, had concluded that the war was immoral and his stories reflected that view. Ward Just, a Bradlee favorite and a future novelist, would write compelling, imaginative stories about its horrors.

Joe Alsop, the columnist, the most determined of hawks and a man of considerable influence at the *Post,* persuaded Ben that a reporter with a more traditional respect for hard facts was needed. On Alsop's recommendation Ben hired Peter Braestrup from *The New York Times* to head the Saigon bureau. The size of the bureau varied from time to time but it would always include at least one member who was emotionally committed to American disengagement. Braestrup remembers it as a refreshing experience.

"We had freedom. You just did your thing. They might bury your story but they didn't attempt very often to impose a superior wisdom on you. They might say, 'Gee, we're not getting very much on this or that,' and they'd put someone else on it to give them the story they wanted, but they'd never tell you to write a story that said X or Y or Z. You were left to sink or swim. It was very unlike the *Times,* where they were constantly second-guessing the reporters."

The permissive approach did not please President Johnson. He took umbrage at the mixed messages and he blamed Katharine.

"He stopped speaking to me, literally, for a while. Even if I saw him in a big group he would not speak to me. I mean he wouldn't say hello."

In the midsixties she heard that someone had told him that she said he had tried to buy her "with dinners" and she wrote him a note

Elizabeth, Agnes, Florence and Bill.

Photo courtesy the Library of Congress

Katharine, at left, felt trapped in a family of strivers. The others are, clockwise from the top, Florence, Elizabeth, Bill and Ruth.

Photo courtesy the Library of Congress

The Meyer family: clockwise from Katharine, seated at left, are Bill, Agnes, Florence, Eugene, Elizabeth and Ruth.

Photo courtesy the Library of Congress

Agnes and her daughters: Ruth, Florence, Katharine and Elizabeth.

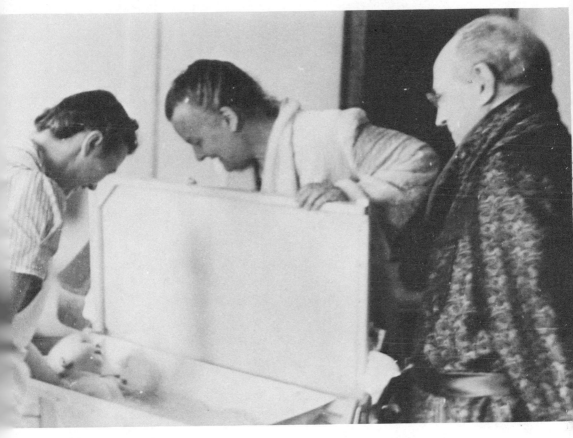

Eugene and Agnes with their newborn grandson Donald Graham. He was
from that time on the designated heir to the *Post*. When Eugene bought the
Times-Herald in 1954 he noted that the paper would now be "safe for
Donnie."

Eugene, his son and grandsons. Donald is standing next to his uncle Bill.

Photo courtesy the Library of Congress

Eugene and grandchildren. Donald is the round-eyed boy with suspenders.

Photo courtesy the Library of Congress

The *Post* city room in the late 1940s was a formal place. Copyreaders and reporters wore coats and ties and were not permitted to leave empty coffee cups on their desks. By the 1960s it became considerably less proper.

Photo courtesy the National Archives

Philip Graham, left, took charge of the paper in 1949, giving it a new and more politically aggressive direction. Cartoonist Herbert L. Block ("Herblock") is second from the right.

Photo courtesy the National Archives

denying it and affirming her friendship and loyalty. He did not reply.

When Johnson fired Robert S. McNamara as Secretary of Defense, she tried again. Chalmers Roberts quotes the letter:

"These times are so difficult that my heart bleeds for you. I think so often of the story you tell of Phil's letter to Jack Kennedy after the Bay of Pigs [in which Phil tried to cheer him up] . . . of course there has been no such parallel event—quite the contrary. And yet, it seems the burdens you bear, the issues you confront, the delicate line you must tread, are almost too much for one human being. The only thanks you ever seem to receive is a deafening chorus of carping criticism. Unlike Phil, I find it hard to express emotion. I can't write in the eloquent words he used. But I want you to know I am among the many people in this country who believe in you and are behind you with trust and devotion."

Again Johnson did not reply. She continued to feel loyal to him but less so to his policies.

She was also moving away from Wiggins. Wiggins was scheduled to retire on his sixty-fifth birthday in December, 1968. In 1967 Katharine hired the man who was to be his successor as chief editorial writer, Philip Geyelin, a diplomatic correspondent for *The Wall Street Journal,* a blueblood from Yale, a friend of Ben's in Paris, and once, briefly, a CIA agent in Washington. He was now, like most of Washington's liberal intellectuals, a dove.

His assigned role was to moderate the Vietnam editorials and to wait patiently for Wiggins to leave.

He did not have long to wait. By now Wiggins and the President were almost the last members of the hard-line club and both knew the end was near. Johnson had already announced he would not run again. In September he called Wiggins at his vacation home in Maine and offered him the post of U. S. Ambassador to the United Nations. It was a reward for loyalty and more of an honor than a job. Wiggins took it with gratitude.

Ben became executive editor and Geyelin editor of the editorial page. Each would be independent of the other and would report directly to Katharine. There was also a new managing editor, Eugene Patterson, who'd won a Pulitzer Prize in Atlanta.

Ben was delighted with his new independence. He was, in his own mind, a simple fellow who put out a newspaper, and a newspaper was not a pulpit.

"I really wanted to get the *Post* out of the 'cause' business. I asked Katharine to split the editorial page off, so no one could accuse me of whatever the fucking editorial policy was. It wasn't in me to preach. I can say somebody's a horse's ass but I can't tell people what to do."

The news columns, however, would not be as pure as he imagined.

He would hire and promote a good many writers and editors who were preachers, even if he was not, and the *Post*'s pages would often serve as a pulpit for certain lifestyles and several causes, some of them contradictory. He would be unconcerned. Politics and ideology bored him. He had his own goals and he had found a publisher who agreed with him, at least up to a point.

CHAPTER

17

"There is something about the Meyers and Grahams," Ben said after he became executive editor. "They have this commitment to excellence." He meant they wanted a paper with impact and a high level of editorial talent, and Katharine showed her commitment with cash. In Friendly's last year as managing editor the editorial budget totaled $4 million. Under Ben it grew swiftly to $8 million. The newsroom staff went up by 20 percent and the number of foreign bureaus doubled.

There were other significant changes.

Wiggins and Friendly had measured people by their ideologies, propriety and gravity; Ben measured them by their competitive success—by their ability to produce a continuing stream of front-page stories.

Ben was building his own team though there was one new member he didn't recruit.

Patterson, the new managing editor, had been Katharine's enthusiastic choice. That did not please Ben, who liked to pick his own people. The rumor was that Howie Simons had been passed over because his nature seemed too gentle, but Simons remained Ben's alter ego.

"We tried to get some people who were not in the *Post* mold— Dick Harwood would not have been hired by Al Friendly; his father was a fundamentalist, traveling, itinerant preacher in Kansas and Tennessee. And look at Lou Cannon, who is really a conservative, and Lynn Downey."

The emphasis was on proven stars. He hired three Pulitzer Prize winners for the home front, David Broder from the *Times,* Nick Kotz from *The Des Moines Register* and Haynes Johnson from the *Star.*

He scattered bright young men all over the globe—Robert Kaiser, Peter Osnos, Peter Jay, Lewis Diuguid, John Goshko and Jim Hoagland.

"It was like building a baseball team," as one recruit recalled. "Not a team for some time in the future but for right away."

Ben created what he called "creative tension." It pitted reporter against reporter, editor against editor, in a daily contest in which the prize was space on the front page. Newcomers, warned that life at the *Post* would not be easy, were often surprised to find how hard it could be. Those who found the pace overwhelming were made to feel unwelcome. Many, including Pulitzer winner Kotz, soon left.

Old hands who didn't fit into the fast-track mold were bumped down to lonely, undemanding, unrewarding jobs. If they didn't like that, they were encouraged to take their severance and go.

Ben ran things directly and through his picked lieutenants—Simons, Harwood and Larry Stern.

Eugene Patterson was ignored.

"He was in an impossible position," one editor remembers. "At news conferences he just stayed on the edge. All he could do was agree with Ben."

He asked Ben to get off his back, but that wasn't the problem. Ben wasn't on his back, he just didn't give him any authority. He left in less than two years.

Ben would agree later that he had never been given a fair shot at doing his job.

The system worked beautifully up to a point. The key men at the top were imaginative and able and the best new reporters were brilliant but Ben was not much interested in middle management and there was a big gap between.

One of Ben's recruits who had worked at *The New York Times* remembers being surprised at the lack of structure.

"You had very weak deskmen, unlike at the *Times,* where the copydesk is a very important piece of the action, where they use the desk to compensate for the weaknesses of the reporters. The deskmen at the *Post,* the copydesk men, were just well-paid drones, and the assignment editors, the people who dealt with the reporters directly, were unimpressive."

Still by the end of the sixties the *Post* was a better paper than it had ever been before.

On the local pages dull writers still filled pages with dull stories, but bright, perceptive young men and women were now scattered around the country and around the world and bright, perceptive stories around the paper. Simons was in charge of the "Sunday Outlook" section—the weekly collection of think pieces—and it bloomed. The national coverage was good and the foreign second only to the *Times*'.

On Sunday, September 7, 1969 (to pick a day at random), there was only one local story on the front page, a tendentious obituary by Carl Bernstein on a judge named Holtzoff, a quick man with a heavy sentence. Bernstein clearly didn't like Holtzoff. Most of the rest of the page was filled with dispatches from far-flung correspondents—from Belgrade, from Brazil and from Hong Kong. At the top Stanley Karnow speculated on what would happen in Vietnam now that Ho Chi Minh was dead. At the bottom a three-column feature by Philip D. Carter on the future of Alaska jumped to a full page.

The first section had stories from San Clemente on the vacationing President Nixon, on Senator Edward Kennedy's Chappaquiddick problems, and on the mayor's race in Atlanta. Judith Martin had a lively story on the Miss America pageant in Atlantic City.

There were also stories on the election of Yassir Arafat as the leader of the Palestinian Liberation Organization, and on Bernadette Devlin in Northern Ireland.

The spread was impressive but the play was erratic. I. F. Stone had said the new *Post* was the most interesting paper in town because you never knew where you'd find a page-one story.

Except for Karnow's front-page story from Hong Kong, there was nothing on Vietnam until page 22, where the wires reported on a Red offensive and Saigon's reaction to truce suggestions and the *Post*'s own correspondents Peter Arnett and Horst Fass told of a night spent at Fire Base Ike.

Their story began, " 'You will hate it here,' the tall, lean Colonel told the young Americans," and it added a few paragraphs later, "The young men who had arrived that morning as replacements for the Colonel's battered battalion were already scared."

It described an unsuccessful night attack by the Viet Cong and reported that two unnamed soldiers would have killed a captured enemy if the company chaplain hadn't intervened. It limited the colonel's observations to his welcoming address and the single statement that "This is a different war, a different Army than when I was here in 1966."

It was heavy on conclusions and light on significant details.

It did not quote the newly arrived replacements. It did not give their names, their ages, their experiences, their economic backgrounds, their training or say where they came from. It offered only the specific conclusion by Arnett and Fass that they were scared, and the implied one that the war was hopeless.

A couple of years earlier (before he was hired by the paper), Ben Bagdikian had written in *Columbia Journalism Review* that the *Post* was "within a lunge of greatness—but it was not great."

Bagdikian gave specific examples of its shortcomings and Mrs. Graham had been impressed. She had written him a thank-you note. "The main charge, that the paper is unedited, is one Russ and Ben and I are already worried about and agree with . . . the charge that we sometimes let opinion creep into the news columns I find painful because I think it a cardinal sin. It is one we're working on."

They would work on and on, but to surprisingly little avail.

If Ben was worried about erratic coverage, it didn't show. He had other things on his mind. One was the women's section—"For and About Women," run for twenty-three years by Marie Sauer, an editor of competence and presence.

Ben decided she and it were out of fashion.

He hired Helen Dudman, a woman of high ability but very little newspaper experience, as a kind of extra editor and gave her the impossible job of redesigning the section while Miss Sauer was still determinedly in place.

By the end of the year they both were gone and on January 6, 1969, Ben junked "For and About Women" and launched "Style." It was intended to be a dazzling combination of fashion, art, entertainment and interpretive news and features, a daily magazine for the sophisticated.

Assistant managing editor David Laventhol, a graphics whiz from the old New York *Herald Tribune,* was in charge. James Truitt, who had been hired by the *Post* after he had written *Time*'s cover story on Phil Graham, was editor. Truitt had been Phil's fair-haired young man, a *Post* company vice-president and publisher of *ARTnews.* After Phil's death he had bounced around the empire and by the time he came to "Style" he was on the edge of collapse. He spent fourteen hours a day on the job and wrote a steady stream of long confusing memos. In six months he caved in.

His wife sued him for divorce and at her urging the court appointed a conservator to manage his affairs. He returned to work after some weeks and was fired.

The third principal at "Style" was Nicholas von Hoffman, an aging flower child, white of hair, thick of waist, who wrote colorful, labored, elitist tirades against members of the lower middle class and their institutions. He had worked with Saul Alinsky as a professional radical in Chicago and had been hired by Ben as a voice of indignant youth though he was perilously close to forty.

He was put in charge of "Style"'s cultural coverage and began by depriving the sitting critics of theatre, movies, music and art of their jurisdictions and assigning reviews to whoever took his passing fancy. He was fiercely resisted and he soon retreated to writing a column called "Poster."

"Poster" was "Style"'s first striking success, though it sometimes seemed too rich to be true. Chalmers Roberts would write that Von Hoffman "had an ear for dialogue so sharp that some felt he must be inventing the words."

He was skilled, often irritating, an advocate who saw people and situations through the eyes of his own ideology. He covered the trial of Abbie Hoffman and other members of the Chicago Seven on charges of conspiring to riot at the 1968 Democratic convention and found clear-cut villains (which was not difficult) and clear-cut heroes (which was). He looked at the jury panel and found crew-cut men and "blue-haired ladies with spiked heels and rhinestone glasses" but, he noted with heavy sarcasm, the panel of "Abbie's peers was not entirely drawn from the lower middle class," since "the prosecution was able to find and knock out one boy who had just graduated from college."

He found that one of the defense attorneys bore a resemblance to Daniel Webster and by contrast offered a sketch of Julius Hoffman, the man presiding: "the teeny judge who bounces up and down on his bench so that he looks like a small girl in an oversized dress playing in her father's chair."

Von Hoffman caught and grossly exaggerated the *Post*'s traditional tone of superiority. In Phil's day the *Post* had been elitist but discreet. Von Hoffman was unbridled. He would describe with snobbish scorn the hairdos and home furnishings of a group of wives of Vietnam prisoners of war, who were vigorously opposed to the Viet Cong. He would deride President Carter as "Jimmy Peanut . . . the gleamy-toothed, bushy-tailed anointed chipmunk of the Lord" and he would in time suggest, apparently seriously, that Ralph Nader was the only Presidential possibility serious people could support.

He was in favor of the "now people" who were "groovy, sexy, beautiful, swinging, mellow, hip and hep" and against those who were "old, ugly, square, plastic and out of it."

He set the tone for "Style." It soon became the voice of the precious few and an affront to many. Katharine Graham worried about it. She was, she told Ben in a memo, "willing and eager to stand still for Nick whom I consider first-rate and worth the gaff and of interest to the young and black whom we need to attract. But I am not willing to use the rest of the section to appeal to one per cent of our readers."

"Style" ran into major difficulties every day. Howie Simons would say that it was "mixed up, identity-crisis-ridden, constantly traumatized and perhaps mismanaged."

But it was original.

It had first-class graphics and, in addition to Von Hoffman, it had solid, witty features by Michael Kernan and Maxine Cheshire's caustic and substantial gossip column, "VIP." It was soon being imitated in newsrooms all over the country. By the end of six months the leadership was gone—Laventhol left to be managing editor of *Newsday*—and there was blood all over the floor. Truitt was followed as editor by Elsie Carper, who was followed by Larry Stern, who was followed by Tom Kendrick, who would finally put it all together.

It would be Ben's greatest personal triumph. It had impact and so did he. He had many pristine qualities—he was a persuader, a cajoler and an inspirer. Sometimes he picked people who did not rise to the challenge and those he quickly forgot. Sometimes he could make a person of unknown talents perform beyond reasonable expectation.

One day in 1969 he made a snap decision that would change both his and the *Post*'s future. He called a young woman on the phone whom he'd never met and offered her a job. Her name was Sally Quinn. She was a slim, unemployed blonde in her late twenties who'd been down on her luck.

When Ben called, she was at low ebb.

She had always been a person of extravagant dreams but now none of them seemed to be coming true.

Her father was a general in the Army, William "Buffalo Bill" Quinn. Soldiers of destiny seem always to have sponsors as well as nicknames. Quinn's was Senator Barry Goldwater and under the Senator's kindly eye he had moved up, up, up, from colonel to brigadier to three-star general.

Sally's mother went amicably along, pursuing status and the social graces. Sally grew up lonely, coddled and resentful. When she was at her father's army posts she was in total command of the troops but when she went to the big East Coast cities she was just another army brat lost in the Pentagon crowd.

When she was seven her mother and father left her alone in an army hospital in Tokyo for six months while she slowly recovered from a ruptured appendix.

"The doctor wouldn't let us visit her," Sally's mother would recall many years later. "Because it upset the children when the parents left."

As a teen-ager Sally wrote a short story about life as a hospital patient called "Dead White."

"Sally said she used to hear footsteps in the corridor and think they were mine and they never were," the mother remembers. "It made me very sad."

In time Sally went to Smith, majored in theatrical arts and finished, in her own phrase, "at the exact bottom of my class."

She tried to crack Broadway and failed—"I didn't want to act enough to humiliate myself day after day"—and she worked for a spell as a flack for a Coney Island animal show.

In 1964 Buffalo Bill's association with Presidential candidate Goldwater brought him embarrassing attention. CBS correspondent Daniel Schorr reported that Goldwater planned to visit the Quinns at their cottage at Berchtesgaden, Germany, where, as Schorr pointed out, Adolf Hitler once had also had a home away from home.

The general had hoped to return to Washington in triumph as Chief of Staff, but he as well as Goldwater was buried in the Johnson landslide. He came home to a formal retirement ceremony instead. Sally was furious.

"There we were alone in a dreary town with no quarters, no orderlies, limousines, aides—no nothing."

She knocked around doing odd jobs.

She was social secretary to Cherif Guellal, the Algerian Ambassador—she "organized his social life"—until the Arab-Israeli war broke out and Algeria called him home. She fell in with a hustling young *New York Post* reporter named Warren Hoge. She did a piece for the *Washington Post* magazine, with the help of Hoge, called "How to Woo Washington Men" but it did not establish her as a journalistic ingenue. A couple of years went by. She worked for Dillon Ripley at the Smithsonian but each found the other uncongenial. She worked as a low-paid staffer in the Eugene McCarthy and Bobby Kennedy Presidential campaigns. She became engaged to Hoge and then disengaged and she went to California, where she spent a few sad, unproductive months with her married sister.

Then she came back to Washington and persuaded her parents to let her give an attention-getting party.

"My father was giving me five dollars a week. I was desperate. I got my parents to stake me to a party, so people would know I was back in town and I could start looking for a job. It was for Barry Goldwater, Junior, who was an old friend, and I had about a hundred people—Tom Braden, Margo and Gil Hahn, and, oh, I can't remember who else."

The next day Ben called and offered her a job on "Style" covering parties. The only newspaper story she'd ever had a hand in was the one she'd done with Hoge and she couldn't write worth beans.

She had, however, less obvious qualifications. The Quinns had moved around the outer circles of Washington society on the basis of her father's military positions. Sally had a cold eye for the rich and socially ambitious who came to town and tried to buy or charm their way to the Georgetown heights.

Her stories poured out free-form and her editors spent hours taking them apart and putting them back together. They were always too long and her rivals on "Style" who had to fight for less space resented her greatly. The stories, however, had a quality all their own. They were sharp, perceptive, vivid and unkind.

She also got along with the boss. She and Ben had a lot in common. They had both spent their youths on the humiliating edge of high, affluent society and they would never forget it.

"I covered parties the way they were, not the way the hostess wanted them to be covered," she would say later. "I covered them the way someone on the 'Metro' section covers a crime."

Her singular career began to hit stride with a sharp-edged piece about a rising young and wealthy political couple in New York City named Carter and Amanda Burden. They would not rise much further.

She covered other New York parties, such as one by well-connected George Plimpton, more gently.

After a while she shifted her attention to Washington and one Sunday she took apart a young Congressional staffer named Steve Martindale, an ambitious bachelor who had met John and Yoko Lennon at a party in New York when they were feeling desperate about gaining custody of Yoko's children. He told them he'd be glad to introduce them to influential people in Washington and they grasped at the straw. They came down and Steve threw a party and his boss, Senator Charles Goodell, came and so did a lot of others from the Hill and the press who wanted to meet a Beatle. When Sally got around to him a couple of years later, Martindale was working for the public-relations firm of Hill and Knowlton and had just pulled a social coup of sorts by giving a party for Joan Braden to which he inveigled a clutch of celebrities he had never actually met.

He did know Mrs. Braden, a close friend of Nelson Rockefeller's. They had met while both were campaigning for Republicans. She had been most kind, giving him inside secrets on how to throw dynamite parties without spending a lot of money. Sally's story considered Steve as a social freak.

"I had watched and observed him for two and a half years and was fascinated, since he had no background and no money. On youth, charm and niceness, he managed to go from nothing to the number-one host. I wanted to find out how he did it. It was like finding the cause of cancer."

Sally's piece went beyond Steve. It offered guidelines to the upwardly mobile. She listed rules for party giving: (1) fill a void, (2) have a sponsor, (3) know whom to invite, (4) master techniques, (5) have persistence, (6) have a thick skin, (7) give productive parties that are fun, (8) plan and work hard, (9) have an emotional need to be a great host or hostess, (10) do it inexpensively, (11) have the right kind of personality.

Steve was very much hurt.

"If I had been Nelson Rockefeller and had done precisely the same thing," he said with absolute accuracy, "no one would have thought a thing about it. Since I wasn't, I had to be after something."

Sally would say later that her story had nothing to do with Steve as a person. Steve would take his drubbing and later say, hopefully, "I'm finally getting along with Ben and Sally."

Sally was soon the most feared social journalist in town. She would often describe some of the less comely celebrities in starkly realistic physical terms. (She was paid back, painfully, after she wrote about Redskin quarterback Billy Kilmer, hinting that he had propositioned her during the interview. Kilmer, asked about it later, said, "Oh, you mean the blonde with the little tits.")

Sally would crush many a butterfly on the wheel and she seemed to have a standard for fairness somewhat below Nicholas von Hoffman's.

She also would be lured into making an ill-considered move toward conquering the strange world of network TV.

Most of the time Katharine left Ben, "Style" and the news columns alone.

Her father had once said she would make a first-class businessman and that was the challenge she took seriously.

She wished to be like him and in many ways she was. She was formally polite, she answered her personal mail, even notes from strangers, and she was also frequently rude. She was remote, apparently unable to remember the names and faces of many of her old employees, often arbitrary, sometimes brutal. She too had a fierce temper.

She had few close friends but cherished the ones she had.

Like her father she had confidants whom she trusted. Most were men. Some were mentors, some were escorts and some were both.

In one respect she was her father's twin: she would make great errors of judgment but she would accept the consequences, reverse her field and start all over.

She had not adopted a long-range plan for personal development when she was young (as he had), but after taking over the paper she began, systematically, building a new Katharine Graham.

She emerged from what writer Judith Viorst called her "groaning and sighing, it's impossible, poor little me" stage, slimmed down, took voice lessons, acquired an interest and expertise in clothes and studied the mysteries of finance and administration.

She allowed herself one silly whirl.

Truman Capote, her New York co-op neighbor at the United Nations Plaza, gave the masquerade of the century in her honor.

There were 540 guests—including fellow media notables William S. Paley, Samuel I. Newhouse and John Hay Whitney; dignitaries from Washington such as Undersecretary of State Nicholas deB. Katzenbach and Defense Secretary Robert S. McNamara; and nondignitaries such as Norman Mailer and Frank Sinatra.

It was held at the white-and-gold ballroom of the Plaza Hotel and she wore a jeweled mask and a white Balmain gown. Everyone wore masks, even the Secret Service men guarding Lynda Bird Johnson, and some masks (though not theirs and not Katharine's) cost $500 or $600.

The guests danced to Peter Duchin's orchestra, drank four hundred bottles of Taittinger champagne and ate $12,000 worth of exotic and domestic food.

Katharine said later that it seemed like "an odd, overaged and gray coming-out party" and she never did anything like it again.

She maintained an active, cool social life—her childhood years of scheduled tennis, swimming and strenuous participation in a variety of group events had left their mark. She entertained and traveled and spent hours talking and listening to prominent people, active, ambitious people. She kept her distance. She apparently found it difficult to be (or at any rate to seem) relaxed and interested with those who lacked the signs and tones of an upper-class background. She would remain a private person and though her name would be linked with a number of men (in some cases by the men themselves), the linkages never rang true.

She could relax with Ben Bradlee and Howie Simons. Simons would say, frequently, that if there had to be publishers, Katharine was the best, but even with them there was a clear detachment. She had been conditioned by a life of wealth and training to regard herself as a responsible member of a ruling elite. Once her husband and her children had been her only business. Now her husband was dead and it was time for her to get down to new business.

She began making large-scale decisions, some better than others.

One wise one was to purchase 45 percent of the Paris edition of the New York *Herald Tribune.*

Americans abroad had been reading it since 1887. When the New York *Herald Tribune* went out of business in the sixties its Paris branch lost its essential news-gathering base. Katharine gave it a new one.

The name was changed to *International Herald Tribune* and John Hay "Jock" Whitney (a guest at the ball), whose family had owned the *Trib,* kept the rest of the stock. In time they would cut in *The New York Times,* which closed its European edition, for slightly less than a third. It was a sound investment all around.

It would be the morning paper for thousands of multinational corporation heads—one reader out of four would be a member of a major board—and, based on its number of subscribers, it would have the highest ad rate in the world.

Its worth would climb from $1 million to $20 million.

Fritz Beebe handled the deal. Katharine trusted him. He had taken over as the Post Company's board chairman a short time before Phil's death and they had learned the business together.

"This company grew like Topsy," she would say later. "I was new and Fritz was new. He and I had a marvelous relationship. He was so decent, so wise; he had a brilliant corporate mind. He saved me."

Some of her decisions did not work out so well and some of her business associates would not remain so cherished.

When she and her advisers decided to build a magnificent new home for the *Post,* they hired I. M. Pei to design it. When he produced plans for a $50 million colossus, some of the executives, such as publisher John Sweeterman, said okay but Katharine said no. She hired a new architect, paid Pei his $2 million fee and soon replaced Sweeterman with Paul R. Ignatius, an ex-Secretary of the Navy. Ignatius had been recommended by her friend and escort Robert McNamara and he was a mistake. One of his jobs would be to deal with the *Post*'s printers and pressmen, who were seething with semi-logical grievances. They were overpaid and underworked but felt with considerable justification that the *Post* regarded them simply as faceless adversaries in a hard and endless war.

When negotiations began, Ignatius decided they were too strong to resist. He kept his regular hours, spent weekends on his farm, and let the next man in line, James Daly, handle them. Katharine was furious. She fired him, though it cost her $150,000.

The *Post* was moving on to greater triumphs and conflicts. Style would thrive but the unions remained angry and would grow increasingly militant and so would Katharine.

CHAPTER

18

The sixties, Katharine and the *Post*'s decade of development, were drawing to a close.

Donnie Graham, who had accepted the draft and gone to Vietnam, returned somewhat disillusioned—"After I was there for a week, I concluded the war was futile"—and became a policeman. It was an exciting but troubled time.

The *Post* was rich. Ben was riding high in the newsroom and Richard Nixon was in the White House. The *Post* did not want him there. Its masthead had proclaimed its independence for decades but it had been independent only in the narrowest sense. It had no formal allegiance to either political party but its publishers had put it to regular partisan use.

Ned McLean had been the incompetent, obedient servant of Harding and Coolidge, and Eugene and Agnes Meyer had helped choose three losing Republican Presidential candidates, Alf Landon, Wendell Willkie and Thomas Dewey.

Philip Graham had been a more successful manipulator, deeply, deliberately and bipartisanly involved in candidate making.

Katharine had given Lyndon Johnson her personal loyalty but, in the end, she had gently disposed of Editor Wiggins, the true loyalist, and had let Ben Bradlee and Phil Geyelin take over the paper. Now the *Post* was closer to political impartiality than it had ever been before but that was not really very close.

In 1968 it endorsed neither Hubert Humphrey, an old friend, nor

Richard Nixon, but its preference was clear and it was not, primarily, a political one.

The *Post* had first become painfully aware of Nixon when, as a freshman Congressman from California, he had pursued Alger Hiss ambitiously and relentlessly. He had been, obviously, a fellow who did not observe eastern establishment rules. One was that people like Alger Hiss were not pursued without very good reason and unattractive plebeian fat men like Whittaker Chambers, the reformed Communist and Hiss's accuser, were not believed without even better ones.

Herblock had fixed Nixon's public image as a sweating, blue-jawed Red-baiter.

The *Post*'s editorial writers had treated him, as Congressman, Senator, Vice President and Presidential candidate (the first time around), with the disdain of the well-bred for the uncouth.

Still Katharine made a new effort. She invited him to lunch with the editors in July and the meeting was polite but not productive. She may have been half willing but he was not. He was a man of deep, lingering resentments and he had no intention of courting the *Post.*

A few weeks later he picked Spiro Agnew, a man with even less elegance, as his candidate for Vice President.

An editorial by Ward Just put the two of them in their places: "Nixon's decision to name Agnew . . . may come to be regarded as perhaps the most eccentric political appointment since the Roman Emperor Caligula named his horse a consul."

It was a nice turn of phrase and, as it turned out, accurate within the rules of hyperbole, but to many ordinary people it seemed yet another example of the *Post* looking down its upper-class nose at the grocer's son from California and the immigrant's son from Baltimore.

Nixon and Agnew won anyway.

The inaugural coverage was extensive and largely objective though the phrase "young protesters hurled sticks and debris at President Nixon's limousine" might have seemed a trifle too detached to some.

There was an arch editorial on the inaugural speech:

"It would be a mistake to read too much into the echoes of Lyndon Johnson in Mr. Nixon's rhetoric for there were also echoes of Adlai Stevenson and Hubert Humphrey and—above all—a wealth of locutions and admonitions reminiscent of President Kennedy's Inaugural address."

The next day there was another. Herblock had announced the day after the election that he would stop drawing Nixon with dark, beardy jowls. Now the *Post* had a little in-house fun: "Mr. Block had indicated on Nov. 7 that (artistically speaking) he meant to give the newly elected President a 'free shave' but thereafter, quite mysteriously, Mr. Nixon more or less vanished from Herblock's work. Thus seventy-four long days and nights went by before Mr. Block fulfilled his commitment. We say 'more or less' because he did turn up on two occasions, once barely discernible in a space suit and once adorned with a tie-on Santa Claus beard. . . ."

Still the *Post* editorial page no longer spoke with a single voice and in February Stephen Rosenfeld gave the new President a little boost. His performance, Rosenfeld wrote, was "deeply troubling to inveterate Nixon knockers" and Nixon sent him a thank-you note.

Katharine made an added effort too; she invited administration people to dine, including old friends such as William Rogers, Henry Kissinger and Daniel Patrick Moynihan, and new nonfriends such as John Mitchell and John Ehrlichman. The nonfriends did not seem grateful and were not asked again.

In the fall Vice President Agnew began denouncing the eastern establishment press. He would get more specific as time went by. After Ohio National Guardsmen killed the Kent State students, he made a mocking reference to "the hysterical [reaction] from the *Post*'s ivory tower."

There was a tempting inclination to dismiss Agnew as a buffoon but the *Post* found to its alarm that his invective appealed to many people.

He attacked it as not so much the promoter of Democratic Party liberal domestic ideology (which indeed it was not) but as a snob paper that regarded lower-middle-class people as probable slobs or even (as in the case of the teen-age National Guardsmen) as possible thugs.

As a countermeasure, Ben appointed Richard Harwood the paper's first ombudsman. Harwood, a man with a clear conscience and a hard nose, did most of his work from within. He counted column inches and found the same counterculture tilt Katharine Graham had noticed in "Style" some months before. He wrote an in-house memo:

"Our standards are subjective and whimsical. They reflect our tastes, values, prejudices, opinions and conveniences. . . . We are a 'white' newspaper in a southern or crypto-southern area of circulation. . . . There are millions of Poles and Italians and Chicanos and farmers and coal miners out there but very few in our newsroom. . . . Our coverage of the New Culture has been so extensive in the news columns, in Style, on the editorial pages, in the literary, art, theater and movie columns—that we may sometimes appear to be a new culture organ."

He also solicited the opinions of other members of the staff.

Peter Osnos wrote: "We are, for the most part, a collection of Easterners, middle class or upper-middle class, well-educated, relatively sophisticated, generally liberal. This shows in our reporting."

William Greider, a reporter on the national desk, offered this view: "Agnew has spoken of Eastern bias but it is really cultural. It turns up in the columns of The Post, Times and other members of the media axis. The core of it is the unspoken assumption that the rest of the country is filled with boobs, simple folks who look eastward for their model of the nobler goals but can be expected to do the wrong thing."

William Raspberry, a wise columnist, who was also a recognized black spokesman, had this to say: "If you were a Martian and read nothing but the Washington Post you would think this city is inhabited by five kinds of people—Georgetown and Northwest whites, black militants at 14th and U, black criminals, black welfare mothers. What is there in the paper for the big, black middle-class out there between 16th St. and Catholic University? What is there in the paper for the white plumber? Practically nothing. These people don't make the happenings so they are ignored and we get a false image of our community."

The *Post* would continue to worry about its image but old habits would be hard to break.

The *Post* would change, though not in the way prescribed. Agnes Meyer died right at the start of the seventies and some of the old *Post* attitude died with her. She had had a full but frustrating life and she didn't want to leave it. She once wrote, "Do anything to me but do not let me die." She had been both an elitist and a social conservative. She had believed in strong discipline for the young and the working classes. She had once been a power in Washington (though never as powerful as she wished to be).

She had achieved status and wealth by marrying Eugene but he had, in the end, turned against her. In his last days, she had written Katharine, she had become "the target of his inner turmoil," and she had added, with a measure of self-pity, "When he was strong I could fight back. That is out of the question now. He conquers through weakness and I am helpless."

The new *Post* would be elitist but permissive. When tens of thousands of young people, most of them children of the affluent suburbs, came to Washington on May Day, 1971, with the announced intention of disrupting the government, the *Post* was not particularly alarmed but a great many simple, solid citizens in Washington and around the country were. The demonstrators disrupted traffic, if not the government, and a few hard-core activists smashed shop and bank windows along Connecticut Avenue.

Tear gas canisters were fired at a crowd in front of the Justice Department and some 12,000 demonstrators were arrested and confined at the Robert Kennedy Stadium a mile and a half from the Capitol. Some were held for thirty-six hours.

The *Post* covered the day's events in great detail (there were nine by-lined stories) and much of the coverage had overtones of sympathy for the disrupters in the street.

The next day an editorial proclaimed that the misbehavior of the young visitors could not be accepted as "an excuse for the prosecutors to set themselves up as judge and jury and to punish people by holding them in confinement, illegally, beyond any period sanctioned by any law or any court. That may appeal to some people as rough and ready justice, and no better [sic] than the demonstrators deserved but to us it is a gross abuse of the principles of equal justice under law, which in turn are fundamental to the very system that the demonstrations were designed to paralyze."

The editorial, though hazy toward the end, made a sound legal point—the courts did in time find the mass arrests illegal and ordered the government to pay a lump sum in damages to be divided among those detained—but to many people there did seem to be some element of rough-and-ready justice involved and the *Post* editorial, like many a *Post* editorial before, would seem one-sided, preachy and patronizing.

The editorials would in time lose much of their faculty-lounge archness and the editors would try earnestly if clumsily to talk to the black bourgeoisie in northeast Washington, if not to the white plumber in the Maryland suburbs. They would hire more blacks, but not a noticeable number of Poles, Italians or Chicanos, and the people in charge would continue to give the impression that deep in their hearts they believed people from the right part of the country, with the right background and out of the right schools, were more equal, more able and more interesting than anyone else.

That obviously did not include the Nixons.

When Tricia Nixon, the older daughter of the President, married a young man named Edward Finch Cox in the rose garden at the White House one drizzly Saturday in June, the *Post* gave the event extensive coverage.

The lead story, which lacked a by-line, noted that the ceremonies had been held outdoors in a light rain at the bride's insistence.

"Several of the guests shielded themselves as best they could and complained of discomfort," the story added.

It went on with a little dig here, a little dig there.

"The bride had looked tense when she first appeared on her father's arm with her train looped over her other arm but she followed his direction to smile at the press stand before descending to the garden."

Alice Roosevelt Longworth, always a *Post* favorite, was given an opportunity to be critical.

"Alice Longworth said that she felt as if she had been sitting on a wet sponge during the ceremony. Asked if she were reminded of her own wedding in 1906, she replied, 'Good God, not a bit. I was married twenty years before Hollywood. This wedding was quite a production.' "

Driving that point home, another story, headed "For $19,000 You Can Have One Too," noted that taxpayers had paid for most of it. Another story listed all the persons of high position who had not been invited.

A third offered the opinion that "The White House Guards for once looked appropriately dressed in their relatively new Graustarkian gold-trimmed white uniforms." The gaudy uniforms had been Nixon's own idea.

The *Post* took a more serious step toward open warfare with the White House a few days later.

CHAPTER

19

On Sunday, June 13, 1971, *The New York Times* began publishing excerpts from *The Pentagon Papers,* a secret, 7,000-page, forty-seven-volume history of America's involvement in Vietnam, compiled in the sixties at the order of Robert McNamara, then the Secretary of Defense.

Fifteen copies had been printed and issued, under careful controls, to the White House, the State Department, and a few former and present high officials.

The *Post* was chagrined and on Monday it began a determined game of catch-up.

Murrey Marder and Chalmers Roberts rewrote the *Times.* Their first story, headed "U. S. Planned Before Tonkin For War On North, Files Show," acknowledged that the *Times* was their source.

On Tuesday the *Post* carried another rewrite plus the announcement that the Justice Department was moving to suppress the publication of further excerpts by the *Times.*

On the sixteenth, U. S. district judge Murray I. Gurfein ordered the *Times* to stop publication. The *Post* had another rewrite plus the information that the FBI was checking on everyone who had access to the report. It was soon apparent that the principal suspect was a former Pentagon analyst named Daniel Ellsberg, an old friend of Ben Bagdikian's. Bagdikian got in touch with Ellsberg and arranged for the *Post* to acquire its own copies of the papers.

Bagdikian flew to Boston, where Ellsberg was holed up, and returned. He arrived at Ben Bradlee's house in Georgetown, carrying 4,400 pages in two satchels, at 10 A.M. on June 17.

Bradlee summoned three reporters, Marder, Roberts and Don Oberdorfer; Phil Geyelin and Meg Greenfield, from the editorial page; and Howard Simons, the deputy managing editor. Eugene Patterson remained back at the office. Two lawyers arrived, from the *Post*'s New York law firm.

The lawyers wanted the *Post* to wait until the courts had ruled. Fritz Beebe, the chairman of the board of the Post Company, arrived and agreed. Bradlee and the editorial people were for immediate publication.

Beebe called Katharine Graham and said he was against publication but "it's up to you to decide."

She said, "Okay, go ahead, go ahead." She would remain aloof but staunch. She seemed determined to give her editors and her paper every opportunity.

The next day, Friday, the *Post* had "The First of a Series" over Chalmers Roberts' by-line, giving its own reading of papers the *Times* hadn't gotten around to yet. Since the *Times* had been enjoined, the *Post* had it all to itself. After the second of the series ran on Saturday, the *Post* was enjoined as well.

Everyone awaited the court's final ruling.

Von Hoffman offered his opinion of the judge who had restrained the *Times* in a casual clause:

". . . Murray I. Gurfein, the grungy Judge who paid Nixon back for appointing him to U. S. District Court by breaking the fundamental law of the nation."

The Supreme Court heard the arguments on July 1 and lifted the order by a vote of 6 to 3.

Patterson, back at the paper, climbed up on a desk and shouted, "We win and so does *The New York Times.*"

In fact both the *Post*'s battle and its victory were more fuzzy than that.

The Supreme Court's split decision (three of the Justices seem to have been grungy by Von Hoffman's standard) did not undo the new principle of prior restraint. It decided that *The Pentagon Papers* did not contain information that was essential to the security of the United States and that it therefore was not necessary to forestall publication.

It did not rule that under the First Amendment newspapers had the right to publish whatever classified documents they could get their hands on.

The *Post*'s role was distinctly different from the *Times*'. The *Times* had decided after months of consideration and preparation to take the risk and publish papers classified top secret, in order to expose the fact that the Johnson administration had deliberately, routinely and repeatedly lied to the American public about the war.

That goal had been achieved when the first *Times* article ran on Sunday. When the *Post* joined in, it added nothing essential.

Some three years later Ben Bradlee would recall the "exact moment . . . I myself confront[ed] freedom of the press as a passionate, personal, immediate reality instead of a glorious concept, lovingly taught but cherished from afar, from a seat in the audience instead of a role on the vital stage. . . ."

It was, he said, the moment when Bagdikian returned with the bags.

Richard Harwood had a somewhat more down-to-earth recollection. "Our main concern was not the public's right to know, it wasn't that we ought to tell people about this dreadful war in Vietnam," he told writer Howard Bray. "We had one basic consideration, and that was here was a hell of a news story and we were getting our ass beaten."

Still the *Post* did, unknowingly, set a mighty train in motion.

President Nixon was outraged at the leak and he ordered an all-out effort to punish Ellsberg.

Three months later a motley band of burglars, led by a former CIA official named Howard Hunt, broke into the office of Ellsberg's psychiatrist in Los Angeles, intending to steal his records. They couldn't find them.

The publication of *The Pentagon Papers* marked a new era.

For years the *Post*'s editors had insisted that their only worthy rival was *The New York Times*. Now they really believed it. Ben had the challenge and a great many troops but he had a lot of distractions.

He could look out from his office and beam or frown on a newsroom full of reporters and subeditors, swarming in and out, night and day, but he found some more appealing than others.

He liked talented people, bursting with energy, who put the *Post* first and produced. The people in the newsroom were just human beings and many were chronically unhappy. There was constant tension and most of it was not what he would consider creative.

The black reporters were, as a group, the most discontented. The women reporters were not far behind. Most of the blacks were new, young and relatively inexperienced. Most of them worked under "Metro" editor Harry Rosenfeld and city editor Barry Sussman, both hard taskmasters.

Rosenfeld, an intense driven man, had been born a Jew in Berlin in 1930. He had been beaten up by Nazis as a child and when his father had been arrested suddenly in the night, his mother took his sister and him and fled to America.

He was loud, aggressive and emotional and he was not a Bradlee favorite. At the daily news conferences he would fight dramatically and often unsuccessfully for front-page space. Once Larry Stern, the national editor, hired a Gypsy fiddler to lurk out of sight until Rosenfeld began his pleading and then step forward, his bow sawing away, making his violin cry. The gathering had a good laugh at Rosenfeld's expense.

Rosenfeld had his admirers as well as his detractors. "What have you done for me lately?" he would shout at reporters, even those who had turned in good stories the day before. The producers were amused and called him Uncle Harry. The others were not and they had other names for him.

When Ben ordered him to tighten up the "Metro" staff, he did. Nine black "Metro" reporters, two of them women, then sent Ben a formal letter of complaint. It shook him up.

Reporters made specific complaints of ill treatment. The letter then went on to more general grievances.

"Mr. Bradlee," it said, "We would like to have written answers to the following questions by Friday, February 11, 1972, by 6:30 P.M.

"Why are there no blacks in top editorial management positions?

"Why are there no blacks on the news desk?

"Why is the African bureau being closed temporarily?"

Ben sent a short reply the next day. "I am against ultimatums on principle. They add one more barrier to the solution of problems that are already hard to solve."

On Monday he and Howard Simons met with the petitioners. Ben still did not answer the questions that had been asked (most were beyond simple answers) but addressed broader issues.

"You are here," he said, "because you feel seriously aggrieved and discriminated against—because you feel that *The Washington Post* as an institution and some of its managers are consciously or unconsciously racist."

He went on to say that those present should speak fully and candidly.

The protesters suggested that timetables and goals should be set for the hiring of additional blacks and the promotion of some already hired. Ben turned them down, saying that for one thing it would cost two million dollars.

He also said he didn't believe in quotas.

"This is a tough league here. Quality, quality—that's the test."

The debate would go fruitlessly on.

To a considerable degree the *Post* management had trapped itself. It had been particularly diligent in hiring blacks and by the early seventies 10 percent of all black newspaper people working for the general, daily press were working for *The Washington Post.*

Some were of high competence, some were not. Many had been hired who did not have the level of experience the *Post* ordinarily demanded.

Some black reporters saw themselves with double responsibilities, as advocates as well as news people. Some white subeditors with black assistants adopted a meek policy of never complaining and doing the more tedious chores themselves.

Rosenfeld said he treated everyone alike.

"Some reporters were incompetent or lazy," he said later. "The fact that they were black was only a circumstance. There were whites who were incompetent and lazy. The fault was in the early decisions bringing on blacks who were inexperienced."

As the discussions went on, twenty-six other black reporters and editors, led by Robert Maynard, sent a more moderate letter to Ben.

It said in part: "On this newspaper . . . and generally in this society, black Americans are painfully aware of the lack of their participation in the writing of the story of America in a time of change. We could not insist that all matters relative to blacks be written and reported by blacks, any more than we could countenance the writing of all stories of women, by women, all Catholic by Catholics, all whites by whites. But the lack of black participation in the shaping of the news about the society in which they play so vital a role has led to unfortunate distortions of the basic posture of the community on such vital questions as crime in the streets and the busing of school children."

One evening Leon Dash, a respected reporter on the national staff, was drinking a few Manhattans at the Watergate bar when he decided to call up Ben.

Ben told him to come out to his house. When he arrived, Ben opened the door and Dash said, "Let's take off the gloves."

Ben mixed drinks and they had a prolonged and angry discussion. Dash complained particularly that city editor Sussman frequently yelled at black reporters. At the end of the conversation, still angry, he shouted at Ben, "We're going to shake your tree."

Ben thought it over and made a formal offer to the original protesters. He said he would hire another black assistant city editor, another black reporter for the national staff and two black trainees.

The protesters, whose number had dropped to seven, turned him down and filed charges of discrimination with the Equal Employment Opportunities Commission.

At this point Ben Bagdikian, who had succeeded Harwood as ombudsman, stepped in.

"Newspaper corporations, like all others, hate to have their linens washed in public," he wrote in his column, "except that laundering significant linen in public is part of the business newspapers are in, a goal frequently forgotten when newspapers themselves get into troubles with unions, inner finances and hierarchical struggles. When blacks' complaints reach formal negotiations and certainly when they come to an apparent impasse, as they seem to be at this moment, this is something a newspaper cannot conceal from a community that depends on the paper and in a city where race is particularly important, just because it is happening to the newspaper itself."

The ombudsman was by definition free to express himself as he wished but Ben was not pleased.

A month later at a conference on "black priorities" in Cambridge, Massachusetts, Bagdikian rather casually suggested that blacks who felt that newspapers were discriminating against blacks would find it more effective to boycott the papers than to denounce the publisher. He pointed out that the *Post* would be particularly vulnerable. He was quoted in an AP story that went out on the national wire.

Ben was furious and he told Bagdikian when he returned that he would not put up with "one of my lieutenants" advocating a boycott.

Bagdikian replied that "I'm not one of your lieutenants. I'm writing for the readers."

Ben demanded he resign and Bagdikian did. Two days later, after thinking it over, Ben backed down and asked him to remain. Bagdikian stayed for a couple of months, found his position increasingly uncomfortable, however, and left.

The local EEOC office ruled in favor of the blacks but the Commission itself decided not to pursue the matter by a vote of 3 to 2.

Meanwhile a group of women reporters and editors also filed a complaint with the EEOC, charging discrimination against women. The EEOC found they were right.

The storms of 1972 slowly passed. Ben had lost one and tied one and he was not a graceful loser. When a black reporter named Joel Dreyfus applied for the job of chief of the *Post*'s Los Angeles bureau he got more than a formal refusal.

"Ever since you joined the paper," Ben wrote, "you have been critical of its managers, their attitudes on racial matters, their personnel policies, their assignments. You have made it clear that you prefer not to become a team player, but to stay outside and try to change the paper in your own image. Editors have invariably respected your talents, if not always your performance. But they have always resented your attitudes. When jobs have opened up that interested you, you invariably applied. When jobs opened up where we wanted you, you invariably turned us down and were critical of us for offering you jobs you considered beneath you.

"This is how you gained the reputation you have among the editors here, the reputation of being a gifted journalist who is also a pain in the ass. All of us would love to have—and will have—as our Los Angeles bureau chief a gifted journalist. None of us want a pain in the ass out there."

Roger Wilkins, who quit his job as a *Post* editorial writer in bitterness, would say that Ben "would rather be clever than decent."

He gave writer James Fallows a detailed sketch of Ben as he saw him.

"It seems to me that Ben never comprehended the women's movement or the black movement. It is clear to me that he never comprehended the agonies that society and *The Washington Post* itself inflicted on blacks who were talented and sensitive enough to be valued employees of the paper. He is not a patient man and the combination of his impatience, his sense of how intractable the problems were and his lack of understanding led him to make anti-black and anti-feminist cracks. These may have been less indicative of his real feeling than of his frustrations. They may make him appear to be a less worthwhile person than he actually is. They did not endear him to me."

It seems a rather accurate picture. Ben was not a patient man and the *Post* was a demanding and impersonal place. Few people, of any race or either sex, felt either secure or appreciated.

Myra MacPherson, a highly respected *Post* veteran, summed up her feeling not as a woman but as an employee: "I sometimes think that if I suddenly disappeared, no one would notice I was gone for two weeks and then they'd be afraid to ask what happened to me."

Judith Martin, who would in time become Miss Manners, would feel frustrated along the way.

"They have a great personnel technique. First they tell you that you should keep on doing whatever trivial thing you're doing, since no one else could do it so well. Then if you persist they start to suggest that you really don't do anything very well."

The *Post*'s days of greatest triumph were just ahead but so were its days of greatest turmoil. There were angry people all over the building.

CHAPTER

20

Not everyone was unhappy at the *Post.*

Bob Woodward, for example, felt perfectly at home and Carl Bernstein had a sense of alienation he enjoyed. The two were not friends though their names would soon be linked forevermore. They had little in common.

Woodward was twenty-nine, divorced a couple of years and working at the *Post* for one. Working was the word for Bob. He had a clear goal in life: he wanted to be very successful. He had gone to Yale, studied hard and written a novel which remained unpublished. The Navy had paid his college tuition and he had owed them a few years' service as his end of the bargain. He served five, reluctantly. Once released, he had gotten a job at a suburban weekly outside of Washington and had started applying at the *Post.* He had been hired and had soon caught Bradlee's eye.

"Who is this guy Woodward?" Ben had asked. "He's all over the paper."

He worked hard on stories that other reporters regarded as dull and was obsessed with stories of misbehavior by public servants. He shook up the city health department and restaurant owners all over town by recounting, in detail, just how careless and venal the city's restaurant inspectors could be. He worked past quitting time and on Saturdays. He loved working at the *Post* and he added to its creative tension.

Ben was more familiar and less smitten with Bernstein. Bernstein was twenty-eight and, like Woodward, divorced.

He was an odd-looking young man, with long stringy hair and irregular features. Women reporters called him Howdy Doody. He had dropped out of the University of Maryland and worked as a copy kid at the *Star* and then as a reporter at the Elizabeth *Journal* in New Jersey. He had a reputation for bumming cigarets, borrowing money and stealing stories from other reporters—at the *Journal* he was known as The Rotten Kid.

He was a determined rebel, a friend of the downtrodden, an enemy of the ruling class, and he liked to do stories about poor people on mean streets, living rich but resentful lives. The *Post* was reluctant to publish them and frequently didn't.

Bernstein appreciated the *Post* as a target worthy of his antagonism. When the staff moved into the new building, he made his own comment on the huge, color-coordinated newsroom and its rows of coupled desks by bringing in a net, a ball and two paddles and converting his desk and the facing one into a Ping-Pong table. Ben was not amused.

There were Woodward and Bernstein in the spring of 1972 with nothing in common except a desire to rise to the heights. Then along came Watergate.

It began on June 17, with a phone call from Joseph A. Califano, Jr., the general counsel of the Democratic National Committee and a future law partner of Edward Bennett Williams'. Williams was the *Post*'s attorney, the DNC's attorney and a close friend of Ben Bradlee's.

Califano called Howie Simons at 8:15 A.M. to tell him that some very peculiar burglars had broken into the DNC's suite at the Watergate the night before.

Simons called metropolitan editor Harry Rosenfeld, who called city editor Barry Sussman, who called police reporter Alfred E. Lewis and Bob Woodward.

It was a fortuitous sequence. Simons, Rosenfeld, Sussman and Woodward were exactly the right people for the job. The three editors were smart, imaginative, daring and committed. Woodward was a human mole who would dig all day and dig all night for the sheer love of digging.

That morning he was sitting at home, vaguely discontented. It was his day off. He rushed to the office and then to the district court, where the five arrested burglars were being arraigned.

Lewis, a short, plump, nervous man, had been the *Post*'s police reporter for over thirty years. He did not write stories, though he often had by-lines. He wore a regulation navy-blue policeman's cardigan on the job and he had excellent personal contacts in the department.

He would play a limited but vital role in the unraveling that was about to begin.

He arrived at Watergate that morning with the acting chief of police and he would be the only reporter to spend the day inside the burglarized suite.

Six other *Post* reporters, including Carl Bernstein, would join the project in the course of the day.

The next morning, Sunday, the *Post*'s remarkably complete story began in the first column of page one under the headline "5 Held In Plot To Bug Democrats' Office Here."

The story established, among other things, that the intruders had come fully equipped with electronic bugs and cameras and that the apparent leader, James McCord, was a former agent of the CIA.

On Monday the nineteenth, according to the memoirs of Woodward, "Deep Throat" would make his first inconspicuous appearance as a "source in the Executive Branch who had access to information at the Committee to Re-elect the President and the White House."

The story, headed "GOP Security Aide Among 5 Arrested In Bugging Affair," revealed that McCord was also the chief security officer for the reelection committee (which would now be known as CREEP). Meanwhile the *Post*'s night police reporter, Eugene Bachinski, had looked in one of the address books the cops had taken from the burglars and found the name Howard Hunt, next to the initials *W. H.*

W. H., as Bob Woodward surmised, meant White House. He did the simple, perfect thing that an instinctive investigative reporter would do. He called the White House and asked for Howard Hunt. He heard the phone ring and the operator say that Mr. Hunt was not in his office but that he might be with Mr. Colson. Charles "Chuck" Colson, an ex-Marine and a former Senate staffer, was the White House aide in charge of "back room" skullduggery.

The foundation of the Watergate story was now in place and Howie Simons was exuberant.

"This is one hell of a story," he announced to Rosenfeld and Sussman.

Ron Ziegler, Nixon's press secretary, disagreed. He had the bad judgment to refer to it, while holding a press conference at Nixon's Florida home, as a "third-rate burglary."

He added, with a measure of accuracy, that "certain elements may try to stretch" it.

When Howard Hunt heard from a *Post* reporter that he and the White House had been tied in, he said "Good God" and left town.

On July 1, Lawrence O'Brien, the chairman of the Democratic National Committee, filed suit against the GOP campaign committee, charging it with responsibility for the bugging attempt. Edward Bennett Williams was the filing attorney.

On July 2, John Mitchell resigned from CREEP, saying he wanted to spend more time with his family.

It was now time for the Democratic and Republican conventions, and the Watergate story disappeared from the pages of the *Post* for almost a full month.

It had not, however, been dropped. Simons instructed Rosenfeld and Sussman to form a continuing Watergate team and Woodward and Bernstein were picked for the job. They would in the coming summer weeks do their most dogged and productive work. Bernstein would dig up the financial connection between the campaign committee, the bugging burglars and a Mexican money-laundering of GOP campaign funds.

His efforts would often amuse reporters at adjacent desks.

"Hey, everybody," one of them would shout when he called a Mexican banker, "Bernstein's talking Spanish again."

His persistence, if not his smattering of high school Spanish, paid off and on August 1 the *Post* had a double–by-lined story headed "Bugging Suspect Got Campaign Funds" and another announcing that Senator Proxmire, Democrat of Wisconsin, had ordered the General Accounting Office to audit the GOP fund-raising operation. Bernstein had discovered that a $25,000 cashier's check, issued to Kenneth H. Dahlberg, the Republican finance chairman for the Midwest, and given by him to Maurice Stans, the overall finance chairman, had wound up in the Miami bank account of one of the burglars. Stans would deny the connection but not very persuasively.

Stans said he gave the check to CREEP treasurer Hugh W. Sloan, Jr., who gave it to G. Gordon Liddy.

Liddy supposedly exchanged it for cash, which he deposited in a proper CREEP bank account. No explanation was offered as to why he would do such a very odd thing.

Liddy, who had already been fired by CREEP, said nothing at all.

On September 1 the *Post* recounted Liddy and Howard Hunt's behavior on the night of the burglary in considerable detail. They had been inside the Watergate when the cops arrived but a lookout stationed across the street had warned them by walkie-talkie and they had escaped. Bernstein and Woodward added a few more fascinating details in the following weeks and on September 20 the *Post* took a pre-election editorial stand.

The final counterattack would now be launched. Chalmers Roberts would quote the view from Katharine's suite that summer and fall: " 'Being so far out in front on the story meant that for months The Post's position was very lonely and exposed. No matter how careful we were, there was always the nagging possibility that we were wrong, being set up, being misled. One of the indications that we were really onto something was the intensity of the pressure to desist.' "

Vice President Agnew indeed soon suggested a setup that was not what Katharine had in mind—that Watergate had been planned by the Democrats to "embarrass the GOP." Other prominent Republicans had suggested that it was just an example of rather ordinary campaign behavior. The *Post* editorial, headed "After The Indictments," said it was not and that "a whole lot of questions . . . remain to be answered . . . before election day."

A friend in the Administration told Katharine that someone within was tapping *Post* phones. She ordered an electronic check that cost $5,000 but it turned up nothing.

Hunt, Liddy and the other burglars were indicted as anticipated and the matter was suddenly beyond the reach of anyone's wishful thinking.

Woodward and Bernstein, who had gotten most of their previous information by digging and deducing, now began to rely completely on inside sources. Most successful exposés depend on inside sources.

The stories that ran from September 29 through October came from a person or persons who knew exactly what the White House was trying to hide. One or all of them may have been the mysterious Deep Throat.

The story on the twenty-ninth said that John Mitchell, while still Attorney General, had controlled a secret campaign fund of between $350,000 and $700,000 to be used to "gather information" about Democrats.

The story was attributed to "several sources."

The night before, Bernstein had called Mitchell and read him the story.

Mitchell exploded.

"All that crap you're putting in the paper? It's all been denied. Jesus. Katie Graham is going to get her tit caught in a big, fat wringer."

The morning story included the quote, except for the words "her tit." It also quoted Mitchell as saying, "As soon as you're through paying Ed Williams, we're going to do a story on all of you."

Katharine absorbed the incident with restrained humor. A friend gave her a small gold wringer which she wore around her neck, once or twice.

On October 6 the *Post* had another inside story. It said: "The FBI has established that an illegal contribution from a Texas corporation had been laundered in Mexico and from the proceeds four Mexican cashier's checks, totaling $89,000, had been deposited in the account of burglar Bernard L. Baker."

A few days later the inside sources opened up a new can of worms.

The headline said, "FBI Finds Nixon Aides Sabotaged Democrats," and the story said that "information in FBI files" showed that the Republicans had stolen Democratic files, forged letters and planted provocateurs in Democratic campaign offices.

It identified the key one as Donald H. Segretti, a baby-faced California lawyer, and it said former *Washington Post* reporter Ken W. Clawson, now a White House aide, had boasted that he had concocted personally a fake letter published in the Manchester, New Hampshire, *Union Leader* which accused Democratic primary candidate Edmund Muskie of making slurring remarks about French-Canadians.

On October 15 the *Post* named White House aide Dwight L. Chapin as Segretti's boss.

The White House began a counteroffensive.

On October 16, Clark MacGregor, the Nixon campaign manager, accused the *Post* of "using innuendo, third person hearsay, unsubstantiated charges, anonymous sources and huge scare headlines . . . to give the appearance of a direct connection between the White House and the Watergate. . . ."

Robert Dole, the Republican national chairman, said the *Post* and Democratic candidate George McGovern were "partners in mud-slinging."

On October 25 the *Post* reported that a witness had told the grand jury that Haldeman was authorized to approve payments from a secret campaign fund. The story was wrong. Ron Ziegler accused the *Post* of "shabby journalism." A few days later Vice President Agnew said the *Post* was "engaged in a veritable paroxysm of individual vendettas against the President."

In the midst of the crossfire the *Post* dedicated its new $25 million building on Fifteenth Street with a bizarre choice of speakers. Once before, when Eugene Meyer had celebrated his eightieth birthday, the speaker had seemed strikingly out of place. That time Vice President Nixon, already an enemy of long standing, had appeared as a substitute for an ailing President Eisenhower. He had muttered a few platitudes and left.

Now the speaker was Nixon's Secretary of State, William P. Rogers.

It is difficult to imagine why Katharine Graham asked him or why he accepted. He had been the *Post*'s lawyer and a member of its board once but he had been replaced by Edward Bennett Williams. He had been, and presumably still was, a friend of hers but not one of the closest.

Everyone was self-conscious. Katharine introduced Rogers by comparing his presence with that of the President of Egypt at a Jewish convention. Rogers in turn blessed the building as "the home of a newspaper with a great tradition . . . that has been strongly enhanced under the leadership of Kay Graham," but he also noted the paper's record in "attacking the Administration of which I am proud to be a part."

Meanwhile the battle raged on. The sudden burst of incriminating stories from the FBI files came at the last crucial moment of the campaign. Edward Bennett Williams, lawyer for the DNC, had close friends in the bureau. The stories produced no significant political results and Nixon won in November by the greatest margin in history.

That, for a while, seemed to be that. A memo was sent around the

Post newsroom saying that Watergate was now over and it was time for reporters to turn their attention to other things, and for six weeks they did so.

Many *Post* people interpreted this to mean that the campaign had been indeed primarily a political one.

If the *Post* was ready to quit, however, the newly reelected President was not. A campaign was launched to strip the Post Company of its television and radio stations. On December 8 the *Post* returned to the fray, firing a not very consequential blast linking Howard Hunt's White House office to the burglars, a connection that had been established for some time.

The White House fought back, apparently unaware that it had already lost the war. The entire American press corps was now covering the beat. The burglars were at last on trial and every day new and damning facts were coming out in the courtroom. *The New York Times* revealed that the White House had paid hush money to the embattled burglars, a fact of paramount importance in defining the cover-up.

James McCord wrote a letter to Judge John Sirica, who was presiding at the trial, spilling more basic beans.

The story now had its own momentum. On April 17, Nixon made a bizarre speech in which he said that he had not realized the seriousness of the charges until March and that he had then ordered a thorough investigation. "Trust me," he seemed to be saying, after most Americans, according to the polls, had already stopped. On April 30 he made another speech announcing that Haldeman and Ehrlichman, "two of the finest public servants I have ever known," had resigned, and implying, accurately, that a third aide, John Dean, who had been speaking freely to the grand jury, had been fired.

Much was still to come: the Senate hearings, the Agnew scandals and resignation, the appointment and futile firing of Archibald Cox as special prosecutor, the tapes, the trials and convictions of Mitchell, Haldeman and Ehrlichman, the looming impeachment and Nixon's own resignation.

The *Post* and Woodward and Bernstein had played their roles and now they would reap the glory—the reporters would write two best-selling books, *All the President's Men* and *The Final Days,* and a movie on their adventures would make them national heroes.

They would almost win the Pulitzer Prize. Ben Bradlee would

persuade the judges to give it to the paper instead. Giving it to the paper was rather like giving it to Ben himself.

Woodward stormed into Ben's office when he heard the news but Ben convinced him that it was all for the best.

"I was mad when I went in there, really mad," Woodward said later, "but he convinced me."

CHAPTER

21

It was spring, 1974, and the sun was shining on the *Post*'s favored few.

Woodward, Bernstein and Bradlee were new and living legends; Von Hoffman was still the guru of the rebellious and affluent young; "Style" was chic and Sally Quinn was poised to conquer network TV. The future would be rougher than they expected.

Sally would describe her experience later in her book *We're Going to Make You a Star.*

It began, more or less, with dinner with Gordon Manning, a CBS vice-president. Manning had been luring her for some time, suggesting that, in her own best interest, she should abandon her still fresh journalistic career and come to the big city and the small screen.

Sally was listening.

Midway through dinner Manning was called to the phone. When he answered he found Ben Bradlee on the line. Ben said simply, "Fuck you."

Manning came back to the table and Sally stayed and listened and found she couldn't say no.

She made a TV pilot with an amiable old television pro named Hughes Rudd and the network said it was enchanting.

She went to Ben, told him she was leaving, and cried.

"It was the only time in my life I have wept in a professional situation," she wrote later.

Ben gave her his blessing and told her there would always be a job for her at the *Post.*

Her new career began going to pieces almost at once.

Clay Felker, the editor of *New York* magazine, called and offered her a job paying the same almost princely salary he paid his top hand, Richard Reeves, and she declined. He then suggested that *New York* do a cover story on her instead. She was willing.

The story was done by a former *Post* reporter named Aaron Latham, who had gained a small measure of fame with an earnest but dull book about Scott Fitzgerald.

From some employees, if not all, the *Post* demanded high loyalty. When it was considering making Latham its New York correspondent, he was dropped from consideration when it was learned that he was also considering the job at *New York*.

It turned out that Latham was now practicing Sally's own kind of jugular journalism.

"I don't do jobs on people, they do them on themselves," she would write.

Latham gave her the same opportunity and Sally did an awful job on herself.

Latham's article (as Sally would note) painted her "as a tough, mean, bitch woman, who had no women friends, who had slept her way to the top to get interviews and jobs, who had used her father's position to wield power, who had considered herself a sex symbol and played it to the hilt and who would scratch and claw anyone, anytime to get what and where she wanted."

Latham wrote that "one evening at a Washington dinner party, Sally Quinn was the center of attention as she verbally measured many of the town's most prominent politicians. The conversation was a Gallup Poll of penis sizes. Then she outlined her theory of how all the best men in Washington screwed beneath themselves. She also said that women in the city like to make love above themselves. It makes a nice Washington compromise."

Sally offered a rebuttal in her book that didn't quite rebut.

The party in question had been at the home of a sometime *Post* reporter named Walter Pincus and someone (not by implication she) had "discussed the alleged sexual problems of one politician." A week later she and Editor Felker had been together at another party at the same house. At that party, Sally said, her hostess, Ann Pincus, "had repeated the story."

"I was there briefly. I arrived shortly before Felker and left to catch the 10 P.M. shuttle back to New York."

She said Latham had been at neither party (he had not said he had) and that she could not remember what, if anything, she had contributed to the conversation (thereby neither denying nor confirming the remarks attributed to her).

Latham and *New York* got Sally off to a poor start.

She was on the cover, apparently just off the plane, sitting on her trunks, saying, "Good morning, I'm Sally Quinn. CBS brought me here to make trouble for Barbara Walters."

Sally would in fact make no trouble for Barbara but a lot for CBS. She would make a press and promotion tour of the country with Rudd, and while Rudd would get a good reception, she would get a disastrous one. She had no training and on the first morning's broadcast she would have a high fever. She would also contribute a series of insensitive ad libs.

A few reviews would be kind. Most were not.

Her TV career would die in a few painful months.

In September, *Time* magazine would announce her engagement to Ben:

"Eight weeks ago he had to relinquish her to CBS. . . . Sally moved to Manhattan and the apartment of her longtime friend Warren Hoge, city editor of The New York Post. But soon she moved out again. [Hoge had also been seeing socialite Amanda Burden.] Now it seems Bradlee, 52, has decided to look after his Galatea, 32. Parted from Toni, his wife of 17 years and the mother of his two children, he plans to marry Sally as soon as he gets his divorce."

Sally bowed out after providing inept coverage of Princess Anne's London wedding (she would blame a number of people for her failures, describing their physical and social shortcomings).

She came back to Washington and moved into the Watergate with Ben. She had two job offers, one from *Newsweek* and one from *The New York Times.* She picked the *Times.* The *Times'* Washington bureau chief, Clifton Daniel, sent her a nice stuffy note: "Congratulations on being the newest member of The New York Times Bureau." There would, however, be a fatal hitch.

Sally had arranged earlier to interview Alice Roosevelt Longworth on her ninetieth birthday. She did and sold the interview to the *Post.*

Sally's piece led the "Style" section on February 12, 1974. It ran over half of the first page of the section and on most of page three.

It was well structured, well written and full of fascinating detail.

A great many people would feel that it took unfair advantage of a very old, garrulous lady. Others would feel it was just what Alice deserved.

It began with an acknowledgment that Teddy's daughter was not universally admired: "There are those who think she is cruel, mean and malicious . . . that she is essentially cold and insensitive to other people's feelings."

The charges were followed by Mrs. Longworth's own rebuttal: "I don't think I'm insensitive or cruel. I have a sense of humor. I like to tease. I must admit a sense of mischief does get hold of me from time to time. I'm a hedonist. I have an appetite for being entertained. Isn't it strange how that upsets people. And I don't mind what I do unless I'm injuring someone in some way."

In the course of a long and fully quoted conversation with Sally, however, Mrs. Longworth would say a number of things that were injurious about a number of people, including, for example, President Nixon's daughter Tricia.

She also had a few things to say about lesbianism. At the prompting of her granddaughter and constant companion, Joanna Strumm, she recounted an incident from long, long ago.

She had been taking a stroll in the White House garden with her friend Margaret Cassini. Margaret had told her that another friend, Alice Barney, was saying horrible things, claiming to be in love with Alice. Alice said she had replied, "I don't think that's nasty. Why, I think that's lovely, so nice, I'm so glad to hear she is."

She added a footnote: "Homosexuality and lesbianism were very fashionable in those days and it was quite acceptable, at least as far as I was concerned."

She also told Sally: "Some things I think are terribly funny. Like dear old men's things hanging all around them. I think that's terribly funny."

To remove any possible confusion, she clarified the point at Sally's prompting; she meant "men's penises, my dear."

She also said that had she her life to live over she would never have married at all.

"No, I never would marry again. I might live with people but not for long. I wouldn't want to do anything pondering or noble or taking a position about someone again. But I might rather just spend a night with them or an afternoon or something."

Clifton Daniel called when he first heard that Sally was writing the story.

"He was in a rage. He admonished me for having done the piece, told me I was disloyal to The Times and said I would always be under suspicion there. 'We at The Times,' he kept repeating, 'are shocked' at what he called my lack of sensitivity for having accepted the assignment. Our relations, he told me, would never again be cordial."

Sally apologized profusely and offered him the piece. He refused. She offered to kill the piece. He said that wasn't necessary. She asked him what he wanted her to do and he slammed down the phone.

He called back ten minutes later, she wrote, and "in a voice tightly controlled but seething with fury" told her to run the piece in the *Post* but "to never, never let it happen again."

The piece ran on Tuesday and a lot of people reacted strongly. But Sally reported that Mrs. Longworth herself thought it was fine. That noon Howie Simons called and offered her her old job at the *Post.* She accepted.

CHAPTER

22

Nineteen seventy-four should have been a wonderful year for everyone. The *Post* was the most famous newspaper in the world.

Jimmy Breslin suggested that high schools should be named after its two most conspicuous reporters and tourists took guided tours of the big, new, impersonal building.

But there was discontent on every floor.

For Katharine, up on the seventh, Watergate had brought fame but not fortune. The *Post* earned $10.7 million before taxes that year and *Newsweek* and the television and radio stations added another $17.4 million but the paper's profits were still below the high level of the sixties. Its net was about 9 percent of revenue and Katharine told a group of security analysts in March that she intended to bring it back to 15 percent.

Her father and husband had been outstanding money-makers and she was still standing in their shadows, not quite certain how to proceed. She worried about her inadequacies as a businesswoman, sought advice from too many people and was constantly second-guessing herself. But she was determined.

Her worries were contagious. The very well-paid executives in the offices nearby knew that when she was in doubt she often fired someone. She was now looking for a vice-president to oversee production and finding it hard to find one. Executives from a half-dozen smaller, less prestigious papers turned her down.

The printers in the composing room were frightened. Computers could do much of their work as well as they and much more cheaply. There were some 770 of them, too many and they knew it. The paper claimed it needed only 250 to put the paper out. Many sat around passing time and others worked on "repro."

Repro was a dead horse around the union's neck. It had been invented by publishers to keep advertisers in line. The advertisers could, if they wished, send over preset ads but the papers would still set new type, proof it, correct it and junk it, and then charge them for the service.

Repro gradually became more trouble than it was worth to the publishers but by that time the unions had grabbed it. It seemed the ultimate guarantee of job security. More and more advertisers used preset ads but the number of printers still grew.

When Katharine hired John Prescott as publisher in 1969, the *Post* had a backlog of two hundred pages of repro a week and as long as there was a backlog the union insisted that any union printer who appeared had to be hired.

Prescott, tall, husky, a gentle-mannered, clever man, set out to get rid of repro and the extra printers as painlessly as possible. His plan was first to make the paper strike-proof and then to persuade the printers to retire or quit.

He bought a computer that could do the work of 115 printers and hid it up on the seventh floor among the executive suites.

He began Project X, sending nonunion *Post* employees to the Newspaper Production and Research Center in Oklahoma City, an institution the *Sunday Times* of London had called "a school for scabs."

They learned among other things how to use the computer upstairs.

In 1973 a dozen printers had been picked to be trained as supervisors and a catwalk was built from the roof of the Pick-Lee House, next door, a building owned by the *Post* and leased to a hotel company. If a strike came, the new supervisors could sleep at the hotel and cross to work high above the picket lines.

Contract negotiations were to begin that fall. In preparation the printers delayed the paper night after night and slipped scathing and occasionally obscene remarks in among the classified.

Prescott was patient. He did not want a strike. He wanted to buy them out, to pay them to retire.

In October reporter William Greider wrote a story on the fears of the printers for the Sunday paper.

He quoted a printer named Eugene Mueller:

"Automation, we talk about this every day. We're talking about people, humanity. How much further can they go? . . . We're human beings, we got problems, we got families. We're not a bunch of wild-eyed radicals."

Katharine Graham came up to Greider in the newsroom the next day and accused him of "romanticizing those bastards." She then turned and walked away.

On a Friday night in November, Prescott cracked down. He fired a printer named Michael Padilla, who, he said, was deliberately holding up production. The other printers stopped working and refused to leave the composing room. The next day squads of U. S. marshals marched them out of the building. The pressmen and the stereotypers left too.

The pressmen, led by James Dugan, were now the union militants. They could not yet be replaced by computers and they were ready to shut down the paper.

On Saturday night Prescott told the union leaders, when asked, that no one was working inside the building. He was lying. Fifty white-collar people from the ad and business offices, trained at Oklahoma City, were busy inside, some as pressmen, some as printers, preparing a limited Sunday edition. The craft leaders, who had spies inside, knew he was lying.

Prescott went back to the *Post* and shortly before midnight phoned Dugan and said, "We're going to go without you."

Dugan led a hundred pressmen to the *Post.* Prescott blocked him at the door.

"We'll run those damn presses," Dugan said. Once inside, Dugan found fifteen nonunion employees in coveralls. They had already "webbed up" five presses with newsprint. When the pressmen came they left.

Dugan said his men would run the presses, as promised, but only if Padilla was rehired. Prescott said that Dugan had not qualified his promise earlier.

"I lied to you," Dugan said.

Prescott backed down.

The unions had won for the last time.

The negotiations with the printers would go slowly on into the new year.

Another negotiation began, this one with the Newspaper Guild. The Guild represented all the other employees in the building. Half the members were in the newsroom, half in the business and advertising departments.

In 1969 the Guild had turned down the *Post*'s final offer and threatened to strike. Katharine had investigated.

"I called up the departments and asked why people were voting against the contract. It turned out not to be economic issues at all. One department had said they were feeling neglected, that some employees didn't even have backs on their chairs for God's sake."

Her conclusion was shallow.

Backless chairs were of no significance in themselves—at the *News,* where morale was chronically high, some chairs were held together by twisted coat hangers—but the people in the *Post*'s newsroom felt unvalued and insecure. So did the people in the other departments. That strike threat had fizzled out but now, five years later, things came to a head.

The point of contention was, on the face of it, wages. Actually to most of the editorial members wages were irrelevant—they had been and would continue to be the highest-paid reporters in the country. Just before negotiations broke off, the *Post* offered a $423.25 top minimum right off and $448.25 in a year, more than had already been negotiated at *The New York Times* or *The Washington Star.*

Many of the commercial members were youngsters with dull, demanding jobs who considered themselves to be passing through. They were ready to strike. So, as it turned out, were the necessary number of people in the newsroom.

So was the Guild's chief negotiator, Brian Flores, a full-time Guild employee who had once been a commercial artist at the *Post.* He walked out on April 8 and announced the strike and the strategy.

No picket lines would be posted, he said, because the Guild did not want to put pressure on the embattled printers.

One pressmen asked, "What kind of a bullshit strike is this?"

The answer by Flores was that the Guild strategy was not to stop the paper from coming out but to deny it "excellence."

"I don't know how long they can stand to have the big by-lines off the front page," he said.

The paper came out the next day, a shortened version but full of news. The editors had written some of the stories and the rest had been supplied by *The Los Angeles Times,* which shares a news service with the *Post,* and by the wires.

It was soon clear that the *Post* could stand to be without the missing by-lines indefinitely.

Early one Sunday morning a committee from the newsroom—Carl Bernstein, Murrey Marder, Bernard Nossiter and Larry Stern—met with Ben and Simons at a hotel without Flores' knowledge. The strike was over by Thursday. It had lasted seventeen days. The *Post* unit accepted the wage offer made before it began.

The *Post* had made a profit on the adventure—it had lost $165,000 in advertising but had saved over $250,000 in wages.

The Guild had been destroyed as an effective bargaining unit at the *Post.* A decade later the Guild leadership and the *Post* unit would still regard each other with suspicion, and contract negotiations would excite few emotions and small ambitions.

The newsroom people would remain discontented. Ben asked George Reedy, once President Johnson's press secretary, to analyze the cause of the strike and perhaps write a book about it.

Reedy, a gentle, low-key man, talked to dozens of news people and some executives. He decided that the wage settlement, offered, rejected and then taken, was irrelevant.

People were resentful and insecure and many believed that the invisible people on the executive floor were out to clip the newsroom's wings. They did not include Katharine Graham. In Reedy's phrase they seemed to think that all would be well if "only the Czarina knew."

Reedy decided not to write a book and he gave his report to Ben in a long letter. He included a personal message.

"The allegation is that you play favorites and glory in pitting people against each other to a point where the office resembles a snake pit."

Ben did not answer the letter.

The summer came and ended and the long-drawn-out negotiations with the printers came to a close.

Prescott made them a two-edged offer they couldn't resist.

If they agreed to drop repro the *Post* would give them $2.6 million to split. They agreed. Some members got $9,000.

Anyone eligible to retire could do so, draw a pension and get a $5,000 bonus. Dozens took the opportunity.

Prescott planned a vacation and his colleagues planned a little party for the day after the printers ratified the contract. They intended to give him $1,400 worth of luggage.

Just before party time Katharine called him to her office. She told him he was publisher no more. She had created a new job for him, one of considerably less importance. He was to be president of a new newspaper division. It meant, as he found out, that he would be more or less in charge of the money-losing Trenton *Times.*

He went back to his own office and had a low-key drink with the boys and the luggage was delivered to his home.

His colleagues would never be quite sure what he had done wrong.

The bonus for retiring printers would be raised to $18,000. By the end of the year there would be only five hundred left and the *Post* would save $3.5 million a year in wages but Katharine wouldn't change her mind about Prescott. He would hang around for twelve months and then leave.

The general conclusion was that Katharine had found him too soft —he had bought the printers out instead of beating them down. Her judgment of men, the theory went, had been conditioned by the determined and occasionally ruthless men who had loomed large in her life. Ben Bradlee was in that mold; Prescott was not.

One reporter offered a more mystical explanation.

"There is the good Queen Kate and the bad Queen Kate. It all depends on how she's feeling that day."

Peace if not contentment now reigned on the seven floors of the *Post* but big trouble was brewing in the basement.

The pressmen were the angriest people in the building and they alone were undefeated.

Jim Dugan, who had traded lies with Prescott at the time of the Padilla confrontation and won, was their leader.

Violence came to the *Post*'s basement early on the morning of October 1, 1975.

The pressmen's contract had expired at midnight; the new shift was at work.

Dugan handed a note to Lawrence A. Wallace, the *Post*'s chief negotiator. It said, "We are willing to work under the terms and conditions of the present contract only as long as meaningful negotiations continue."

Then he and a few strategists stepped across the street to the Post House bar to consider their next move.

At one-thirty Dugan phoned Wallace to say the union was ready to continue negotiations in the morning.

Later he returned to the *Post* and called a chapel meeting. He said the time had come to strike and just about everyone agreed. He left to get the placards that had been prepared.

About 4:30 A.M. John Hover, the pressroom foreman, noticed a sudden quiet.

The presses had stopped. He stepped out of his office and saw pressmen scampering up the ladders and across the huge machines. As he moved forward, two men stepped from the shadows and grabbed him and a third beat him around the head.

A dozen men were up on the presses slashing the electrical wiring and the rubber blankets that cushion the plates, and smashing the gauges that control the flow of ink. Flames roared around one press, licking the lead plates in place on the cylinders.

The work of destruction was over in minutes. The men who had done it ran. The men holding Hover let him go.

He staggered to his office, blood rushing from a deep cut over his right eye, and called John Waits, the night production chief, on the phone.

"There's a riot down here," he said. "They beat the shit out of me."

Waits called general manager Mark Meagher, who was asleep in his office. Meagher called Katharine Graham at her home in Georgetown and her son Donald at his home in Cleveland Park.

The Grahams drove to the paper and found firemen, policemen and pressmen milling around in the dawn's early light.

The pressmen's strike had begun, and though the pickets would remain on the line through half the coming winter, it had already been lost.

As one pressman put it later, "We were like a sandlot team playing in the big league."

The *Post* had not assumed that the pressmen would beat up the foreman or cripple the presses—in that it was just lucky—but it was prepared.

Some 150 white-collar people from the advertising and commercial departments, trained in Project X, had been standing by early in the evening ready to run the presses but they had been sent home when the pressmen came to work.

They were ready to come back.

The *Post* had also hired the J. Walter Thompson public-relations firm to shape public opinion. It was soon shaped. The agency prepared an album of glossy photographs of the mutilated presses and distributed them widely. It estimated the damage rather vaguely at between one million and two million dollars. It was much less.

The *Post*'s chief negotiator, Lawrence Wallace, said later, "We had the big propaganda machine."

If the machine faltered, the pressmen themselves were quick to give it a hand.

They seemed proud of their achievements.

The *Post*'s Guild unit met that afternoon, around the corner at the old red-brick African Methodist Episcopal Church, and Brian Flores, the local executive secretary and the architect of the disastrous Guild strike, asked the 650 members present to "support our brothers in labor."

Don Oberdorfer, a reporter who had covered the war in Vietnam, replied:

"They ask us to consider the future of the Guild. What about the future of the paper? Last night a bunch of guys who call themselves a union tried to destroy *The Washington Post.* I'm not about to stand on a picket line with a bunch of guys who went out there with crowbars and torches and tried to wreck our newspaper."

The members voted overwhelmingly to continue to work.

The pressmen, totally misunderstanding the impression they were making, remained self-satisfied and aggressive. A picket followed Jules Witcover, a middle-aged, nonathletic reporter, one night and beat him unmercifully, blacking his eye, chipping some of his teeth and fracturing his jaw.

A minority of Guild members did not cross the picket line.

The *Post* had never been beloved by Washingtonians but it easily won the contest for the public's sympathies.

It also won the contest on production. On October 3 two leased helicopters landed on the *Post*'s roof, picked up photocomposed pages and carried them to six nonunion newspapers, one 115 miles away. They printed a twenty-four-page paper, loaded it on trucks, and sent it back to shopping-center parking lots in the Washington suburbs where dealers were waiting.

The emergency paper was a professional piece of work, crammed with news and features.

On Monday, October 6, the first of the damaged presses was back in working order and it printed 100,000 copies of another limited edition.

On November 7, forty-one of the working Guild members wrote Katharine an anguished note. They said the newsroom had the oppressive atmosphere of an armed camp and they said some Guildsmen who were working were doing so, in part at least, because they "fear reprisals if they don't work, despite your pledge that there will be no reprisals. Their bosses have led them to think otherwise. . . ."

Katharine sent a somewhat nonresponsive answer ten days later. The pressmen, she made clear, would never return. To accept them back, she said, would be the "ultimate act of irresponsibility on our part. . . .

"I could not myself in good faith preside over a building or an enterprise in which people who had worked faithfully and to the point of exhaustion for the company were in continuing physical danger from fellow employees, in which those who committed the acts of violence resumed their control of a whole section of our building. . . ."

The Thursday before Thanksgiving the *Post* had 184 pages, plus a 104-page food supplement printed at the Miami *Herald* and trucked north.

On December 10 Katharine Graham stood in the newsroom and made an emotional speech outlining the *Post*'s terms for settling the strike.

If the pressmen did not accept them that, as far as the *Post* was concerned, was the end of the union.

The *Post* would permit only those pressmen who had not been involved in the violence to come back. Base pay would be increased from $14,500 to $22,500 and the work force would be reduced by attrition. The company would control manning and schedules. In turn the union members would be given $400,000 to divide among themselves.

Katharine clearly did not expect the pressmen to accept her terms.

The helicopters returned to the roof that afternoon, this time carrying nonunion pressmen recruited from around the country.

There were bitter but futile reactions. Some two thousand pressmen and sympathizers marched to the *Post* building and burned Katharine in effigy. Charles Davis, one of Dugan's key lieutenants, carried a placard that showed how little the pressmen understood about public relations.

It said, "Phil Shot The Wrong Graham."

The Guild members met for the fourth time and voted again to keep working.

George Meany of the AFL-CIO, who had been involved in peace efforts, pointed out that the *Post*'s latest offer was less appealing than the one it had offered before the strike. The pressmen turned it down 249 to 5. Meany later told *Post* reporter Robert Kaiser that he had asked Katharine Graham what she would have done if the union had accepted and she had said, "Slit my throat."

A few faint rumblings were still heard. Nicholas von Hoffman, who had avoided crossing the picket line by sending his columns in by messenger, spoke his first public word on the strike. Mrs. Graham's decision to bust the pressmen, he said, was "as socially and politically reckless as the pressmen destroying the presses. . . . By breaking with its own past, The Post breaks with the liberal solution without offering any other but dire conflict." He was, of course, wrong. The days of union dire conflict were past. There was nothing reckless about Katharine's decision.

The AFL-CIO's executive committee issued a statement, presumably for the record. It said, "It is clear that The Post management wanted a strike, hoped for a strike and long planned to replace union members with scabs. . . ."

Most of the few Guild members who had joined with the strikers now slipped back to work. In mid-February the printers who had been locked out when the strike began were allowed to return. The pickets would walk their weary beats for additional weeks but to no avail. The unions were no longer of consequence at the *Post.* A year later a stock analyst would tell a meeting of security salesmen that in breaking the pressmen the *Post* had made a gift to all the newspapers in the land.

It had also increased its own profits beyond any reasonable expectation. Mark Meagher would say simply that the gain was staggering.

CHAPTER

23

The *Post* had problems within, but it looked great from without, bigger and better than life. It was clever, sassy and daring and it had pushed Nixon out of the White House.

Compared with it, *The New York Times* seemed ineffectual. Katharine Graham was the perfect publisher; Ben Bradlee, the ultimate editor; Woodward and Bernstein, reporters of genius.

If there were discontented people upstairs and down, the ones in the newsroom at least had a sense of sharing the glory.

The people at the top tried to keep things in perspective but there was a giddiness in the air and even enemies came to pay their reluctant respects.

One spring day twenty young White House fellows, all ardent Republicans, made a scheduled visit to the *Post*'s seventh-floor conference room.

They were working for Gerald Ford but they remembered Watergate.

A nervous young woman led them in to where the paper's big guns were sitting elbow to elbow behind a long table: Harry Rosenfeld at one end, Bob Woodward at the other, Haynes Johnson, Ben Bradlee, Howard Simons, Katharine Graham and David Broder in between.

Their shepherdess asked the first question: "What does the *Post* do best?"

Katharine answered in a soft, earnest voice.

"Gosh. It's almost impossible to answer. I think that we do best

—if I had to sum it up—I'm extremely involved in the delivery of quality news to a mass audience. I think we do as well as we can."

She gave a little chuckle and patted Howie Simons on the shoulder. "We're perfect."

The visiting fellows did not laugh and the rest of the questions were searching, argumentative, and sometimes mean.

How fair or unfair had the *Post* been in its pursuit of Watergate and Nixon?

Katharine talked about the former President and his men.

"They were very personal about me and about Ben Bradlee. I think they were trying to undermine the credibility of the paper, and I think they did very well. Most people didn't believe Watergate. It makes me laugh now. When you think that the government of the United States was trying to destroy a news company, it blows your mind."

The fellows looked resentful and unpersuaded.

"I think you are very powerful," one young man said in a low, angry voice.

"Not nearly as powerful as any department of government," Rosenfeld said, bridling.

Ben interrupted. "I suspect we are more powerful than we like to admit," he said softly.

Katharine had the last, reflective word.

"It may be that the press has too much power," she said. "Yes, Watergate brought down a President, and that was too much power."

The fellows left, still smoldering. The *Post*'s leaders followed, looking a little self-conscious but pleased with their performances.

It was carnival time and the most glittering of the *Post*'s people were enjoying the lights and noise.

Robert Redford and Dustin Hoffman were making a movie based on *All the President's Men.* On April 11, 1975, "Style" devoted its front page to the movie in the making. The story, headlined "When Worlds Collide: Lights!, Camera!, Egos!" had three by-lines, Tom Shales, Tom Zito and Jeannette Smyth, and it began with three quotations, from Robert Redford, from a "publicist" for the film, and from Ben himself.

Ben said, "I think the movie could have an important impact on people who have a stereotyped view of newspapers. It may reinforce those stereotypes, or it could show them that we strive very hard for responsibility."

It would, in fact, replace the old stereotypes with some brand-new ones.

The story was written with a gee-whiz air and it described how "the movie people . . . have been in and out of The Post for months in an effort to soak up authenticity, rub elbows with newspaper people and learn the routine of a daily newspaper."

The exercise was not, however, simply a bath for the actors. It had the self-conscious residents in a sweat as well.

"Beneath this fuss . . . lie questions that gnaw at the editors and reporters alike. . . . Normalcy is disrupted, simple privacy invaded, and ironic conflicts generated as two disparate worlds—the entertainers and the working press—meet on the press's turf."

There were quotations galore.

" 'For some it's a battle of glamour,' says Sally Quinn, frankly glamorous herself, 'and the movie people have found out they're losing.' "

The story jumped to a full page inside and ran on and on, searching souls.

Carl Bernstein, trying hard to be profound, said, "I think there's a great similarity between the movie business and newspaper business. We're all voyeurs." (Actors would seem more like voyees. Perhaps he was thinking of audiences at X-rated movies.)

Ben said, "There's a fantastic amount of interest in this story. Everybody around town is talking about who's being cast as whom. I'm somewhat depressed by the interest because it tends to judge us not for what we put out as a newspaper but how other people make us look."

Harry Rosenfeld told a reporter, "We usually dish it out; now we may have to take it," and then thought better of it. He called the reporter back to "clarify" the quote, and when the reporter seemed reluctant, he said, "If that shows up I'm not going to be like these tolerant guys around here. I'll personally throw your desk out the window. Your career is at stake, friend."

The reporter used both quotes.

Ben returned with another slice of philosophy: "The question you have to decide is, Is there any potential service to journalism that this is a good movie? [Or at any rate that was how he was quoted.] So do you get involved? I mean we're a little bit pregnant now. Journalists should be in the audience, not behind the footlights, but I don't know if we can have it both ways. The press has a profound effect on life in America. If we're going to support the people's right to know, then we're going to have to support the people's right to know about us."

The people took it in stride but fame had come to the principals and they would never be quite the same again.

It came most abundantly to Ben.

He was fifty-three years old and for him every age was a critical one. He had played a role for years: the aristocrat who would fight anybody in the barroom; the Georgetown socialite with a touch of crass who drove to black-tie dinners in his pickup truck; the office jock who passed idle moments in his glass-enclosed office tossing a miniature ball through a miniature hoop.

He was still slim and energetic and a sex object, living now with Sally, who as the reporter has noted was self-consciously glamorous.

He too was surrounded by his own myth and something of a fixed target.

His book *Conversations with Kennedy* came out that spring. It was excerpted in the *Post* and celebrated with an office party.

Staffers could and did buy it on the spot at a special price, $3.05. Ben autographed their copies after asking a good many of them their names. The party was resented (though Ben could not figure out why) and the book was clobbered by critics (and he couldn't understand that either).

Garry Wills opened his review in the *New York Review of Books* with a quotation from Castiglione:

" 'I think the conversation which in every way the Courtier must try to make pleasing is that which he has with his Prince; and although this term "conversation" implies a certain equality which would not seem possible between a lord and a servant, still we will so name it for the present. Therefore, in addition to making it evident at all times and to all persons, that he is as worthy as we have said, I would have the Courtier devote all his thought and strength of spirit to loving and almost adoring the Prince he serves, above all else devoting his every desire and habit and manner to pleasing him.' "

Wills went on:

> Mr. Bradlee . . . presents himself as a chronicler of slight events, and chitchat. As a friend of Jack Kennedy, he felt it his duty to give the off-duty President a way of relaxing and gossiping (often about

women with special emphasis on breasts). Castiglione would have approved. . . . But it is clear Kennedy got more than the latest jokes from his sessions with Bradlee. . . . The President called Bradlee on Saturday morning to find out what Newsweek would be running in its Periscope feature next week and—from other similar sources—to inform Bradlee what Time would be carrying on its cover. Bradlee cleared stories with Kennedy (a cover treatment of the family) and warned him of breaking features (the use of "flechettes" in Vietnam). Bradlee got the exclusive White House story on rumors of an earlier Kennedy marriage—but only by agreeing to let the President approve the final version—the problem of journalistic ethics seems not to have bothered Bradlee (or anyone else). . . .

Bob Woodward reportedly did not read Ben's book because he had heard bad things about it and was afraid they were true. Ben hinted that he had done it mostly for money; his wife had divorced him and he had to support the kids. Sally Quinn would say that Ben had written it that way on purpose, to show the perils and temptations of Washington reporting.

Ben's world would never be the same. He was not a man who took criticism lightly. There was a touch of hubris in the air.

Triumphs are often traumatic and they were for Ben. He had arranged that the Watergate Pulitzer went to the paper, which meant in effect to himself.

He and Katharine beat the Guild in the spring and the pressmen in the fall. Then came the movie. The days of triumph were also days of strain, and his ability to see other points of view grew less. He was feisty as ever and more sensitive. Criticism by insiders seemed acts of disloyalty and by outsiders impudence. He wrote more nasty notes, some to associates, some to strangers. He kept old enemies and made new ones.

James Truitt was a senior enemy. He had had a breakdown while editor of "Style" and had been fired abruptly. He believed, with some logic, that Ben had double-crossed him and after moving to San Miguel de Allende, Mexico, he began an abusive correspondence. In February, 1976, he seized what seemed a chance for revenge.

He told *The National Enquirer* that Bradlee's former sister-in-law, Mary Pinchot Meyer, had had an affair with President Kennedy. He intended apparently to embarrass Ben, whose otherwise candid book,

Conversations, had not mentioned it. There were other revelations. He said that Ben's ex-wife Toni had found her sister's diary after her death and had turned it over to James Angleton, then chief of CIA counterintelligence. Angleton, a friend of Mary's and a CIA associate of her former husband's, Cord, had supposedly destroyed it.

Ben was on vacation in the Virgin Islands when the *Enquirer* story ran. Howie Simons and Harry Rosenfeld called him and persuaded him that the *Post* could not ignore it. The *Post* ran a slightly defensive but complete rehash, quoting Ben.

Truitt continued to write angry letters until he killed himself.

Ben's new enemies included Reed Irvine, the founder of Accuracy in Media, or AIM.

Irvine would insist that he wasn't an enemy, just a critic, but he bombarded the *Post* with accusations of slanting and suppressing news.

Ben reacted with outrage. He finally ended his side of the exchange with a note calling Irvine a "miserable, carping, retromingent vigilante." It was a notable example of Ben's letter-writing style—retromingent describes an animal who urinates backward. It didn't shut up Irvine and it didn't answer many serious questions he had raised.

From a distance Ben still seemed a man who could handle a crisis a day without feeling burdened but up close it was clear that he was getting tired.

He had one critic, a former *New York Times* reporter named Barney Collier, who decided that despite his proper Boston background Ben was "rootless." In 1975 Collier published an odd, unstrung book called *Hope and Fear in Washington (the Early Seventies): The Story of the Washington Press Corps.* He wrote a good many devastating things about a good many people, including Sally Quinn (who tried to stop publication), and the book was often unfair but Collier sometimes threw light on the private thoughts of public people. He included an off-guard conversation with Ben which showed Ben in a light that most of his enemies would find startling. It had taken place a couple of years earlier, when Sally and Ben were first living together.

> It's nine o'clock in the morning. Ben Bradlee hasn't had any restful sleep in so long he can't remember the last time.
> I say, "You look tired."

"I am," he says.

"Your left eye is drooping."

"I know. It's a nerve inflammation. I noticed it a year ago. I thought it was a brain tumor or a stroke. The doctor said no, but they put me on warning about my health."

He puts his feet up on his desk. He wears a small-sized loafer that isn't polished. He says, "I was on the bathroom floor throwing up all night."

He makes it sound glamorous.

I ask, "Was Sally with you?"

"No, she went back to New York."

"Then you were alone."

"Yeah. And I had to get up this morning to take my kid to school."

"Your children are living with your wife?"

"Yeah . . . but I go over there and pick 'em up in the morning."

"Why?"

"I get to see 'em that way."

"None of them live with you?"

"No." And then he says, "Barney, I want to keep away from that."

"Are they making it hard on you, Ben?" I ask.

"Sure they are," he says.

I ask, "Who's doing it to you?"

"You know who," he says.

"No, who?"

"All the ones in Sans Souci. All over town. It's the big topic. It was in *Newsweek* and *Time* in New York. People in the business. I can't go into a bar in New York without people knowing about it."

"What do they say?"

"Nasty things. You know. What you'd expect."

"Doesn't anybody wish you well?"

He shakes his head.

"How about your friends?"

"Yeah, my friends."

"Do you have any friends?"

"Of course I have friends."

"A lot of friends?"

"No, not a lot."

CHAPTER

24

Watergate would be the *Post*'s most significant milestone and it would also be a millstone. Katharine would remain aloof from the celebration and from the principals. She would seem relaxed around Woodward, a proper Yalie, but would never warm up to Bernstein. She wrote the two of them a rather qualified note of congratulations:

"... All things considered, it's miraculous. I consider all the things we must concede—incredible amounts of luck, sources willing and even finally a few eager to talk and help—I concede the role of the courts, grand juries and Congressional committees—We didn't bring him down—those institutions and holders of office did, as we all keep repeating—But I believe if the story, pre-election and post-, hadn't continued McCord might well not have written his letter. I concede by that time too you had been joined and sustained by other reporting —But it was still an extraordinary gutsy hard, brilliant piece of journalism—and I want to say this to you both despite all the accompanying crap that has fallen all over us and especially you. Lastly, you've both made it fun and we've all kept the demon pomposity in moderate if far from complete control. The sound of our own voices, while listened to by us with some awe and even some admiration, is receding. And if it isn't there are all sorts of stark realities before us to restore balance and defy hubris."

Watergate made the two reporters national heroes and millionaires and put them in the hopeless position of trying to match it for the rest of their lives.

They wrote a second book, *The Final Hours,* an account of Nixon's last twistings and turnings. Like the first, it was written with the assistance of a Simon and Schuster editor and was an odd mixture of fact and fancy.

It opened with a vivid scene, a meeting between Nixon and Henry Kissinger on the eve of Nixon's resignation.

"There was the President in his chair, as he had seen him so often. Kissinger reflected on the fact that he really didn't like the President. Nixon had made him the most admired man in the country, yet the Secretary couldn't bring himself to like his patron."

Who told this to Woodward and Bernstein? It could hardly have been Nixon so the source must have been "the most admired man in the country." Was Kissinger a reliable witness? Would he give Woodward and Bernstein a full, accurate, uncensored sweep of his innermost thoughts? Weren't the thoughts as presented self-serving?

There were other quotes and thoughts from the past and the private conversations of other people. Many denied both the quotes and the conclusions.

Ray Price, Nixon's speech writer and the former chief editorial writer for the New York *Herald Tribune,* said he was appalled at the distortions and had tried to prevent them. "I tried to convince Bernstein to drop all his preconceptions. The President was not bonkers nor was he 'out of control.' "

John Osborne of *The New Republic* said the book was "on the whole the worst job of nationally noted reporting that I've observed during 49 years in the business."

Nevertheless the celebration went on. It reached a climax in April, 1976, when the movie made from their first book (the making of which had so excited "Style") was previewed at the Kennedy Center.

The evening had a slightly surrealistic tone. The film was shown to an audience of movers and shakers. A thin line of leftover strikers stood outside with their wives and sympathizers in the brisk spring night, singing "Pressmen Shall Overcome" as self-conscious Senators and Congressmen walked by.

Autograph seekers swarmed around Robert Redford and ignored Woodward, Bernstein and everybody else.

The guests went upstairs by elevators to a huge marble hall.

Redford, Dustin Hoffman, Woodward, Bernstein, Ben Bradlee and Sally Quinn and most of the other important people went inside

La Grande Scene, the Center's pretentious French restaurant, where they remained for the rest of the evening.

Katharine and Donnie stayed outside with the lesser lights, who were drinking champagne and eating lobster, quiche, pastries and ices. Katharine looked her regal best, with soft brown hair and sad brown eyes, in a simple blue gown, pale and cool as a Necco wafer. Donnie stood beside her, clean-cut and smiling. One by one and two by two, friends, statesmen and courtiers approached and spoke and she replied in her soft, clipped, patrician voice. Perhaps she was not entirely at ease. The movie had been made without her personal approval or cooperation and no one had played either her or Donnie.

It was an oddly awkward, not quite festive evening. The *Post* people outside, the lesser editors and executives of solid, anonymous competence, seemed pleased to be there (but not to be outside). The hero of the night, Redford, accompanied by Woodward, emerged from La Grande Scene at one point and made a slow, smiling circuit of the hall. The outsiders smiled back sheepishly.

For Woodward and Bernstein it was a first climax to be followed by more adventures. Bernstein went off to conquer new worlds. Woodward would stay. Both would marry second wives, father children and be divorced again.

Bernstein announced his intention of writing a definitive book about the Joe McCarthy era, based on his parents' experience, but he would not get it done.

He would write a long piece for *Rolling Stone* about the involvement of newspapers with the CIA. It was interesting but it did not provide evidence of deep involvement.

He became ABC's Washington bureau chief amid much fanfare but did not learn much on the job and found it increasingly hard to assert his authority. He was eased out and made a kind of special, unattached TV reporter.

Woodward worked harder and did better, at least for a time. With the help of researchers and a boyhood friend named Scott Armstrong he put together a book on the Supreme Court called *The Brethren,* an odd and ignoble work, gossipy and inaccurate. Anthony Lewis, of *The New York Times,* demolished it in the *New York Review of Books* and Renata Adler tore the tatters to shreds in the *Times'* own Sunday review section. It would, by and large, receive an unfavorable press.

The criticism hurt. The *Legal Times of Washington* reported that

Woodward and Armstrong believed that *The New York Times* had conspired against them and that its denunciation had "cost us at least $800,000" on the paperback sale.

Still Woodward would take it more or less in stride.

He told a *Washingtonian* writer that the reviews "were about what I expected" but he also said that Ms. Adler, who had just received a law degree from Yale, was "just ignorant and picky."

Through it all he kept right on working and it was generally agreed that he worked his second marriage to death as he had his first.

His wife, Francie Barnard, told a reporter that Woodward had behaved in the same overachieving way when he was courting her in 1974.

"I felt like I was a project—I had the right credentials—and he just wore me down."

He had other projects ahead. With two marriages and three moneymaking books behind him, he was ready to move into management at the *Post*.

Sally's CBS connection was gone but not forgotten.

She wrote a book about her misadventures, *We're Going to Make You a Star*. It came out in 1975 and it had some virtues. It was clearly written, extremely candid, and it moved rapidly but it struck a whining note, like a small child on the edge of a tantrum.

Sally couldn't believe how mean everyone had been to her.

"Instead of sympathy for being caught in a corporate disaster and for my own lack of experience, I got destroyed, almost in a personal way, by the majority of the critics and reporters."

She complained about irrelevant personal attacks and then, a few pages later, described a woman TV critic as "enormously fat . . . with a moustache and black hair . . . her tiny eyes squinting behind folds of fat."

The book was denounced by critics almost without exception. Free-lancer Ann Chamberlain, a friend of Katharine Graham's, demolished it in the *Post*. Sally moved on to bigger things, partly of necessity. She had gained fame by breaking social butterflies on the wheel but now most of them hid when she came to call.

She wrote a piece on Senator Goldwater, the old family friend.

"Barry Goldwater is tired. Sick and tired. And not just physically either. . . . When he arrived at the [Republican] Convention Hall he found that nobody had bothered to tell him about or give him the proper credentials. They wouldn't let him in."

It was too vivid and it upset her parents.

When Jimmy Carter came triumphantly to town, Sally assumed her role as the defender of the real elite and focused on Smith Bagley and his wife, Vicky. Smith, the grandson of Reynolds tobacco, aluminum and all that, had arrived in the middle of the Presidential race and established himself as Carter's advance guard.

"There are a lot of rich people floating around," Sally wrote, "people who have tried desperately to make it socially in Washington, throwing lavish parties, wearing designer clothes, joining the right committees, to no avail. But the Smith Bagleys had something else. They had Jimmy Carter. Or so everyone thought. Which was all that mattered.

"Many people who have met Vicky Bagley find her one of the most ambitious young women they know."

She went on in rather mysterious fashion, suggesting that the Bagleys didn't really have Jimmy in their pocket but then quoting the President as saying, yes, indeed, they were good, old and close friends.

Sally had implied that the Bagleys had "tried desperately" to attract attention but in fact they had refused to be interviewed by her, and their lawyer had even written the *Post* asking them not to run the story.

She had been humiliated in New York but not humbled. She was back on her own turf and ready to strike. But no one would cooperate.

She tried her hand at rewriting Tom Wolfe, in a piece headed "Viva La Causa! Radical Chic Revisited."

"Manhattan's affluent liberal 'do-gooders' " who had gone underground when the "oh so hideous expression 'radical chic' crept into popular usage" were now back at the old stand raising funds for Cesar Chavez. The story had the impact of pure grape Kool-Aid. The next day she had a page-and-a-half follow-up interview with Cesar, a gentle nonsophisticate.

He was, she decided, "making a comeback in the fine American tradition of Judy Garland, Frank Sinatra, Muhammad Ali and Ruby Keeler."

She soon found a new and bigger victim—the oil-rich Arab. She found one in London and delivered a three-part series that began with an article headed "The Empire And The Chic of Araby."

It began:

"Upstairs in the casino of The Playboy Club, Ismail Baluch had just lost 50,000 pounds ($86,000). Not as much as his Arab friend sitting next to him who was still smiling after losing 170,000 pounds ($292,000), but still Baluch had enough gambling for one night. And he was in a good mood. It was time for some dinner. Some pretty women, some good wine, some fun . . . a large corner table for eight was reserved. . . . Next to him he seated Amira, the belly dancer, his old, old friend of seven years and the singer he had also befriended. They ordered champagne and caviar and the most expensive foods and wines. . . ."

In the next installment Sally gave Amira more attention.

". . . Amira knew her talent. At one point she danced on top of Baluch's table, knelt on the table in front of him and wiggled. He took a wad of bills from his pocket and stuffed 500 pounds down her breasts. He gave a reporter another 200 pounds to do the same. . . ."

To round out the picture, Sally described Baluch in some detail:

"Baluch is short and dark skinned with a huge black mustache but very little black hair left on his head. He has dark, dancing eyes and a dazzling set of white teeth which he displays quite frequently since he is almost always happy. . . ."

The series was a remarkable display of racist reporting but it had a more familiar ring. Sally hadn't found a new target. Baluch was simply an exotic version of the upwardly mobile new-rich Washington hosts and hostesses that she had cut her journalistic teeth on.

Who did he think he was?

There was still, however, a shortage of victims—she could only do Arabs once and what other group could she attack with impunity?—so she now began to write about her heroes.

The first was Peter Jay, the new British Ambassador who was the son-in-law of the British Prime Minister James Callaghan. Sally was enchanted with Jay.

She was even more enchanted that fall when she and Ben were among the first American journalists to go to Cuba. Fidel Castro had a few small failings, Sally found, but nevertheless he knocked her for a loop.

"Part of Castro's charm," she wrote, "exasperating as it is at times, is that he can convince someone, at least for the moment, of something they do not believe. In fact he can actually make it sound logical when he says that the press should be a tool of the State and Party. . . ."

When Castro threw a party for the press in New York a year later, Sally went with Ben. It was very exclusive. Katharine Graham was there, Henry Grunwald of *Time,* Lester Bernstein of *Newsweek,* Roone Arledge of ABC, Barbara Walters, Mike O'Neill of the New York *Daily News,* Frank Mankiewicz of National Public Radio, and Joe Armstrong of *New York* magazine. Abe Rosenthal of *The New York Times,* who had been offended by Castro's remarks on Israel, did not show up.

The party was to be secret and totally off the record, but the rule was relaxed and a couple of days later Sally told the world the inside story.

Castro, she found, still had that little-boy charm.

At first he seemed nervous and a little shy and then one of his aides confided that he had never given a party before.

When the guests assembled in a rather empty room he began moving chairs and got into a tug-of-war with one of the guests, Sally wrote with awe-struck delight, "when the guest suggests that a head of state shouldn't be carrying chairs around."

He had, however, matured.

"He is calmer, mellower. He is less up-tight about the U. S., even about the CIA, which admittedly tried to assassinate him at least once. Before, when he spoke of the CIA, it was with total outrage. Now it is with ridicule, contempt."

The demon news people naturally asked questions.

> The subject comes up about how many troops the Cubans have around the world and where they are. It soon becomes a game of Botticelli with the guests guessing names of countries and Castro getting more coy with each passing moment.
>
> The next go-around is naturally about the recent blow-up over the Russian brigade in Cuba, how it all happened.
>
> This is a subject he has been waiting to get into all evening, and he does not hesitate to name Zbigniew Brzezinski as the villain of the whole Cuban brigade affair.
>
> . . . [He said] that military personnel have been there for seventeen years with the same structure and [that they have] the same function that they had for the past seventeen years.

Sally closed with a sentimental note.

"At dawn . . . [the] plane will whisk Fidel Castro away with yet another title to add to the string of credentials—revolutionary, president, international statesman—and now host."

Castro was a reliable favorite but he wasn't around very often and Sally wrote fewer stories.

She needed new worlds to conquer and decided to give marriage a whirl. She and Ben were joined in a brief but elegant ceremony in October, 1978. The joining took place just as Pope John Paul II was assuming his office and the unfriendly office joke had Ben saying, "Sure, I'll marry you, Sally, the day there's a Polish Pope."

It was an unfair appraisal. Ben needed Sally just as Sally needed Ben.

Fame affected the *Post* as well as its people.

That spring it set out to prove Watergate was no fluke and that it was as willing to destroy a Democratic Congressman as a Republican President.

Representative Wayne Hays, Democrat of Ohio, was the chosen target—an unpolished, brisk, openly self-indulgent, machine pol from the Midwest.

He was powerful—chairman of both the House Administration Committee and the Democratic campaign committee—and vulnerable.

Representative Philip Burton, Democrat of California, had called him the meanest man in Congress. His colleagues treated him with deference since he allotted Congressional office and parking space, as well as campaign funds, but they didn't like him.

The lesser folks of the Hill didn't like him either. He had ruled that the barbers who gave Congressmen subsidized haircuts could no longer accept tips and he had taken stools away from the operators of the automatic elevators in the House office buildings, so they couldn't sit down on the job.

He was, on the other hand, remarkably generous to himself.

He was not surprised by the *Post*'s attack but he wasn't ready for it either. He had told friends that Bob Woodward was out to get him but it turned out to be twelve other reporters.

The first front-page story, by Marion Clark and Rudy Maxa, ran on May 23. It was headlined "Closed-Session Romance On The Hill, Rep. Hays' $14,000 A Year Clerk Says She's His Mistress."

It began in the manner of *The National Enquirer:*

"For nearly two years Rep. Wayne Hays (D., Ohio), powerful Chairman of the House Administration Committee, has kept a woman on his staff who says she is paid $14,000 a year in public money to serve as his mistress. . . .

" 'I can't type, I can't file, I can't even answer the phones,' says Elizabeth Ray, 27, who began working for Hays in April, 1974, as a clerk. . . ."

The story said Miss Ray appeared at her "luxuriously appointed office in the Longworth House Office Building . . . only once or twice a week for a few hours.

" 'Supposedly I'm on the Oversight Committee . . . but I call it the Out-of-Sight Committee. . . .' "

Two reporters would go to Ohio to cover the hometown angle and ten others would prowl the Hill. There would be front-page stories on each of the next thirteen days and on most days there would be one or two inside as well. They were written with obvious zeal and free of any suggestion of objectivity.

One, for example, would say without supporting evidence that Hays had made "the power of intimidation . . . an art form" and that his reputation as "the meanest man in Congress, the House bully from whom no one is safe, has grown and grown. . . ."

The series brought Hays down. He resigned first from one committee, then another and finally from Congress. He was a bully and no great loss. He had intimidated State Department bureaucrats. In granting Congressional fringe benefits he had a liberal standard for himself and his allies and a tougher one for everyone else.

But the *Post* had behaved like a bully too. A single hardworking reporter probably could have dug up a wealth of persuasive, significant and less sensational evidence of the misuse of power. Miss Ray's story should have been a relatively minor part of the whole.

Hays felt aggrieved and he had a point.

Post reporters, editors and publishers had known and left unreported many sexual and nonsexual scandals involving politicians—including the identities of President Kennedy's and Johnson's in-house mistresses—who, with the *Post*'s aid and approval, had gone on to glory.

There were other signs of the *Post*'s poor judgment and bad management.

"Style" had many excellent writers but it wasn't using them well. Its front pages were often given to routine reviews of minor artistic events.

It had been charged earlier with ignoring the lives and interests of Washington's ethnics and blue-collar workers and its hundreds of thousands of middle-class blacks. It now tried to give the blacks some attention. Jacqueline Trescott ground out frequent dull stories on such subjects as black society parties and sorority balls. They greatly resembled the stories about white social events that had appeared in "Style"'s predecessor, "For and About Women."

Writers with acceptable peeves or quirky points of view were encouraged to give them vent.

A man named Wilkes, who had spent a year with a carefully selected average American family, wrote a book about it. The man in the family, forty-three, was a foreman in a die-cutting company, the woman a not quite contented housewife. They had several, varied children.

It was reviewed on "Style"'s front page by Colman McCarthy and Dorothy Gilliam, side by side. Neither of them said much about the contents of the book.

McCarthy, a former Trappist lay brother, was the *Post*'s liberal Catholic spokesman and Gilliam was the spokeswoman for blacks.

McCarthy liked the book because of "the large addition it makes to the shamefully small knowledge we have of families." Gilliam despised the family (called the Neumeyers in the book) because it had moved to the suburbs when blacks moved into its old city neighborhood. (The man, however, had also stood guard over a house being built in their new neighborhood by a black family when vandals damaged it.)

In Mrs. Gilliam's opinion the family was clearly racist, and Wilkes, the author, was probably a racist too or, as she put it, "The fact that he still found the Neumeyers the average family appears to bestow Wilkes' tacit approval of their racist attitude."

Some of "Style"'s first stars were flickering. Nicholas von Hoffman was having an identity crisis. He had begun as the angry not-quite-so-young man in the late sixties when middle-aged men and women (even those the same age as Nick) were inclined to feel guilty. The world was a frightening mess and who was to blame? He assured them that they were.

Herblock was a power in his own right and his work brought the paper much prestige. He disagreed with the paper's endorsement of Eisenhower in 1952 and continued to draw cartoons critical of Eisenhower which the *Post* refused to run.

Photo courtesy the National Archives

Katharine and Philip Graham on board the ocean liner *United States* in 1956. That spring was probably the high point of their life together. The purchase of the *Times-Herald* had made the *Post* secure and put it on the road to immense power and profits. But Phil's swift emotional decline lay just ahead.

Photo courtesy United Press International

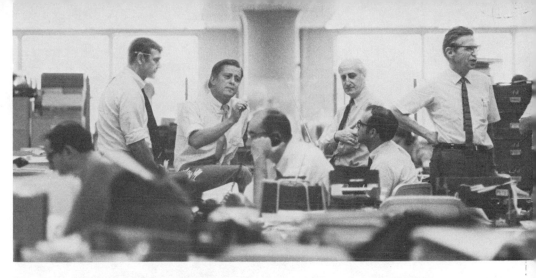

The *Post* newsroom of the 1970s. Ben Bradlee and his top staff members would change the shape of the paper. Some of them, shown here from the left, are Dick Harwood, Bradlee, Ben Bagdikian, and Chalmers Roberts. The seated man looking at Ben is Haynes Johnson.

Photo courtesy Dennis Black

Sally Quinn, "frankly glamorous." Ben hired Sally sight unseen after she threw herself a well-publicized party.

Photo courtesy Washingtonian, *photographer John Boden*

Katharine Graham in 1974. Few employees thought she could become a good executive. But she transformed the paper, taking it from a loosely structured family-owned enterprise into a professional, publicly held corporation.

Photo courtesy Washingtonian, *photographer Barbara Hadley*

Donald Graham, right, enjoys hiring old college friends. Here he is with one of them, Andy Beyer, who covers the track for the *Post*.

Photo courtesy Washingtonian, *photographer Diana Walker*

A Georgetown party given for Shirley MacLaine. From the left: Sally Quinn,
Jerry Rafshoon, Mrs. Herman Talmadge, Ben Bradlee and Hamilton Jordan.
Photo courtesy Washingtonian, *photographer Diana Walker*

Bob Woodward and Carl Bernstein in the *Post* newsroom.

Donald Graham holding a press conference after *Post* reporter Janet Cooke had to return her Pulitzer Prize when her story was exposed as a fraud.
Photo courtesy Washingtonian, *photographer Mimi Levine.*

In time, as the world grew calmer and readers more reflective, his tirades became first familiar, then absurd.

By 1976 he was in a difficult position. He could remain routinely indignant or develop a softer technique, perhaps as a wise old (or at least older) man. He tried both.

In the latter role he suggested that prisons might be abolished.

"Some people are considering the idea of giving up on punishment and substituting for it a system by which criminals would have to work to compensate the victims of their crimes. . . ."

He did not develop the thought. Since the average convict has limited legitimate skills, an indentured felon might find it difficult to get a job that would both support him and permit him to pay his indemnity. If, for example, a court decided that a mugger owed his victim $25,000 and he could earn only $150 a week, he would have to pay him $50 a week for five hundred weeks, roughly ten years, even without interest. It seems possible that the mugger might not stay on the job. He might even go back to mugging and, if he was caught, get even deeper in debt. Perhaps Von Hoffman intended that the mugger should work directly for the muggee on weekends, mowing his lawn or polishing his silver.

He was even less logical (and more irritating) when he played the old Nick.

In May he took a long, unfriendly look at the refugees from South Vietnam. They had, of course, from his point of view been on the wrong side.

"There is a new national unity," he wrote, "in the resentment at the thousands of smarmy fugitives Ford and Kissinger have air-freighted in here—again the fait accompli without Congressional permission—to put a tax on the public purse or to form another revanchist clique lobbying for a return to another China, another Cuba. . . ."

Von Hoffman would fade away, first from "Style"'s front page, then from the pages inside. In a few years he would be gone. No one would explain who had decided to cut him adrift but things hadn't been the same since the day he'd decided to say a few words about Katharine's handling of the pressmen's strike.

"Style" was having trouble finding itself.

CHAPTER

25

Many, perhaps most of its readers considered the *Post* slanted. Some thought it was really a tool for the CIA.

Others thought it was a tool for the radical left.

The first group found a spokesperson in Deborah Davis, who wrote a poor book called *Katharine the Great.* She concluded that Watergate had been arranged by Richard Helms, the CIA director, and James Angleton, the chief of counterintelligence. She said Angleton had slipped his deputy, Richard Ober, into Richard Nixon's confidence.

Ober, she said, was the only man in the nation with access to classified information at the White House, the FBI, the CIA and the Committee to Reelect the President. He had set Nixon up, she said, and then given the incriminating evidence to the *Post.* He thought he was doing Ben Bradlee a favor, she said, but his boss, Angleton, saw it as the "ultimate dirty trick" since "Bradlee would take all the risks, and either Bradlee would succeed in getting rid of Nixon or Katharine Graham would have to salvage her newspaper by getting rid of Bradlee."

It was an improbable scenario. It was true that Angleton no longer liked Ben—"He thinks I'm a traitor," Ben would say—but it would have been a strange dirty trick to give him the information that would win the *Post* a Pulitzer Prize and establish him as a legend. Ben and the *Post* did take big risks in pursuing Watergate but they were not tricked into taking them.

It does seem possible that someone in the CIA was the *Post*'s Deep Throat and that it was done as part of a planned maneuver. It seems also possible that the *Post*'s source was at the Democratic National Committee. Bradlee consulted his close friend Edward Bennett Williams every inch of the way. The Democratic National Committee sued the Republican Party and Williams had begun gathering depositions three days after the break-in. Whoever gave the information to the *Post* gave it not as a favor but because the *Post*, a Washington newspaper with enormous influence, was the logical recipient.

If the CIA did contribute, the *Post* and Ben were strikingly ungrateful.

When Angleton was forced out of his job by Helms's successor, William Colby, the *Post*'s sister publication, *Newsweek,* reported that a team of CIA "mole hunters" had once suspected Angleton of being a Soviet agent. It added that "no investigation-surveillance, bugging or wire tapping of Angleton was ever authorized" and that the suspicions had been dismissed by his superiors (which meant Helms) as "too circumstantial and speculative." The story quoted Colby as saying that the mole accusations were "not a factor" in his dismissal— a careful phrase that stopped short of saying that the thought had never crossed Colby's mind.

The *Post*'s handling of Richard Helms was no gentler. In the fall of 1979, Helms pleaded "no contest" to charges that he had twice lied to a Senate committee about CIA activities in Chile. His lawyer was Williams. Williams announced that Helms had agreed to plead "no contest" to two misdemeanor charges and the Justice Department had agreed to arrange a suspended sentence.

Williams slipped Helms into court for sentencing and was obviously trying to avoid publicity.

The *Post* gave the story a banner headline.

Philip Geyelin, once a CIA man himself, considered the matter on the editorial page as well, though he did treat Helms somewhat more gently.

"We are not saying that Mr. Helms should have been let off scot free. The integrity of testimony under oath to a Committee of Congress needs to be upheld as a matter of principle. But neither do we think he should have been prosecuted more severely. . . . There was, in short, no way for Mr. Helms to meet the double standard in the case. . . ."

The publicity had a negative effect on the sentencing judge, who announced that he did not feel bound by the Justice Department arrangement. He did go partway—suspending the two-year prison sentence he gave Helms but making him pay a two-thousand-dollar fine.

A few days later the *Post* had another Helms story. It said he had formed a consulting firm which would help Iranian businessmen in the United States. It also noted that since Helms had been the U.S. Ambassador to Iran after leaving the CIA he might "possibly embroil him[self] with U.S. regulations governing conflicts of interest for former Federal employees."

A few weeks after that, the *Post* would give Helms an even nastier rap.

Tom Braden, an old CIAer and an occasional columnist on the *Post*'s op-ed page, gave a private testimonial dinner for Helms to which Averell Harriman, Stuart Symington, Robert S. McNamara and Henry Kissinger came.

The *Post* gave an astringent page-one report.

The high point, it said, "was the brief and melodramatic speech of Robert McNamara . . . who wanted all in the room to know: whatever Dick Helms did, whether it was over the line or not, the former Secretary of Defense supported him fully. The moment of fraternity moistened some eyes around the table."

The case against the *Post* from the other end of the spectrum was more direct. It was launched by Reed Irvine of Accuracy in Media in a series of letters questioning the paper's coverage of the killing of two million Cambodians by Cambodia's communist government.

The exchange began in the spring of 1978 with a letter from AIM protesting the *Post*'s failure to run a story on a press conference by a former Cambodian official named Pin Yathay. Yathay had given a detailed account of government atrocities.

In his letter to Katharine Graham, Irvine said:

> One hears a variety of speculative reasons for the behavior of The Post with respect to Cambodia. Some think that it is a case of bad conscience. The theory is that journalists who helped turn the country

over to the communists, confident, as The Times put it, that "life would be better for most," are now reluctant to dwell on the fact that life has become a hell. Others think that a leftist mentality is to blame—a mentality that holds that when eggs are broken in the name of "revolution," attention of the public should be diverted from the broken eggs and focused on the lovely omelet that is being prepared.

A third theory that is strongly held by some of my Asian friends is that this is merely a reflection of racism. People with brown skins, they say, are different from us. They really don't know what human rights are and being indifferent to their suffering is not the same as being indifferent to the suffering of Europeans or even Latin Americans.

Katharine replied that no story had been run on the press conference because in the opinions of editors Larry Stern and Peter Osnos the charges of atrocities "did not add substantially to the already large body of reportage from Indo-China and other points which had been carried in The Washington Post on a continuing basis since the present Cambodian regime took power."

Irvine made a long reply.

He had checked on all the stories the *Post* had run in the previous year, and, he wrote:

"There is not a single Washington Post story that deals with any specific eyewitness account of the murder and starvation going on in Cambodia. I count only three stories that discuss the agony of the Cambodian people more than glancingly. And two of these are strongly diluted with arguments either that the horror has been exaggerated or that the U. S. bears heavy responsibility for what happened or for comparable crimes. . . . Balancing the three articles which deal with the agony we have reports . . . on Pol Pot and Teng Say which basically express the replies of these perpetrators of the Cambodian genocide to the charges made against them."

A short time later, the AIM newsletter ran a detailed account of Larry Stern's role in the noncoverage.

Katharine wrote Irvine objecting, saying the article was "reminiscent of the methods of Joe McCarthy."

Irvine replied:

"We simply, carefully laid out the facts about the way The Post had treated certain news stories and about the apparently incorrect explanation that was given to us for the failure to carry one story. We suggested that you ought to be curious about this and should try to get from Mr. Stern a more accurate explanation of what he based his decision on. I have never met Mr. Stern and I have spoken with him only briefly three times in my life. I know him only through his works and through those brief conversations. You no doubt are much better acquainted with him, and perhaps therefore you can provide a better explanation for the facts that we have described than I can."

In July he wrote Katharine again, listing and analyzing the stories the *Post* had carried on Cambodia and concluding that "there is reason to believe that the biases of your staff influence the way in which the news is reported or not reported. I wonder if you would not agree that a greater diversity of views among those covering Cambodia would have produced better coverage."

The dispute reached a kind of emotional climax in the summer of 1979, when Stern died suddenly while vacationing on Long Island, apparently of a heart attack. He was playing tennis when he complained of having been stung by a bee. The fatal attack came moments later. At a memorial service a few days later a Cuban official named Teofilo Acosta, identified as the first secretary of the diplomatic mission to the United Nations, gave the eulogy. AIM would later identify him as the Washington station chief of the Cuban Directorate General of Intelligence, Cuba's equivalent of the CIA. AIM would argue that Stern's close association with Acosta reflected his biases and that he had not been the objective editor he should have been.

Stern had worked for the *Post* for decades and had held most of the top editorial jobs at one time or another. He was among the best-liked newspaper people in Washington but a great many persons considered him to be an ideologue who let his beliefs affect his professional performance. The most damning description of his approach to the news came as a message of praise and farewell from a friend, Alexander Cockburn, in *The Village Voice:*

". . . Larry's heart and head lay on the left side of the political bed. He was not one of those pallidly objective souls who need a route map to get from a gas shortage to Exxon headquarters, or who feel incapable of making up his mind 'until all the facts are in' and until all the evidence has been judiciously assessed. . . . Larry knew what the facts were going to tell him long before he discovered what they actually were and the route map he carried with him through his life showed the eternal landmarks—the rich man in his castle and the poor man at his gate. . . ."

CHAPTER

26

On January 10, 1979, Katharine Graham made her son, Donald, aged thirty, the publisher of the *Post*. She would remain as chairman of the board. She also gave him her good wishes.

"My whole goddamned life has been a soap opera," she said, "and I don't want him to inherit it."

Don responded with characteristic modesty. "Today, as in the rest of my life, my mother has given me everything but an easy act to follow."

He added: "The uniqueness of my mother's story is that she had something dropped in her lap. She had to fill in without warning and she performed brilliantly. We aren't much the same."

He was right. He was not his mother's clone.

Katharine saw herself as a businesswoman and felt slight kinship with the editorial people. "I take a lot of flak when I talk about profitability," she told one writer. "They [meaning the people in the newsroom] get up pretty tight at the mention of M-O-N-E-Y. They think I'm some heartless bitch . . . profit making is my priority. If it weren't I goddamn well shouldn't be here."

Donald was more interested in the actual gathering of news and in the people who gathered it. He would send nice notes to those who did it well. Donald and Katharine would work together in the coming years, roughly as equals. When they disagreed, Donald would usually prevail.

Mark Meagher, the business manager, would remark that they seemed more like business associates than mother and son. Katharine would almost agree.

"It's tougher to be the son than the mother. Both of us have a lot of respect for the other and we make our relationship as close to a regular business relationship as we both want to. It is and it isn't."

She had given Donald a mixed bag of assets. The *Post* was her achievement. She had made it immensely profitable and given it a new professional respectability. Donald inherited a paper that was written and edited by a large, competent staff and though it was still often unfair it was no longer systematically so.

Katharine had changed some but not all of the basics. The *Post* was still a vehicle of power, designed to destroy political enemies and exalt political friends. It was still cold, a prestigious but anxious place to work. Katharine had changed herself, significantly but not completely. She had begun as a shy, middle-aged woman with grave doubts of her own abilities, had examined herself with detachment and had become a perfect model of a woman manager and a heroine of the feminist movement. *Ms.* magazine had written admiringly in 1974 that she had "outgrown her tolerance for silliness, thrown off a life-long cloak of diffidence and come to accept the heady fact that, within reason, she gets to do whatever she wants."

She learned to relax with courtiers and other members of the ruling class. She did not learn to hobnob with her underlings though she did invite little groups of staffers to lunch in the executive dining room.

"The lunches were entertaining because she was entertaining," one guest remembers. "She was like a grande dame and she told marvelous anecdotes in her deep-throated, gravelly-voiced way but she behaved as if she was following a script, even when she moved forward to shake hands. It didn't seem spontaneous. It's as if she'd been packaged."

She came to believe it was pleasant to work at the *Post,* which it was not. "At . . . the *Post,*" she told one interviewer, ". . . there's a rather great, healthy irreverence that makes working a lot of fun." She would never understand how much fear there was around the newsroom.

She was free to do whatever she wanted but her nature hemmed her in. *Ms.* noted that she fretted about her hair and that she lay awake nights "to redo my mistakes."

She was often rude, particularly to those below her in the social or economic scale, although her friends say her conduct was simply a manifestation of her shyness. Ben Bradlee could make her laugh out loud and perhaps her regard for him was based, to a large degree, on that.

He saw her as the Queen, Donald as the young Prince, and himself as senior, confidential adviser. As the time for succession approached, he watched with care. He told a reporter:

"She had the bends for a while. She worried unnecessarily that people would forget her. First she toyed with doing it in early 'seventy-eight. Finally I said, 'When are you going to do it?' She said, 'None of your business.' So I knew she'd made up her mind. It was a bigger deal to her than to anyone else. I think Donnie was dying to be publisher but he would have deferred to her for years. It's not in his nature to rebel."

When Donald succeeded, Ben offered, *pro forma,* to resign. Donald said he could stay as long as he wished.

Donald began with a flourish. He replaced Phil Geyelin, the editor of the editorial page, with the deputy, Meg Greenfield, and the editorial pages would soon achieve a new, continuing excellence—breadth, depth, grace and logic. They would display a dedication to truth and fair play.

The rest of the paper was Ben's and it would not fare so well. He had shaped it in his own image. It was daring, impulsive, impatient, insecure, flashy, entertaining and competitive. Sometimes, like Ben, it was ruthless.

One reporter who came and went said Ben had made the *Post* a great big college newspaper. Its emphasis was determined each day by the ambitions and opinions of competing reporters and editors and shifting winds. Its philosophy seemed to be that (as Oscar Wilde once put it) nothing succeeded like excess. There would be a growing recklessness and arrogance and, every now and then, staggering misjudgments. A notable one took place in the spring of 1979.

As the year began, the world seemed to be the *Post*'s oyster. When something went wrong, the *Post* saw it as an opportunity.

That May its most popular comic strip, "Doonesbury," moved to the *Star* and Larry Stern had had a daring idea—the *Post* should create a new and better strip of its own, one that would put "Doonesbury" in the shade. Ben was persuaded and he called a young artist named Hatley Mason up from Roanoke, Virginia.

Hatley, twenty-two, had recently graduated from Virginia Commonwealth University's school of art, the best in his class, and had gone to work at a Roanoke paper. He had aspired to work for the *Post* and sent up his portfolio. He was summoned to Washington and invited to breakfast at the *Post*'s executive dining room. He arrived and found Ben; Larry Stern; Sally Quinn; Richard Cohen, a new "Metro" columnist; Henry Allen, a "Style" writer; and Bob Martin, the art director, waiting.

"I came in thinking I was going to be interviewed for a job. It was all very top secret. Bradlee looked over my portfolio and said, 'Well, we know the kid can draw,' and then he told me he wanted to make me a cartoonist."

Henry Allen had prepared some sample dialogue. The committee told Hatley that the strip would not be just a "Doonesbury" replacement but a further development, one that "would show what happened after the Woodstock generation turned into modern Washington bureaucrats and businessmen. Bradlee wanted a strip that would be just as successful as 'Doonesbury' or more so."

The plan was that the breakfast group would meet each week and feed ideas to Henry Allen and Hatley. The goal was to have the first strip in the paper June 15, the last day "Doonesbury" would run. Days went by and reality edged in. The weekly meetings were dropped, Allen and Hatley were given creative autonomy and the deadline was pushed forward.

The strip, as it emerged, revolved around the tepid adventures of Hilary and Lester, young, faddish and affluent. They worked in some vaguely professional capacities, probably for the government (or possibly at the *Post*), and they had proper, preppy friends, including a young black man named Peabody who was a slightly stuffy conservative and who apparently was intended to be an amusing reversal of the usual stereotype of the hip, radical black counterculturist.

Larry Stern, the prime mover, died suddenly in August, before the strip was published. At that time Ben was still trying to decide to publish it or not, although *Time* magazine had already announced its genesis. Stern's death may have been a deciding factor. Hatley believes "one of the reasons it was published was because of Larry's memory."

It was slipped into the paper one day, without fanfare, though

Time readers and many others knew it was supposed to be "Doonesbury"'s rival. It was not. It had many problems, one of which was that its humor was precious and limited.

"It was definitely elitist," Hatley said in retrospect. "It assumed that people would be interested in people like the people at the *Post.* The people were a little too normal and we leaned a lot toward social issues; Peabody and the other characters were trying to make statements rather than trying to be funny. We were always struggling with the problem of wanting it to seem realistic, like something that could occur, while needing to have silly situations in order to be funny."

By the spring of 1980 the strip was syndicated in eighty-five papers, including *The Los Angeles Times* and the Chicago *Tribune,* but it was losing instead of gaining. Bradlee had set a syndicate goal of over one hundred and he called a meeting to say that it had missed it but he still hadn't made up his mind what to do. A few weeks later Hatley took a month's advance strips down to the printer and the printer told him that the strip had been canceled. The next day he saw Ben and Ben apologized for not telling him directly.

Hatley would say later that he still thought highly of Ben but he was disappointed.

"It just seems like Bradlee could have handled things better."

He also reached a conclusion about the *Post.*

"It is just a corporation that prints a newspaper."

Nineteen seventy-nine was a year of change.

Bob Woodward had been put in charge of "Metro" and it was assumed that he was being prepared as Ben's successor but he had his built-in limitations—Robert Redford has called him, only half in jest, a "humorless workaholic"—and they would hinder him as a deputy managing editor.

He had a sense of humor, but it was not one that charmed everyone.

Scott Armstrong, the co-author of *The Brethren* and a boyhood friend, told writer Richard Lee that Woodward "was fun to be with on a rainy day. He would think of some bizarre trick, generally having to do with people being revealing about themselves."

This brand of horseplay still surfaced now and then. Woodward brought a belly dancer to a party given by staid and proper Donald

Graham, and the dancer danced for a long, long time before an embarrassed and captive audience.

Woodward seemed insensitive to other people's tastes and sensibilities. In *The Brethren* he told improbable and spiteful tales about the Justices of the Supreme Court. It would not seem to occur to Woodward that the dignity of the Supreme Court is an important part of the dignity of the nation, that truth is an essential part of reporting, and that even belly dancers and Supreme Court Justices have feelings.

He was a compulsive worker and a compulsive driver and apparently he had come to believe that his gifts were greater than they were.

As the "Metro" editor Woodward had over one hundred reporters and editors working for him. Each had strengths, weaknesses, ambitions and fears and a great many had families. Many had much greater experience than he. Woodward seemed to assume that they would follow his direction on all things, even when they knew more about the subject than he did.

On one occasion he pulled Jonathan Neumann, a Pulitzer Prize-winning investigative reporter he hired away from the Philadelphia *Inquirer,* off a story on the alleged hoarding of oil by large utilities and its alleged cover-up by the Department of Energy. He told Neumann that it was "not our job at 'Metro' to look into the oil story." Neumann asked sarcastically if it would have been their job to look at Richard Nixon. Woodward was not amused.

He took himself and his job very seriously. He assumed that when he came in on Sunday anyone he might want to talk to would be there too or available on short notice. He frequently scheduled meetings with staffers on their days off.

He was not imaginative. He saw news as primarily scandals, usually about people in public office. A story with a trivial example of non-, mal- or misfeasance would be better than any story with no scandal at all.

He was a hard taskmaster but did not seem to be particularly concerned about the implications of the stories he ran.

Under him the "Metro" section became more readable and more exciting but it developed its own eccentric editorial policies. Stories and columns frequently expressed the writer's own opinions. In the process it undercut the whole paper's credibility and lost many readers' respect.

Meanwhile "Style" continued its reckless ways.

The fiasco of the year came on Wednesday, December 19, 1979. That day "Style"'s front page carried the first of a three-part series by Sally Quinn.

The headline said, "The Politics Of The Power Grab: Nine Rules Of Notoriety.

The subhead said, "Brzezinski: Seeking The Limelight In The Shadow Of State."

The articles were intended to demolish President Carter's national security adviser.

The first began with an introduction in italics:

> *Zbigniew Brzezinski was first approached for an interview last June.*
>
> *Shortly after the request Brzezinski began calling to negotiate the terms of the interview.*
>
> *"I am by nature extremely shy and modest," demurred the highly publicized Brzezinski in the first phone call.*
>
> *He flirted briefly with the idea of an interview, stopping just short of a promise. Then, responding to a suggestion that the reporter would sleep better knowing the interview was sewed up, he responded, "I would sleep better knowing that you sleep better."*
>
> *He was only warming up.*
>
> *The second phone call came on a weekend early in July. The profile was to be of him and his wife Muska. "We are not the kind of people who like all that publicity," he said.*
>
> *The interview the week before in Women's Wear Daily, which had him posing nude from the waist up, was just a fluke, he explained.*
>
> *"So you want to do an interview with me and my wife? Isn't that sexist? Or maybe just sexy," he giggled. "Husbands and wives have their own separate careers, you know ... and maybe more than that separate.*
>
> *"I'll wait and see who else you are going to decapitate."*
>
> *The third conversation took place at the end of July.*
>
> *"So," he said, "you want to find out what I'm really like. How are you going to find that out? You'll have to come and live with me. There is no other way."*
>
> *His invitation was greeted with laughter.*
>
> *"No," he said, "I'm serious, my wife will be out of town.*
>
> *"Muska will be in Europe for the first three weeks in August," he said.*
>
> *He was reminded that the reporter was married.*

"Ha," he snorted, "don't worry about that. I'll just talk to your husband about it. I can take care of him."

It was suggested that a one-hour interview was all that was asked for.

"No," he replied firmly. "You'll just have to come out here and live with me. That's the only way I'll do it."

The actual story began on a no-longer-appropriate note of mystery. "His name now is almost a household word. His face—the pale skin, the squinting eyes, the narrow beak-like nose—is instantly recognizable. . . ."

It turned out, as the reader already knew, that the subject was not Henry Kissinger. After several more put-downs, Sally grew solemn and announced her purpose in writing the articles. It was, as it turned out, almost a scholarly one, though confusing.

Brzezinski, she wrote, was "a fascinating study in the politics of the power grab in Washington, a study in how it should be done but more important, how it should not be done," a sentence that defies clear interpretation.

He was, she said, atypical of Washington's power people, at best a limited success and remarkably unloved.

"Even men who have been despised in some quarters in Washington during their careers will inspire loyalty or affection or admiration in some group, no matter how small. Not Brzezinski—at least on the basis of over fifty interviews with foreign policy experts, government officials and Washington observers. Which is why this becomes such an interesting case. Here is a man in one of the most potentially powerful positions in Washington with one major constituent. The President."

It seemed, as one read on, that Brzezinski was not even an interesting example of failure. The story ran two full pages, filled, for the most part, with pointless anecdotes (Brzezinski once asked the Iranian Ambassador to rush some caviar over to the White House for a lunch for Shirley MacLaine) but it had a crusher at the end.

The last seven paragraphs said:

The national adviser enjoys himself in the limelight.

A reporter for a national magazine recently went to the White House to interview Brzezinski.

The interview was very jolly. A great success. Not surprisingly Brzezinski was pleased with himself, exuberant.

So exuberant that as the reporter was leaving he began to joke around and flirt with her.

Suddenly he unzipped his fly.

The photographer who was with them took a picture of the unusual expression of playfulness.

Shortly afterward the reporter received a photograph of the private moment they had shared, captured for eternity. It was inscribed by Zbigniew Brzezinski.

The reporter was not identified. It was, as it turned out, Clare Crawford-Mason of *People*.

Mrs. Crawford-Mason had interviewed Brzezinski a year before Sally's story ran. Sally's version of what happened would turn out to be almost totally inaccurate.

The interview had gone well. The *People* photographer, Terry Arthur, had taken a great many pictures and Mrs. Crawford-Mason had sent a selection of prints to Brzezinski. She had also sent a note asking if he would autograph one for her.

A few days later Sally Quinn and her editor, Sandy Rovner, were visiting Mrs. Crawford-Mason when two signed photos arrived from the White House. The first showed Clare and Zbig standing relaxed, face-to-face, with him in his shirt sleeves, his thumbs in his belt, grinning. He signed it, rather mysteriously, "I really shouldn't."

The second picture showed them shaking hands at the end of the interview and he had signed that, "Thank you very much."

Sally, Sandy and Clare spent some minutes trying to figure out what the inscriptions meant. They decided, Clare remembered, that they were to be read in sequence, as a before-and-after joke. In the first Brzezinski does appear to be more or less leering and it might be assumed by the imaginative that he was about to make some kind of romantic overture. The second inscription then would be a prankish pretense that he had. Actually he hadn't.

Some months later, Clare recalls, Sally called her and asked her if she would try to persuade Brzezinski to give her an interview. Clare tried to no avail.

Some months after that, on December 18, 1979, Sandy Rovner called. She said Sally was doing a story on Brzezinski and wanted to know the wording of the inscription on the photograph. She had, apparently, forgotten that there were two. Clare said that she would rather Sally left her and the photos out of the story and she said that since the photos had been signed at her request, she would have to have Brzezinski's permission before she could give them the exact wording.

The next day Sally's first story ran with the strange statement that Brzezinski had unzipped his fly.

Clare read it and was aghast. Two hours later Sally called. She was giggling. She said she had made Clare a celebrity and asked if she could borrow the picture so *Post* readers could judge for themselves what it showed. Clare refused. Meanwhile, Brzezinski had also seen the story and he and Presidential press secretary Jody Powell went to see President Carter. Carter was furious. The *Post* was called and asked to send a representative to the White House. "Style" editor Shelby Coffey and a *Post* lawyer went. The White House counsel, Lloyd Cutler, met them and demanded that the *Post* run a full retraction. The *Post* representatives, who had not yet seen the photos and who were apparently locked in euphoria, said no. Clare was also summoned to the White House. She brought the pictures with her. The first showed, as it had always, a grinning man in his shirt sleeves with his thumbs in his belt. The second showed him shaking hands. Clare said positively that nothing improper had happened and nothing improper had been said.

The next day the *Post* ran a grudging apology, on the front page of "Style":

"Correction. In yesterday's story about Zbigniew Brzezinski, it was stated that at the end of an interview with a reporter from a national magazine—as a joke—Brzezinski committed an offensive act and that a photographer took a picture of 'this unusual expression of playfulness.' Brzezinski did not commit such an act and there is no picture of him doing so. A photograph of Brzezinski and the reporter was made and Brzezinski autographed it at the reporter's request. The poses, shadows and background of the picture create an accidental 'double entendre' which Brzezinski refers to in his caption. The magazine reporter states that nothing in the interview or the autographed picture offended her. The Washington Post sincerely regrets the error."

The apology was misleading.

Time magazine ran the picture and to the eye of the ordinary reader the "poses, shadows and background" do not suggest a double entendre at all.

Zbig's inscription (or caption, as the *Post* said)—"I really shouldn't"—was certainly a mild one.

Ben rushed to Sally's defense despite the apology. He said the story was a "son-of-a-bitch of a good story" and that the picture (this was before *Time* ran it for all the world to see) was "very suggestive." Later he told *Post* staffers that Brzezinski deserved the story, true or not. A few weeks later, the *Post* nominated Sally for the Pulitzer for her efforts that year. She did not win.

Brzezinski thought of suing but was dissuaded. Sally's three principal victims were herself, Ben and *The Washington Post*.

It was now finally time for Sally to put her hatchet away. She would, in the manner of the rider thrown from a horse, try again. She would write a few more stories and then announce that she was taking time off to write a novel.

CHAPTER

27

On April 14, 1981, the *Post* announced in a discreet front-page story that one of its writers had won a Pulitzer Prize.

"Janet Cooke of the Metropolitan staff of The Washington Post won the 1981 Pulitzer Prize in feature writing yesterday for 'Jimmy's World,' the story of an 8-year-old heroin addict in Southeast Washington."

The story went on:

> Cooke told the story of a third generation heroin addict, aged 8, who sat calmly in a living room chair while his mother's lover injected heroin in his arm. . . . The story, the Pulitzer board said, "was met by a wave of shock and disbelief" but social workers and teachers confirmed that heroin was being used by others of Jimmy's age. The story also led to a fruitless search for the boy by District of Columbia officials who once threatened to subpoena Cooke for his identity [sic].

> Cooke wrote the story on assignment for the city desk in September, 1980. At that time she was a member of the District Weekly staff. The 26-year-old reporter, a native of Toledo, came to The Post in January, 1980, from the Toledo Blade. She is a graduate of Vassar and the University of Toledo.

Inside on page C-six, the *Post* had a full-page house ad. The top third showed Miss Cooke, an exceptionally pretty woman, standing on the roof of the *Post* building, posed against the city skyline, her hair blowing in the wind.

The rest of the page carried a reprint of the story, describing a scene in which the eight-year-old has heroin injected in his veins by "Ron."

Ron, the mother's boyfriend, was described as "27 . . . recently up from the South," and the one who first "turned Jimmy on."

"He'd be buggin' me all the time about what the shots were and what people was doing and one day he says, 'When can I get off?' Ron says, leaning against the wall in a narcotics haze, his eyes half closed, yet piercing."

Jimmy was quoted as saying that though he was not much interested in school, "I pretty much pay attention in math because I know I got to keep up when I finally get me something to sell."

It said further that "Jimmy wants to sell drugs, maybe even on the District's meanest street, Condon Terrace, S.E., and some day deal heroin, he says, 'just like my man Ron.' "

Two days later the *Post* had another front-page story announcing that the Pulitzer had been withdrawn:

"The Pulitzer Prize Committee withdrew its feature-writing prize from Washington Post reporter Janet Cooke yesterday after she admitted that the award-winning story was a fabrication."

It said that Ms. Cooke had made up Jimmy, his mother and Ron. It said Jimmy was "based on a composite of information about heroin addiction in Washington gleaned from various social workers and other sources."

Her admission followed revelations that certain statements she had made in an autobiographical report to the Pulitzer authorities were also false. Cooke had said that she was a magna cum laude graduate of Vassar College and held a master's degree from the University of Toledo. Cooke resigned from The Washington Post yesterday.

"It is a tragedy that someone as talented and promising as Janet Cooke, with everything going for her, felt that she had to falsify the facts," said Benjamin C. Bradlee, Executive Editor of The Washington Post. "The credibility of a newspaper is its most precious asset, and it depends almost entirely on the integrity of reporters. When that integrity is questioned and found wanting the wounds are grievous and there is nothing to do but come clean with our readers, apologize to the Advisory Board of the Pulitzer Prizes and begin immediately on the uphill task of regaining our credibility. This we are doing."

The *Post* also had an editorial optimistically entitled "The End Of The Jimmy Story."

It painted a sentimental picture of the *Post* as a principal victim of the hoax.

"In truth, just as readers may feel maltreated by publication of the 'Jimmy' tale and all the subsequent hullabaloo it created, so we at this newspaper feel at once angry, chagrined, misused ourselves, determined to continue the kind of aggressive reporting Miss Cooke's story only purported to be and determined also to maintain and honor the highest standards of straight and fair reporting. We feel, as well, something else: enormous sorrow for the burden this young woman created for herself and deep hope that she will find her way out of trouble. . . ."

It ended on a note of something close to self-congratulatory cheer:

"You may be plenty sure that there will be lots of self-examination, that the episode will be written about and explained in this paper and that more of the skepticism and heat that our colleagues traditionally bring to bear on the outside world will now be trained on our own interior workings. One of these episodes is one too many."

In fact the end was not in sight.

First there came a rush of letters to the editor, a few of which seemed to feel that the truth of the story was not in itself of great importance.

"Janet Cooke's story is a myth. And her error was in submitting it as news. But let us not lose sight of the fact that it is a very powerful myth—an extremely well-written myth—and that it reveals great truth. We all know that 'Jimmy' exists."

The great majority of the letter writers were not so forgiving. One said, "Frankly, I don't understand The Post's embarrassment, shock and dismay. . . . I have always read The Post half believing. . . . Are we to believe there really was a 'Deep Throat'? Come now."

Another wrote that "The Post seems to be the most arrogant newspaper in the country and I do not believe that the 'Jimmy' story is an isolated case. In an ocean of 'confidential' sources there are undoubtedly others."

Another said: "[Your] apology does not wipe out two terrible wrongs perpetrated by The Post. The lesser of these evils was the publication of a sensational story—defamatory to an entire community—without first checking out the accuracy of the story.

"Even more appalling was the callous disregard by The Post of the value of a human life. For at a time when The Post allegedly believed that 'Jimmy' really existed, it refused to disclose his identity to authorities who wanted to try to save the poor child. Instead The Post sanctimoniously preached to us about the First Amendment to the Constitution and elected to stand by and allow an eight-year-old child to go down the drain. How shameful! And how distressing that in such a short period of time a once-great newspaper should evolve into a filthy rag."

The next Sunday, the nineteenth, the *Post* ombudsman of the moment, Bill Green, launched a counterattack.

It covered three pages and was divided into a half-dozen sections.

One toward the end was entitled "The Ombudsman: After The Agony, The Reappraisal."

It began on a personal and revealing note:

"I wrote this story of 'Jimmy's World' after being invited to do so by The Washington Post's Executive Editor, Ben Bradlee. It is important to understand the verb 'invited' because if I had been assigned to do it, that would have violated the relationship The Post has maintained with its Ombudsman for over a decade. The central idea is autonomy for the person who sits in this chair. Without it the Ombudsman would be a fake like 'Jimmy.' "

Mr. Green protested a shade too much. A more independent ombudsman might have taken it for granted that he would report on the case and to such an ombudsman Ben's invitation might have seemed an impertinence.

Green began with a section entitled "The Players: It Wasn't A Game." It gave the names, ages and staff positions of twenty-two reporters and editors mentioned in the report. Its sole purpose seemed to be to heighten the drama of "full disclosure."

The next section was headlined "The Reporter: When She Smiled, She Dazzled; When She Crashed . . ."

It began with an account of how Janet got the job.

"On July 12, 1979, 11 days before her 25th birthday, Janet Cooke, a reporter on The Toledo Blade, wrote a letter to Ben Bradlee. It was the kind of letter he receives daily. 'Dear Mr. Bradlee: I have been a full time reporter for The Blade for slightly more than two years and

I believe I am now ready to tackle the challenge of working for a larger newspaper in a major city.' "

Attached to the letter was a résumé and copies of six stories Cooke had written for the Toledo *Blade*. One thing caught Ben's eye: the résumé said Ms. Cooke was a Phi Beta Kappa graduate of Vassar in 1976. Ben underlined that and sent the clippings and résumé to Bob Woodward.

After much consideration the *Post* offered Ms. Cooke a job on "District Weekly," a Thursday section that went only to subscribers living within the boundaries of Washington, D.C. She produced fifty-two stories in the next year and made a generally favorable impression on the "Weekly"'s editor, Vivian Aplin-Brownlee. Toward the end of the year she spent weeks preparing a story on heroin use in the city. Ms. Aplin-Brownlee decided that the story would be more appropriate for "Metro," the general local-news section, and sent Janet to city editor Milton Coleman.

Janet brought her notes to Coleman and in the course of the conversation said that she had heard about an eight-year-old boy who was an addict. Coleman told her to find him. If she did, he said, she'd have a front-page story. Janet returned two weeks later to say she couldn't find the boy but a week after that she returned again and said she'd found another eight-year-old addict and had talked to his reluctant mother. Coleman was excited. He said that she could promise the mother that she would remain anonymous.

Janet came back in a few days and said she had visited the mother at her home and interviewed her, the boy and the mother's boyfriend. She turned in a first draft of a story, thirteen and a half pages long.

Janet said that during her interview the mother's boyfriend, "Ron," had paced the room with a knife in his hand and had told her he would come after her if her story caused him any trouble.

Coleman was very much impressed although he was also very much in the dark. He would never press Janet to tell him the identities of the principals. At one point Coleman saw the name Tyrone on a memo written by Janet and decided that that was Jimmy's real name. Janet also told him the name of the elementary school she said Jimmy attended and the general neighborhood in which she said he lived.

That was all he was told but later, when reporters voiced doubts about the story to their editors, they were told that Coleman knew the child's identity.

Coleman's bosses, Woodward, Howard Simons and Ben, followed the development of the story with excited interest but none of them checked to make sure that Coleman knew who Jimmy was. Coleman said one or more of his superiors might have asked him if he believed the story but none asked him for the child's name. He said his attention was "concentrated on the story and formulating it."

"Howard said she should deal with me and tell me the child's identity; it never occurred to me that she could make it up."

Simons did take an active interest in one aspect of the story—the protection of the reporter from any move by Ron—and just before leaving for a Florida vacation he gave Coleman a message to give to Janet.

Coleman delivered it.

"I said she had written a story that is certain to be controversial. You have seen a crime and may be subpoenaed and if you refuse to reveal your sources, you may be found in contempt of court and have to spend time in jail. Before the story goes, if you don't want to face that, we won't run it. Think it over, tell me in the morning."

No one seemed to have considered the fact that the crime Janet said she had witnessed had an eight-year-old child as its victim and that by allowing the mother and her boyfriend to remain unidentified, the *Post* would be shielding them at the expense of both the boy and society. Janet returned the next day and said she wanted the story to run, and it ran, one Sunday in September. The same day the Los Angeles Times–Washington Post News Service moved it out to three hundred clients.

The reaction was extraordinary. The *Post*'s phones rang for four days. Readers were outraged. The story was described as racist and criminal. The callers wanted to know about Jimmy, what was being done to save him.

The police chief ordered a massive hunt for Jimmy. It would go on, fruitlessly, for two weeks.

Green, the ombudsman, would say in his report that "it would be difficult to overestimate Washington's compassion for 'Jimmy' or its anger when The Post refused to reveal his identity."

There were also people who immediately doubted that there was a Jimmy at all.

One was Vivian Aplin-Brownlee, Janet's old editor, who had not seen the story until it was in print.

She would later tell the ombudsman:

"When I first read the story I was astonished. I thought it was going to be about the use of heroin that causes skin ulcers. . . . I never believed it and I told Milton that I knew her so well and the depth of her. In her eagerness to make a name she would write farther than the truth would allow. When challenged on facts in other stories, Janet would reverse herself but without dismay or consternation with herself. I knew she would be tremendously out-of-place in a shooting gallery. I didn't believe she could get access. No pusher would shoot up a child in her presence. Some of Jimmy's language didn't ring true. What 8-year-old in Jimmy's circumstance would make a connection between math and drugs."

Coleman told Ms. Aplin-Brownlee that he still believed the story.

"I didn't have to ask why. He believed it because he wanted to believe it."

David Maraniss, the deputy "Metro" editor and a close friend of Janet's, read the story on vacation and found it implausible.

Dr. Alyce Gulialtec, director of Howard University's Institute for Substance Abuse and Addiction, whom Janet had interviewed, told *Post* reporter Patrick Tyler that she didn't believe any addict would "fire up" in front of Janet.

Janet's roommate, Elsa Walsh, who knew Janet to be physically timid, didn't believe that Janet would go into such a household.

She would say later, "My own instincts told me it was wrong. She would have real trouble going into the 'Jimmy' setting. When I tried to put what I knew of Janet together with the story itself they wouldn't fit."

Ms. Walsh went through Janet's extensive notes and found no mention of Jimmy.

The doubts either did not reach the people at the top of the *Post,* or if they did, they did not impress them.

On October 7, Donald Graham wrote Janet a long note:

> With all the turmoil of the last weeks, it's important that one say the basic thing: not only was that a very fine story in Sunday's paper a week ago, it was only one of many you've done in the last year.
>
> The Post has no more important and tougher job than explaining life in the black community in Washington. A special burden gets put on black reporters doing that job and a double-special burden on black

reporters who try to see life with their own eyes instead of seeing it the way they're told they should. The Post seems to have many such reporters. You belong very high up among them.

If there's any long-term justification for what we do, it's that people will act a bit differently and think a bit differently if we help them understand the world even slightly better. Much of what we write fails the first test because we don't understand what we're writing about ourselves.

You seem to have much more than the common measure of understanding and the ability to explain what you see. It's a great gift.

And you went through your tests of last week with what seemed to me world class composure. Sincerely, Don.

The Mayor of Washington and the police chief, who had combed the city for the child for seventeen days without finding a trace of Jimmy, had perhaps the biggest doubts of all. On October 15 Mayor Marion Barry said, "I've been told the story is part myth, part reality. We all have agreed that we don't believe that the mother or the pusher would allow a reporter to see them shoot up."

After the Mayor's statement, Ben went to Woodward and Coleman and asked if there was anything that should be rechecked. They told him no.

The Post reacted to the police's skepticism and to the department's failure to find the child by trying to find not Jimmy but some other child addict. Coleman assigned six reporters, including Janet, to the hunt.

Janet worked with Courtland Milloy. Milloy soon grew suspicious. "We were supposed to be finding another kid. But I'll tell you the truth. I wanted to find Jimmy. So as we drove around I circled through Condon Terrace, the general area where Janet said he lived."

Janet said she couldn't find the house. Milloy asked her if it was to the right or left. She said she didn't know. They drove around for seven hours.

Milloy told Coleman about his growing disbelief. Coleman would explain later that he did not give Milloy's doubts too much weight. "I thought part of his doubting might be jealousy. But also I got the distinct impression from him and from Janet that he was concerned with our making sure the child was identified and turned over to authorities. My concern at that time [was] for protecting the reporter on the story."

Coleman said he did, however, relay Milloy's doubts to Woodward and Simons.

Woodward said the incident should have alarmed him but it didn't.

Coleman said, "I voiced my concerns to Howard and he said in so many words they were legitimate. But he urged me to find the most creative way to examine them, stressing that I more than anyone else had to stand by the reporter, [that] at the point that I even began to hint to her that I thought she had not been truthful, her trust in me would be destroyed."

Coleman soon had other grounds for suspicion. Simons had told him to make a personal effort to find Jimmy, to go with Janet to the house where she'd said she'd had the interviews. Coleman told Janet about the plan. The next day she came to him and said she'd gone alone to the house and found it vacant.

Meanwhile Janet was working on another story. She told Coleman that she had interviewed a fourteen-year-old prostitute and her twenty-year-old pimp.

Woodward and Coleman had, however, grown a shade more cautious. Woodward wanted Coleman to meet the young woman before Janet proceeded. He would say later that he wanted to protect Janet from more staff criticism. Janet kept arranging times and places for meetings but they all fell through.

Mrs. Aplin-Brownlee heard about it and told Coleman, "She's about to do it to you again. Why would a fourteen-year-old hooker and her twenty-year-old pimp sit down with Janet in a restaurant in Georgetown?"

Coleman was now infuriated with Janet. He went to Simons and told him what had happened. For the first time Simons had doubts too. He did nothing about them.

"All I had was a hunch and the fact that she had ducked the visit. How do you prove a negative?"

On November 17, 1980, Elsie Carper, the assistant managing editor for administration, sent out a memo asking for nominations for seventy-three separate newspaper awards. The Pulitzer Prize, with twelve categories, was, of course, the big one. Coleman and Woodward went to bat for Janet's story. It would eventually win in the feature story category but it would be the *Post*'s only entry for local news reporting. In the feature category the *Post* had four nominees—

Sally Quinn (Ben's wife), Myra McPherson, Henry Mitchell and sportswriter Tom Boswell.

Janet and the others filled in the standard *Post* bio form and attached it to their entries. Janet's differed substantially from the information she'd put in her résumé. In the résumé she said she spoke French and Spanish. She now added Portuguese and Italian. In the résumé she said she'd won an award from the Ohio Newspaper Women's Association. She now said she'd won six from the Association and another from the Ohio Associated Press. In the résumé she said she'd graduated with honors from Vassar and had gotten a master's degree from the University of Toledo. She now added a year of study at the Sorbonne.

While the nominations were being considered, doubts about Janet and Jimmy peaked in the newsroom.

Jonathan Neumann, the *Post*'s leading investigative reporter and himself a Pulitzer Prize winner, told David Maraniss, the deputy "Metro" editor, that he didn't believe the story.

"A number of people felt strongly that it should not be nominated because it could disgrace us," he said later.

Maraniss, who had had doubts all along, reread it and decided he didn't believe it either. He went to Woodward and suggested Woodward reread it.

Woodward said he'd stick with the story.

He would later explain his decision with a singularly revealing remark.

"I have used the phrase 'in for a dime, in for a dollar.' "

He also said, "I believed it, we published it. Official questions had been raised but we stood by the story and her. Internal questions had been raised but none carried a specific and none about her other work. The reports about the story not sounding right, [about] her personal life [told by men], two she had dated and one who felt in close competition with her. I think the decision to nominate the story for a Pulitzer is of minimal consequence. I also think that it won is of little consequence. It is a brilliant story—fake and fraud that it is."

The Pulitzer decisions were made on April 3 and two members of the advisory board called Ben Bradlee to tell him what they thought was the good news. Janet had won.

Ben called Woodward and Coleman and together they called Janet, who was in New Haven, Connecticut, on a story. When she said she couldn't believe it, Ben repeated the message.

The official announcement came on April 13. The Toledo *Blade* ran the Associated Press story in its first edition. Later in the day an editor noticed that Janet's biography, as carried by AP, didn't jibe with his own recollection. He told the AP man, who checked and found that it was indeed inaccurate: Janet did not have a master's degree from the University of Toledo. He called the New York AP office and someone there checked and found that Janet hadn't gone to the Sorbonne either. AP called Janet, and Janet said the bio as presented by the Pulitzer people was correct. AP executive editor Louis D. Boccardi called Howard Simons just as Dixie Sheridan, assistant to the president of Vassar, was calling Ben Bradlee. They both pointed out biographical misstatements.

Simons called Woodward, Coleman and Tom Wilkinson, the assistant managing editor for personnel, and told them to come to Ben's office. Wilkinson brought Janet's personnel folder with him.

They decided to begin by checking out Vassar. While they were checking, Coleman took Janet out for a talk. They went to the bar of the Capital Hilton and ordered two ginger ales.

Janet insisted she had graduated from Vassar with honors. Coleman said he'd call Vassar. Janet said, "I don't see why it is so important. The Vassar record is just me. The 'Jimmy' story is something I did."

Coleman called Vassar and talked to a clerk in the registrar's office, who said Janet had never graduated. He talked to the clerk's boss, who said the same thing.

Janet said they were wrong.

She called her mother in Toledo and talked to her for fifteen minutes.

She went back to the bar and told Coleman that Vassar was right, she'd gone there for only a year and had then entered the University of Toledo, where she'd graduated with a bachelor's degree.

He asked if the rest of the résumé was accurate—if she spoke French and Spanish and had gone to the Sorbonne. She said it was.

He asked her about Jimmy and she said the Jimmy story was true.

Coleman called Woodward and gave his report. Ben told Coleman to bring Janet back to the *Post* to a large, vacant office on the eighth floor.

Ben and Woodward went there and found Janet sitting on a sofa, crying.

"You get caught at the stupidest things," she said.

Ben asked her to speak in Portuguese. She couldn't. He asked her if she could speak Italian. She said no. He spoke to her rapidly in French. Her answers were stumbling and nonresponsive.

Ben said she was like Richard Nixon—she was covering up.

She still said the Jimmy story was true. She said Jimmy's real name was Tyrone Davis, that his mother's name was Candi Davis, her boyfriend was Robert Jackson Anderson and that they lived on Xenia Street.

Ben told her she had twenty-four hours to prove that there really was a Jimmy.

Woodward told her he didn't believe there was. He said he was going to prove that she lied "if it's the last thing I do."

Ben sent Coleman and Janet to Xenia Street.

After some time Coleman called back and said Janet couldn't find the house. He was now totally convinced she was lying. She insisted she was not.

Woodward, Wilkinson and David Maraniss went through Janet's 145 pages of notes and listened to her taped interviews. There was no mention of Jimmy.

The editors called Elsa Walsh, Janet's roommate. She drove to the *Post* and came to the office. She told them she had never believed the story.

Coleman and Janet met Woodward, Maraniss and Wilkinson in the fifth-floor conference room.

Maraniss would say later that Janet "looked awful. Her eyes were glassy, her face contorted and she seemed not to know what word would come out before she said it."

Woodward told her that her notes proved she had concocted the story. He said he could take her through them and show just how she had put it all together.

"This is getting too cruel," Janet said finally. "All I have left is my story."

She said again that the story was true, but she added, "I have to believe the story."

Woodward and Wilkinson left the room.

Maraniss sat alone with Janet and held her hand.

She said, "I was afraid I was going to be left alone with you. The first time I saw you today, I thought, Oh boy, he knows and I'm going to have to tell him. I couldn't lie to you. I couldn't tell them. I never would tell Woodward. The more he yelled, the more stubborn I was. Wilkinson represents the corporation. It means so much to Milton. You guys are smart, Woodward for the mind, you for the heart."

Maraniss smiled and she asked why.

"Because I had a tremendous surge of empathy for you, refusing to submit to the institution in an absurd situation. You were so strong not to give in. The institution will survive."

Woodward, Wilkinson and Coleman came back in and Maraniss told them it was all over, Janet had confessed. The three editors hugged and kissed her and then left to spread the word.

She and Maraniss talked on. She said she hated Ben Bradlee because he had compared her to Nixon.

Early the next morning Ben broke the news to Donald Graham.

Bill Green, the ombudsman, told the story of Janet and Jimmy with odd flourishes. He praised the editors involved for being a number of irrelevant things. Coleman was a "rangy, tall man, deceptively quiet," who jogged a lot and who "pursues news as though it's his quarry" and whom "admiring colleagues regard as highly competitive." Woodward was a "tough, determined and persistent administrator," Ben "luminescent" and Simons "philosophical."

He told the tale in fragmented parts, with many digressions along the way. He sometimes seemed to be recounting not an extraordinary failure but a kind of wonderful adventure in which some remarkable people went astray for a while but won through in the end.

He reached some remarkable conclusions.

It was, he said, "a complete systems failure and there's no excuse for it," and that was certainly true.

He said, ". . . the scramble for journalistic prizes is poisonous. The obligation is to inform readers, not to collect frameable certificates" and he suggested the *Post* should consider not entering contests.

He asked if race, the fact that Janet Cooke was black, had anything to do with her hiring and rapid rise. He said maybe. He pointed out that Milton Coleman, the key editor in the case, was also black and so were "two of her strongest critics, Vivian Aplin-Brownlee and Courtland Milloy."

He decided that race "may have played some role" and he also decided that "professional pride and human decency were deeply involved in the story." It is hard to see what he meant by that. The professional pride and human decency seem to have been displayed almost exclusively by those, inside and outside the paper, who spoke out against the story—the cops, for example, and Jonathan Neumann and Courtland Milloy.

He also decided, apparently, that the Jimmy business was just one of those things and that it had nothing much to do with the system of "creative tension" that pitted reporter against reporter and editor against editor.

"To believe that this mistake, big as it was, challenges the honesty of any other story in The Post . . . is overreaching. It won't wash. There is no evidence whatsoever that this kind of thing is tolerated at this paper. . . ."

He wound up obsequiously.

"The Post is one of the very few great enterprises in journalism and everybody associated with it ought to be proud of it."

The same day Haynes Johnson, a Pulitzer Prize-winner himself, addressed the question on another page in the paper. His column was headlined "Hoax" and he found that there were lessons to be learned that Mr. Green had missed.

> I believe today's young journalists, those of the age of the Janet Cookes, are the best prepared intellectually and educationally, the most professional, serious and dedicated ever to grace American newspapers. But I also believe fundamental values of the news business are in jeopardy.
>
> Entertainment and gossip intrude into the news process, and sometimes overwhelm it. The mystique of "investigative reporting" and its cloak of anonymous sources is becoming a license for distortion. No source—ever—is so confidential that I, as an editor of a critical story, should not be privy to it. If the reporter chooses not to accept that condition he is welcome to work elsewhere. Certain techniques of the so-called "New Journalism" (an arrogant term when it was first adopted literally a century ago and equally pretentious now) are eroding public trust in the reliability of reporting.
>
> Example: An article some years ago in New York magazine, pur-

porting to be a profile of a prostitute and her pimp, turned out to be "composite" characters and the quotes "composites" of supposed interviews and the practice was defended then as a way to a greater truth. The "docudramas" that pollute television mask as believable accounts of historic episodes when they are not; if Harry Truman didn't actually say it, well, make up his quotes anyway.

We are in danger of losing sight of what should be journalism's most valued tradition, crafted painfully over the years—that of looking at news with the hardest of skeptical eyes.

CHAPTER

28

The *Post* was wrapped in a new confusion but business had never been better. For over twenty years it had had a morning monopoly in a huge area of affluent newspaper readers and its afternoon competition had been fading.

When Eugene Meyer bought the *Post* in 1933 it was the least of five papers.

Phil Graham bought the *Times-Herald* and it was the first of three.

The *Star* bought the *News* in 1972 and then there were two.

It was a lopsided rivalry. Three families, the Noyeses, the Kauffmanns and the Adamses, had owned the *Star* for more than a century. Two of them, the Noyeses and the Kauffmanns, took turns running things. Samuel H. Kauffmann, company president from 1949 to 1963, was the one who ran them into the ground.

Robert Cleveland, who controlled the Adams family stock, said he was a "man of enormous strength of personality. He didn't think anyone was any damn good but Sam Kauffmann. He was the board [of directors]. . . . He tended to treat the other generations like a bunch of kids and none of them built any self-confidence."

A Kauffmann family member said, ". . . on the surface he was secure, glib and attractive. Underneath he sure as hell was shot through with guilt and insecurities. He was unable to deal with anybody else except in terms of dominating a situation and showing off."

He was also a poor judge of realities. He thought the *Post* would be lucky to hold 5,000 of the *Times-Herald*'s 253,000 circulation. It held 180,000, giving it a 143,000 advantage over the *Star.*

Kauffmann refused to believe the paper was in trouble. Editor Ben McKelway (the only nonfamily member ever to hold the job) suggested the Sunday paper be beefed up with a new magazine for young people and a week's listing of television programs.

Instead Kauffmann built a new $15 million plant in an inaccessible part of southeast Washington, making it more difficult to get papers to the expanding suburbs.

He became seriously ill but kept tight control. He became totally deaf and would preside at business lunches reading snippets of the conversation scribbled on a child's magic slate by whoever sat next to him, and doing most of the talking himself.

When he died his son, John H., called "Golden Boy" by the staff, bought the *News* for $5 million.

Most of the 200,000 people who read the *News* bought it on the streets and had the *Post* or the *Star* delivered at home. The *Star* picked up little circulation and most of the *News'* staff. They missed the principal editorial asset, Tom Donnelly.

Donnelly, a columnist who wrote on life, books and the theater, was very talented and very fat. A *Star* executive agreed, reluctantly, to pay him the salary he'd gotten at the *News* but said he would have to lose fifty pounds before he went on the payroll since he would then be covered by the paper's health insurance program.

Donnelly went over to the *Post,* where Ben offered him $50 a week more than he had been getting without asking him to lose an ounce.

The Kauffmanns and Noyeses stumbled along until 1974, when, after prolonged negotiations, they sold the *Star* and its television station to a Texas millionaire named Joseph Allbritton.

Allbritton hired James Bellows, once of the New York *Herald Tribune,* as editor and Bellows remade the paper. His most notable innovation was a spritely gossip column called "Ear." The paper became more readable but less reliable and it continued to lose enormous amounts of money. Bellows quarreled with Allbritton and resigned. A short time later Allbritton sold the *Star* to Time, Inc. He kept the TV station and made millions on his adventure. Time announced it was prepared to spend $60 million making the *Star* competitive with the *Post.* It would spend the money but it wouldn't reach the goal. When it introduced a new section, the *Post* simply followed suit. It was like a rich poker player outbetting one who was almost broke. In the fall of 1981 Time-Life gave up the ghost of the *Star.* The *Post* bought the building and the presses but got the ads and circulation free. The *Post* stock, which had been climbing for two and a half decades, would leap.

CHAPTER

29

After Janet confessed and Jimmy collapsed, the *Post* had promised there would be a "lot of self-examination" and there were three positive steps though they were not necessarily the result. Maraniss replaced Woodward as "Metro" editor and Woodward became the head of a special unit for investigative reporting.

When Time, Inc., finally gave up on *The Washington Star,* and the *Post* became the only major paper in a vast area, the editorial pages were greatly expanded to include a full page of letters to the editor once a week. They were part of the editorial section and free from control by the news departments.

When Green finished his term as ombudsman, Robert J. McCloskey, a former State Department official, took his place. Under him the post would take on new force.

These were positive changes but the sections of the paper that most needed change—"Metro" and "Style"—changed least. Two tendentious "Metro" columnists, Dorothy Gilliam and Richard Cohen, hit new highs in upside-down reporting.

When a member of the Washington City Council, who was white, decided to withdraw from the race for council chairman because he thought a white couldn't be elected, he was persuaded by his black opponent to change his mind. Mrs. Gilliam expressed her outrage in her column. She saw the whole maneuver as a trick to keep blacks from voting for blacks. Despite her strenuous efforts the white councilman was elected, along with the black Mayor. When Washington's chief of police suspended thirty-nine police trainees when tests showed they had been using marijuana, Cohen mounted an implausible and —as it turned out—erroneous attack.

"Survey after survey indicates," he wrote, "that a rather small percentage of young people have never, but never, used marijuana. Such a person is probably not fit to be a police officer. What we do not need on the streets is the law enforcement equivalent of a virgin.

"Yet this is precisely what the District of Columbia is seeking. It wants police recruits who have not once in the last seven years availed themselves of the weed known as pot. It has tested its police recruits with a urine test that detects marijuana use going back maybe seven years. As a result the Police Department suspended and threatened to fire thirty-nine recruits."

Cohen had apparently picked up the idea that the tests checked back for seven years from an earlier, inaccurate story in the *Post*. It was not true. A second story, which ran the same day as his column, partly corrected the mistake. It quoted Dr. Richard Hawks, of the National Institute on Drug Abuse, who said that the tests (which were 95 percent accurate) checked back no more than two months.

The last, compelling word on the subject came in a letter to the editor signed by Maurice T. Turner, the chief of police.

It said:

> Bear with me a moment while I explain why "being a cop in Washington" is nothing like being a newspaper columnist. As a condition for appointment to and continued employment with the Metropolitan Police Department, one must have character—in the sense that one's behavior demonstrates moral strength and conformity to the standard of conduct expected of a man or woman to whom society entrusts its police powers. These standards are embodied in laws, regulations and departmental policies, violations of which automatically expose officers (and recruits) to formal, internal discipline and may result in a fine, suspension or termination (whether or not civil or criminal liability also exists).
>
> By contrast, a columnist apparently can compose a mixture of misinformation, pedantry, and crude analogy, call the product journalism, and present it to the public with little fear of just repercussions piercing the First Amendment shield.
>
> I have placed 39 recruits on administrative leave pending the outcome of our investigations of the fact that their urine tested positive for

illicit drug usage within three to ten days prior to the examination. No one can argue that this is not proper subject matter for coverage by The Post; however, The Post's readers deserved better analysis than they received in one recent issue.

Richard Cohen's column demonstrates what a columnist can do. Among other things, the work is predicated on misstatements of fact (also evident in the companion news article).

Contrary to Cohen's assertions, we are not conducting an investigation either limited to marijuana usage or its "episodic [use] in the distant past" nor do we necessarily reject a police applicant whose background check reveals minor indiscretions or "experimentations."

Further, I believe this community holds belief in and expects its government to conform to higher standards than espoused by Cohen. "Hypocrisy" or no, we recruit non-criminals for police officers. Surely I am not alone in rejecting the notions that the "use of marijuana . . . has nothing to do with a person's ability to perform as a police officer" and my scoffing at logic that would suggest, with minimal extension, that we recruit at penitentiaries in order to find subject matter experts.

In sum, conduct "ordinaire" is unacceptable in law enforcement; too much is at stake. Our judgment, our credibility and our liability routinely are evaluated by judge, jury and public at large (including The Post). Fortunately good, honest, hard-working cops are not "rarebirds" nor are responsible journalists.

Cohen's baseless tirade was not unique. Many people at the *Post* seemed almost to be in the business of promoting their own opinions. Columnists and feature writers traditionally have been allowed to express themselves more freely than reporters. This is at least partly because their job is often to provide entertainment. An ability to entertain (and Cohen, for example, can be entertaining) does not necessarily mean that the practitioner has sound grasp of logic or an innate and governing sense of fair play.

"Style"'s writers, for example, had gotten less reliable and more opinionated.

When the *Star* collapsed, the *Post* grabbed its stars. Diana McLellan, the producer of "Ear," turned herself into a corporation, and Ben bought its services. He did not like "Ear" (which had told many Ben-and-Sally stories) but he recognized its popularity. Some years earlier, he had tried to overpower it with "Gossip Column," by Nancy

Collins. It had been turgid instead of spritely and cautious instead of daring and it soon disappeared.

"Ear" began appearing in the *Post* four times a week and one day it contained an item that would rear back and smack the *Post* in its credibility.

The item said that while the Reagans were staying at Blair House before Inauguration Day, Nancy Reagan had told friends that she wished that Jimmy and Rosalynn Carter would clear out of the White House. It said that the Carters soon found out about it, because Blair House was bugged and they had heard a tape of Nancy's very own words.

Mrs. McLellan put the item at the end of a Sunday column. Shelby Coffey, the editor of "Style," saw it and decided it deserved better display. At his suggestion Mrs. McLellan made it the lead item in her Monday column.

Coffey also read the item over the phone to Ben and was told to proceed as planned. It was a poor decision and one that brought a torrent of criticism.

The most telling came from the Carters, who threatened to sue for libel.

The *Post* and Ben then scurried around trying to build a quick defense. The source, it turned out, was, more or less, a writer named Dotson Rader, who was, among other things, a close friend of Ruth Carter Stapleton's, the President's sister. Rader had told friends that he heard the substance of the story first from Mrs. Stapleton, then from other members of the Carter family. He had, apparently, repeated it to Nancy Reagan, who, it was said, had told friends.

Ben went up to Princeton, New Jersey, and talked to Mr. Rader at great length. Mr. Rader did not hold firm. The best underpinning for the story that emerged was that, maybe, someone had taped Nancy without her knowledge. No one would take responsibility for saying that Blair House actually had been bugged.

The *Post* then delivered an extraordinary editorial, headlined "FYI (For Your Information)." It said:

> There are a lot of "we's" at The Washington Post, but the one you are about to hear from comes about as close as you can get to being the basic, collective "we"—the voice of The Washington Post. This is the space, after all, where funless earnestness and even grandiosity are

not accidental as they may be when they turn up elsewhere in the paper: We have an actual mandate on the editorial page 1) to speak for the paper as an entity, unruly though the entity may be, and 2) to get dead serious about it.

We are dead serious now. The subject is Jimmy Carter, The Ear column and The Post. Mr. Carter and Rosalynn Carter are upset about an item that ran in The Ear column last week. That item, which was accurately sourced, made a relatively modest point that had, nonetheless, a momentous implication for those who read it casually. The point was that a story was circulating (various unnamed bearers of it were alluded to) that Blair House had been bugged while the Reagans were staying there during their pre-inaugural/post-election visit to Washington; it was reported to be by virtue of a tape of such eavesdropping that Mrs. Carter learned that Mrs. Reagan wished the Carters would leave the White House sooner than scheduled—a story, incidentally, that we recall Mrs. Reagan herself denying at the time.

It was one thing, however, to read that item to say that such a tale is circulating and being given currency by estimable public figures who repeat it—and quite another to conclude from this that the place was in fact bugged and that the Carters did in fact perpetrate such a scheme. We weren't there. But everything we know about the presidency of Jimmy Carter suggests otherwise, that it was false. This newspaper took plenty of editorial exception to various actions and policies of that administration. This is no secret to anyone, the former president included. But it always did seem to us and still does—especially as the values involved are being eroded in present-day Washington—that Jimmy Carter was courageous and right in his refusal to play the bugging-taping game, in his insistence on rejecting the precedents for White House invasions of anybody's privacy it wished. Mr. Carter's distinction in this area was real . . . and he can hardly be blamed for wishing to see it maintained.

Perhaps it is foolish to expect people to read newspapers with rabbinical or juridical care, to sift out the fair from the unfair or the justified from the unjustified inferences that can be drawn from a collection of words, even when those words don't add up to what an angry subject thinks they do. The best we can do here, because we feel as strongly as Mr. Carter does about the importance of what he tried to do on this score while he was in office, is to be as blunt and clear about what that Ear item said as we know how. It said there was a rumor around. There was. Based on everything we know of the Carter instinct and record on this subject, we find that rumor utterly impossible to believe.

The rumor around the *Post* was that Donald Graham had written the editorial himself.

It did nothing to still the critics.

One letter writer noted that the editorial had said that while the rumor was "accurately sourced," the *Post* found it "utterly impossible to believe. . . .

"This raises troubling questions about the editorial policy of The Post. What responsibility do you accept for the accuracy of the material you report?"

Another suggested that since the *Post* apparently believed it could save its face by pointing out that it had only said that a rumor was circulating, it might print other rumors such as "that The Post did not run a certain political ad because a politico favored by The Post requested The Post to drop it."

Another said, "I suggest that you consider whether a responsible newspaper should report rumors—especially when you admit you didn't believe this one."

Another asked if the *Post* would have informed its readers that it found the rumor about the Carters "utterly impossible to believe" if "you had not been threatened by a suit by President Carter."

Anthony Lewis in *The New York Times* took the *Post* editorial apart:

"If there were a Pulitzer Prize for lamest newspaper explanation of the year, that editorial would win going away. Readers of 'The Ear,' however expert at penetrating its coy style, would surely have thought that the paper had some evidence for the bubbling report. After all, the item said that 'one little tattler in the Carter tribe' had described listening to the tape. Perhaps the editorial anticipated a legal defense to be argued by The Post. But the courts are not likely to hold that someone who merely reports a rumor from unidentified sources—a false and damaging rumor—is immune from libel actions. Nor would such an argument exactly improve the public image of the press. In order to win a libel suit, Mr. Carter, as a public figure, would have to prove that the writer or editors of the item published it knowing it to be false or in reckless disregard of its truth or falsity. In other words, the state of the publisher's awareness would be a crucial fact. And two years ago the Supreme Court held that a libel plaintiff, in order to make his case, may demand detailed answers from the defendant about what he knew when he published.

"Who was 'one little tattler'? Who were 'Rosalynn's close pals'? Did the writer of The Ear actually talk to any of those people, or did she rely on second-hand rumor-mongers? The answers to such questions could determine whether the item was published in reckless disregard of the truth."

Lewis ended his column by noting that a Carter libel suit would be a wonderful case, but he hoped he wouldn't sue. "He has made his point," Lewis wrote, "about The Post's irresponsibility and arrogance."

When her contract was up the following fall, the *Post* refused to give Mrs. McLellan a new, long-term one and she went to the Washington *Times,* the *Post*'s low-circulation rival, where her column, renamed "Diana Hears," seemed more at home. Arrogance was a word that had been associated with the *Post* for decades, and Mrs. McLellan's departure did not change that. It was a word that would be used more and more frequently in the months to come.

CHAPTER

30

"Style" had other wayward writers, most of them *Post* veterans.

Tom Shales, the TV critic, a clever writer, provided a singular example of slanted reporting in April, 1982.

Bill Moyers of CBS produced a documentary about poor people suffering hardships through the confusion and maladministration of federal government programs intended to help them survive.

It was called *People Like Us.*

John J. O'Connor, the TV critic of *The New York Times,* praised the program and noted that Mr. Moyers was virtually the only network correspondent "allowed to bring a personal vision and voice to his reports."

The program reported four examples of truly needy people who had fallen through the "safety net"—a cerebral palsy victim who'd been cut off Social Security rolls; the mother of three children forced to give up a low-paying job and go back on welfare; a mother who had been caring for her paralyzed daughter at home and who was now committing her to a hospital; and a priest who said the number of people coming to his church for free meals had doubled in the preceding year.

The cases were not presented as the direct results of actions by the Reagan administration, as indeed they were not, but the program did challenge Reagan's assertion that there was a safety net that would take care of the truly needy.

O'Connor quoted Moyers's concluding remarks: "There's no

question but that Federal programs which help the poor are riddled with waste and fraud. So are programs that help the middle class."

Shales's reaction to the program was remarkably different.

His column began:

> Tonight's edition of CBS Reports, "People Like Us," could mark a turning point in American public opinion toward the Reagan administration and cavalier treatment of the poor. This could be the most influential network documentary since "Teddy," the 1979 Roger Mudd interview that effectively killed Sen. Edward M. Kennedy's chances for the Democratic presidential nomination the following year.
>
> Though probably not intended as a direct attack on administration policies, the effect of "People Like Us" is to alter one's image of President Reagan from that of a well-meaning boob to something more along the lines of callous cad.
>
> Neither Reagan nor any of his army of gray spokesmen and ax-wielding henchmen is seen on the report . . . but it is difficult to watch the program's four stories of hardship and destitution and not invoke the visual memory of the President romping in the surf outside Claudette Colbert's house in Barbados, and the distressing symbolism that goes with it: The President splashes about in the lap of luxury while Americans go hungry. Even the people on this program, victims of Reaganomics all, are reluctant to say a word against him, but the program leaves one feeling that a very fragile bubble is just about to burst.

The letters-to-the-editor columns were soon running over.

One writer said, "I am dismayed that The Post would print this vicious and insulting article on the President of the United States." He added a point that went to the core of much of the paper's one-sided pulpiteering. "The Post is a very liberal paper. Many of us are middle-of-the-roaders and some are conservatives. The Post is not serving this large group of people very satisfactorily."

There were also internal voices to be heard. The new ombudsman, Robert J. McCloskey, had, it developed, a somewhat unexpected tilt toward fairness and objectivity. He would be the first *Post* ombudsman to be directly and publicly, if usually gently, critical of the performances and attitudes of some of the paper's privileged people.

In February, Bob Woodward, back to reporting, had a story, under the headline "The Unvarnished Haig," which gave extended verbatim quotes from private high-level State Department meetings.

Secretary Alexander Haig was shown speaking very freely about the policies and diplomats of other countries.

There were once more outraged letters to the editor. One noted that "during Watergate The Post abhorred the break-in and the secret taping and the cover-up. But in printing the Haig staff meeting material, The Post obtained secret taping or notes of the meeting from a source who remains under cover and in essence has printed the fruits of surreptitious entry in the government's inner confidences.

". . . The Post's use of others to 'bug' staff meetings makes them The Post's agent and establishes The Post as a principal. Remember The Post's righteous indignation at anyone 'bugging' the National Democratic Committee headquarters? Now it is all right for The Post to 'bug' Alexander Haig. . . . I hope The Post will shape up and live by civilized standards."

Another said: "We are evidently supposed to believe that we must choose between Soviet-style suppression and tolerance of irresponsibility as demonstrated by Bob Woodward. In fact, if high government officials who are trying to do their job—not to commit crimes or misdemeanors—cannot have confidential staff discussions, their ability to function effectively becomes altogether questionable. . . . Nothing in the First Amendment compelled Mr. Woodward or The Post to publish the story that so clearly violates the public interest."

McCloskey treated the matter in one of his first columns.

He said that "the critics are right in saying that something reprehensible occurred here." He did falter, however, in ascribing blame. He quoted Ben Bradlee, without comment. Ben said that "anything that shows the thinking process of the man in this powerful position, as this story does, merits publication."

McCloskey then concluded that "it is too much to expect a newspaper not to print material like it" and decided that "the villain of this piece is somewhere in the State Department."

McCloskey would pick up a further shade of independence as he went along.

On May 19 he considered the letters of protest against Tom Shales's preview of the Moyers documentary and scolded him, though mildly and in general terms.

"All critics . . . function within limits. Generally this means that critics avoid competing with the topic under review, thereby leaving no opening for the charge that the critic is a hit man working on targets of convenience. The writ accorded a critic carries with it a firm requirement for relevance and fairness. It is exceeded if one takes advantage by simply letting off offensive steam."

Shales did not take the lesson to heart and he returned to the pulpit in May with a remarkable piece of doublethink attacking an article in *TV Guide*. The article, entitled "Anatomy of a Smear," had shown convincingly that a CBS documentary on General William C. Westmoreland had been deliberately slanted against him. Shales had ignored the substance of the article and focused instead on the fact that Walter Annenberg, the publisher of *TV Guide*, was a conservative Republican and a close friend and supporter of President Reagan's.

This time the most effective protester was Ben's old nemesis Reed Irvine, of Accuracy in Media.

The *Post*'s letters column gave him all the space he needed. Irvine wrote:

> I find it strange that The Post failed to tell its readers anything about the substance of the charges that TV Guide had leveled against CBS News and its attack on Gen. William C. Westmoreland in the documentary, "The Uncounted Enemy: A Vietnam Deception," though The Post ran a 2200-word article by Tom Shales on the story.
>
> 1) One of the chief witnesses against Gen. Westmoreland, Sam Adams, was paid $25,000 by CBS News and was given a rehearsal prior to his on-camera interview. CBS News standards require that all such interviews be spontaneous and unrehearsed except in rare cases when approval is given by the head of CBS News, and the audience is informed that the interview was not spontaneous.
>
> 2) Gen. Westmoreland, when interviewed by Mike Wallace, said at least ten times that the number of Vietcong thrown into the Tet offensive proved that the Army estimate of Viet Cong strength was overstated, not understated, as the CBS program contended. That argument was not aired. Instead, Mr. Wallace told the viewers just the opposite.
>
> 3) Gen. Westmoreland was shown confidently asserting that the enemy infiltration rate from the north in the fall of 1967 was 20,000 a month and Mr. Wallace used that to make the point that Gen. Westmoreland had falsified the figures when he said the rate was 7000 a month. The full transcript shows that he expressed uncertainty about the figures and said he would have to check his records. He did so and wrote to Mr. Wallace to say that the lower figure was correct. Mr. Wallace ignored the correspondence and used the incorrect figure to convict Gen. Westmoreland of lying.

4) Mr. Wallace explained to Gen. Westmoreland that he had not interviewed his top intelligence officer, Gen. Phillip Davidson, a key figure in the case CBS was making, because Mr. Davidson was "very, very sick." Mr. Davidson was in good health and told TV Guide CBS had never tried to contact him.

5) CBS created the impression that Gen. Westmoreland had ordered his staff officers who were negotiating order-of-battle estimates with the CIA, not to permit the estimated strength to go above 300,000. The head of the MACV delegation, Gen. George Godding, had told CBS that was not true, and Col. Gains Hawkins, one of the negotiators, told CBS four times that he had not been given any numerical ceiling. CBS used Mr. Hawkins and an officer who did not even represent Gen. Westmoreland's headquarters in an effort to buttress the charge that there was a ceiling.

6) The producer of the program, George Crile, had his mind made up that Gen. Westmoreland was guilty of doctoring intelligence data before he began his investigation. He edited the interviews to support that view and killed entirely, important interviews such as the one with Walt W. Rostow, that demolished the argument.

Mr. Shales did not mention these or any of the other serious charges leveled against the CBS News. Mr. Shales devoted 825 words to the fact that TV Guide is published by Walter Annenberg, a friend of Richard Nixon and Ronald Reagan, and to the supposed implications of that fact.

On a WRC talk show, Mr. Shales explained that he had not bothered to check out the accuracy of any of the stories presented on another CBS program, "People Like Us," because CBS News is a prestigious organization, and it was not his job to question its veracity. Apparently Mr. Shales believes that anyone who questions the veracity of CBS News must be impelled by ulterior motives. But shouldn't the readers of The Post at least be told of the evidence TV Guide uncovered? Is not The Post aiding a cover-up by CBS News of a serious scandal?

Another letter writer noted that Mr. Shales had written that articles such as the one in *TV Guide* "may help bring about a chill on investigative reporting" and asked, "What does he think the TV Guide article was, anyway?"

CBS was not as partisan as Shales. It had Burton Benjamin, its senior executive news producer, investigate the charges and he compiled a sixty-two-page report. The network issued a 1,300-word memorandum signed by Van Gordon Sauter, president of CBS News, but it took extraordinary steps to keep the actual report secret.

The memo admitted that the documentary had violated several of its own rules for fair play and that statements had been distorted, material transposed and, in four instances, answers from several questions combined so as to appear a single answer. The network did say that it was "standing by the documentary."

Shales was outraged at CBS. He felt they were yielding to pressures.

A *Post* editorial took a different view, underlying the paper's increasingly split personality.

It was headed "CBS Looks Hard—At CBS." It listed the specific flaws acknowledged by the network and praised its decision to appoint a new vice-president to hear future complaints of bias. It said, without mentioning Shales by name, that some people had suggested that "dark clouds of corporate or commercial pressure" were hovering and had criticized Sauter "for answering at all."

It concluded that CBS had done what it should do. That in issuing its report it was practicing "the only credible kind" of journalism.

Reed Irvine was less impressed.

He said that Sauter in his memo had "softened and substantially altered the major premise of the documentary." He added that it was "unconscionable" that the full report was never released.

General Westmoreland wasn't impressed either. After CBS made some limited efforts at reconciliation he sued for $125 million.

Sometimes "Style"'s chosen targets seemed merely personal.

In June, 1982, there was a front-page profile of Nancy Dickerson, once television's leading lady of news, who had retired from NBC in 1970.

She was returning to the tube with a two-hour documentary on President Nixon's departure from office ten years before. It was produced by her own company, The Television Corporation of America, and entitled *784 Days That Changed America: From Watergate to Resignation.*

Reviewers in general would consider it a substantial production, rather well done. The "Style" piece, by a free-lancer, Richard Lee, was headlined "Dickerson's Return—The 'First Lady' Of Network News Looks To The Future With A Watergate Retrospective."

It began on a mean and personal note.

Nancy Dickerson is smiling, but the smile is tight and forced. Actually, Nancy Dickerson is very ticked off, very ticked off indeed.

She gets up from her desk, a willowy, well-tended auburn-haired lady in her mid-fifties, looking very chic in a black and white checked Bill Blass suit. She paces the floor, then rather pointedly closes the door of her office, lest her executive assistant or assistant producer, working down the hall, overhear what she is about to say.

Why is Nancy Dickerson ticked off? Well, she reminds [the reporter that] the reason she had agreed, finally, to do the interview was to publicize her documentary. . . .

This is what she had agreed to talk about, she reiterates. She feels deceived, she says, and strongly suggests the reporter may have misrepresented himself.

"I've refused numerous requests for interviews, because I don't want to talk about my personal life," she declares.

"All these people you've been talking to," she goes on, "my friends, my ex-husband, people I worked with at NBC, asking them if this show is a comeback for me, asking if my emeralds are real . . ."

The story went on to no obvious point. The interviewer had indeed, apparently, talked to many people and, apparently, none of them had anything derogatory to say about Nancy. There were, however, suggestions of tales that could have been told if only Lee had found someone willing to tell them—as he put it, "she had left NBC for reasons about which there is still occasional speculation in media circles. . . ."

Why had the *Post* run this story of insinuation without substance? Why was the *Post* (or Mr. Lee or possibly both) mad at Mrs. Dickerson? There was a faint suggestion that one or the other didn't like some of her political associations. She had once been very close to Lyndon B. Johnson but she had made new friends as time went by. As the story said, her social career was "climaxed probably by the glittering dinner given in January, 1981, for President-elect and Mrs. Reagan's close California friends, the Armand Deutsches. . . ."

A bit earlier, "Style" had another random victim. The story was illustrated by a touched-up photograph across the top of the front page showing a quiet suburban street behind sketched-in bullet-shattered plate glass. The story, by Stephanie Mansfield, was headlined "Mother Kills Child; Sorrow Shatters A Neighborhood."

It was by way of being a closer look at a tragedy which had occurred in an upper-middle suburban neighborhood two months earlier. A woman had shot and killed her ten-year-old daughter and then had shot herself. She had survived but lost an arm.

The story seemed to have mixed purposes—to be trying to measure the impact of the tragedy on the neighborhood and particularly on its children; and also to be trying to fix the blame, perhaps on the neighborhood, perhaps on individuals. It focused with some particularity on the husband.

It began: "The neighborhood was shattered. . . . Now [the woman in question] sits in the Washington Hospital Center's psychiatric ward charged with second degree murder. Her left arm has been amputated. [Her husband]—who some believe did not pay enough attention to his wife's mental illness—is trying to rent the house, the bedroom walls scrubbed clean of bloodstains by friends. He has not seen or spoken with his wife. The fashionable neighborhood is angry. And guilty. Some knew [the woman] suffered from depression. . . ."

The story rambled on, full of elusive signs and portents.

There was a strong suggestion that the woman had objected vigorously to the husband's having a shotgun in the house. It was this gun she had used. A neighbor was quoted by Ms. Mansfield as saying, "There was an argument over the gun. She told him to get the gun out of the house. He refused. She said 'we don't need it.' He just totally ignored it."

There was a significance suggested in the fact that the child had written a macabre story for her school paper.

"The story, which some parents say eerily foreshadowed the child's own violent death, is titled, 'The Thing In The Woods.' It tells of a young husband and wife who buy a haunted house, one 'that every tenant who lived in died before the lease was up.' "

In the story the wife rode into the woods.

"She started to breathe very hard. She hyperventilated. After a few hours the husband began looking for his wife. He called the police and described the woman as 5 feet 6, weighing 110 pounds, blond hair and blue eyes." Ms. Mansfield pointed out in her article that this was a "near perfect description" of the mother. The story ended, "She had been killed by a thing which left deep claw marks on her face. There were globs of flesh hanging out. It was a gruesome death."

The child's story had not, in any sense, foreshadowed her own death.

Ms. Mansfield's story drew a great deal of outraged mail.

One neighbor asked, "Why must your paper reopen all the pain and fear that everyone involved with the family suffered?"

Another said that Ms. Mansfield "grossly misrepresented the kind of article she was planning . . . she said she was going to write a story which focused on the support people in a community affected by such a tragedy give to one another. She assured me she was not writing a story on the . . . family."

A mother whose child was in the same class pointed out that the story the child had written for the school paper had been a Halloween assignment and that that particular issue of the paper had "many such stories." She accused Ms. Mansfield of including it simply to "compile a maudlin case study."

The *Post*'s omsbudsman examined the complaints and quoted another neighbor's summation:

"I imagine that each one of our lives has an episode that might not fare well if subjected to public scrutiny, especially if the 'facts' upon which the judgment is made are supplied by those who choose to see only that which supports a preconceived notion. This type of writing, so common now in The Washington Post, is designed to titillate rather than inform."

The ombudsman added his own conclusion:

"Is a newspaper entitled to ransack a family's affairs and defend it as someone else's right to know? I think not."

CHAPTER

31

The Washington Post is written for the ruling class, the trendy and what Nicholas von Hoffman called the hip.

Its writers often express approval or disdain and seem to assume that the readers share their animosities and adopt their conclusions. Its opinions are quirky but they usually fall within the established boundaries of what, for lack of a better label, is often called the liberal point of view.

The fall of 1979 had been an unfortunate season for the opinion makers. The worms had begun to turn and the chickens came home to roost.

That October, "Metro" editor Bob Woodward and reporter Patrick Tyler had focused on William P. Tavoulareas. Mr. Tavoulareas was president of Mobil Oil and, as Ben Bradlee would later acknowledge in court, a tough cookie.

He had been brought to Woodward's attention earlier by an anonymous note which suggested that he and his son Peter were engaged in improper business behavior. Woodward pursued it vigorously. Had it named an executive in a favored business (a department store president, for example) or an office holder who voted properly, it might have been ignored, but the *Post* seemed to consider presidents of big oil companies natural suspects. As Alexander Cockburn had written of his late friend Larry Stern, some *Post* reporters and editors didn't need signposts to lead them from a gas shortage to big oil headquarters.

Woodward had dug in vain and put the note aside. That fall he brought it forth again and gave it to Patrick Tyler. Tyler had worked for Eugene Patterson, the *Post*'s former managing editor, at the St. Petersburg *Times* and he had recommended him to Bradlee as a young man with brains and guts. Tyler reminded Woodward of himself.

Meanwhile a less favored reporter on an organ of less renown, Sandy Golden of the Montgomery *Journal,* a weekly in a Washington suburb, went to see a specialist at Johns Hopkins about his eyes. The doctor, Philip Piro, had been married to William Tavoulareas' daughter and he had grievances against her family. When he found that Golden was a reporter he told him a strange tale.

It was about William Tavoulareas and his son Peter's involvement in Atlas Maritime Company, which used Mobil ships to transport Mobil oil and made a great deal of money. The suggestion was that the arrangement benefited the son but not Mobil's shareholders.

The tale and the newspaper stories that grew out of it had other implications for Mr. Tavoulareas senior.

"They said my son is an idiot and incompetent and everything he had done, I had to do for him," he later said in court.

Golden told the tale to his editor at the *Journal,* who said that whatever it was, it was beyond that paper's scope.

Golden then used it as bait to try to get a job with *The Washington Post.* He called Woodward and got his secretary. He told her, cautiously, that he "had a lead on an international oil company" and a few days later Patrick Tyler called him back.

Golden bargained with Tyler. He said he would exchange the story for a job. Tyler said no and Golden finally settled for a promise of a joint by-line. He then set up another interview with Piro, and Piro repeated his story in front of Tyler.

As the two reporters were driving back from Baltimore, Tyler said, "It's not every day you get a chance to knock off one of the Seven Sisters." He meant one of the big oil companies and he would say later that he was just kidding.

He added however that he had learned nothing of value from Piro and he told Golden that the joint by-line deal was off. Golden, very upset, said that he would take the matter up with Woodward, but when he tried he still couldn't get through. He decided to work on the story alone, in competition with Tyler and the *Post,* and arranged a month's leave of absence from the *Journal.* In the next few weeks he found and interviewed John Comnas, an original partner in Atlas Maritime Company who had been eased out after Peter Tavoulareas learned the ropes and who was presumed to be angry with both father and son. Golden also interviewed Peter Stockton, an investigator for the House subcommittee on energy and power, and he talked to two public-relations men at Mobil. A few days later Mobil issued a press release saying that Golden had failed to tell them he was working with Tyler and the *Post* (which he was not) and that "this kind of procedure . . . diminishes the public's confidence in the reportorial process."

Golden tried to sell his story to *The New York Times, The Washington Star* and the Associated Press with no success, but when Tyler found that Golden was still working on the story he grew alarmed and offered to give him a credit line on the *Post* story if he would lay off. Golden, whose month of leave was running out, agreed.

The first story appeared in the *Post* on November 30 with Tyler's name at top and Golden listed as a "special correspondent" at the bottom. It said that Tavoulareas senior had set up Atlas for his son's benefit and that it "did millions of dollars in business operating Mobil-owned ships under exclusive no-bid contracts." It said Atlas dealt with Mobil through Samarco, a company which Mobil helped organize but which "existed largely on paper." The story was overly long and not particularly interesting. Some people at the *Post* thought it had been given a great deal more attention than it was worth.

Golden had made no contribution to it at all, a point he would later emphasize.

"I had no role in writing any portion of any draft or of the final version. I never saw the drafts. I had no role in editing." A second story, with only Tyler's name attached, appeared on December 1 and quoted allegations about the Tavoulareases made by Representative John D. Dingell (Democrat of Michigan) to the Securities and Exchange Commission. The Commission would find the charges insubstantial.

On December 4, William Tavoulareas, flanked by a couple of Mobil vice-presidents, came in to the *Post* to complain.

Ben received them in his office.

"I like to handle those first meetings alone," he said later. "If the reporter involved is there or the editor, you generally get bogged down in detail. . . . I like to take the measure of the person, the measure of the complaint, lay the groundwork."

Mr. Tavoulareas made an impression on Ben.

"He had a reputation as a tough guy and someone who is not scared of muscling the press a little and he has been known to sue, so I was paying particular attention to what he said. He started denying . . . the general allegations of the story and he was particularly interested in the documents [of the House subcommittee]. He said he didn't think it was fair for us to have documents of the Congress of the United States, to have documents that he didn't have."

Ben, by his own testimony, had remained respectful but adamant.

"I had been told I would like him and I did. My general purpose was to listen to what the complaint was. I said we could not give him the documents. We had received them under conditions that we would not reveal them, we would not reveal the source, and we would not give the documents away. . . . Everybody was friendly and he asked me at one point . . . 'Haven't you ever done anything for your son?' and I said, 'Yes, I certainly have.' The feeling [at the *Post*] was that there was nothing to retract. There was nothing to apologize for."

There was, however, something, in Ben's phrase, to add.

On December 7 the *Post* ran an unsigned article headed "Documents Support Mobil Chief On Issue Of Funds." It said that Atlas money, not Mobil money, had been used to buy out John Comnas.

Ben Bradlee had also written Tavoulareas a letter in which he said that "since we are writing history on the run, we make errors from time to time."

The Tavoulareases were not mollified. They filed a suit against the *Post* charging libel and asking for $150 million in damages.

After exhausting and expensive preliminaries, the case came to trial in the summer of 1982. The *Post* took a poll to determine whether it or Mobil had the better public image, and on the basis of it chose to have a jury trial.

At the trial Tyler admitted that he had made the remark about knocking off one of the Seven Sisters and that he had also asked Dr. Piro if they could find someone to "rifle the safe" at William Tavoulareas' New York home. He said that on both occasions he had been joking.

There was evidence that Representative Dingell's letter to the SEC had been prompted, at least in part, by information from Tyler and Golden.

Witnesses contradicted many specific points in the articles and John Walsh, Tavoulareas' lawyer, accused the newspaper of "ignoring the truth each time it stood in the way of the central theme."

The *Post* covered the trial extensively, occasionally with less than total objectivity. At one point a *Post* story had gone beyond the evidence to say that the Securities and Exchange Commission had been critical of the setting up of Atlas even if it hadn't prosecuted. John Walsh complained.

"It goes beyond all reason," he said, "the ability of one party to communicate to the world at large and perhaps to the jury."

Judge Oliver Gasch agreed. "Reporters ought not to print stuff that doesn't occur in court," he said. "It is just common sense and common ordinary decency, it seems to me. I am not going to declare a mistrial, but this kind of stuff is irritation."

He asked the *Post* attorney to convey his displeasure to Ben Bradlee.

By the time the case went to the jury, the *Post* had spent or committed an estimated one million dollars and the Tavoulareases two million dollars.

Judge Gasch gave the jury extensive instructions about the laws of libel. He pointed out that since William Tavoulareas was president of Mobil and therefore "a public figure" he would have to meet difficult standards to prove he was libeled.

"It is not enough for William Tavoulareas to prove the defendants did not conduct a thorough investigation of the facts, or that they were negligent in the way they wrote or edited the articles. . . . [He] must prove that the defendants had a high degree of awareness that the articles were false or probably false and that they recklessly disregarded whether the articles were false or not. . . . You must be convinced that they intentionally printed false information or acted with reckless disregard for the truth."

The six-person jury deliberated for more than eighteen hours and found Tyler, Golden and *The Washington Post* guilty of libeling the father and awarded him $2,050,000. It also found Dr. Piro guilty of slander and ordered him to pay $5,000 to the father and $1,000 to the son.

Most of the award to Tavoulareas, $1.8 million, was in punitive damages, which meant in Judge Gasch's phrases that the jurors chose "to make an example" of the *Post* "as a punishment for outrageous conduct."

The *Post,* which had relied on its poll, was amazed.

Its lawyer, Irving Younger, said "the jury made a mistake." A few days later Donald Graham told a group of *Post* editors that there was no lesson to be learned from the experience, that the *Post* and its people had handled the Tavoulareas stories just right.

The stories may have been handled with a high degree of caution and professional skill.

William Greider, who oversaw the editing, emphasized that there was nothing reckless about the process.

"We were very careful with that story, exceedingly careful. We went over and over it and [Tyler] went back to the typewriter."

The story was "lawyered" by the *Post*'s attorneys and they had concluded that it was libel-proof.

It seems probable that had the *Post* chosen to be tried by a judge instead of a jury, it would have won. It didn't, and the jury—people who read it every day of their lives—spent more than two working days considering the *Post*'s reliability and decided that it had displayed a "reckless disregard for the truth."

There were lessons to be learned and the principal one may have been that many, perhaps most, of the millions who read the *Post* do not accept it as a fair and impartial reporter—that a significant number of them believe it judges some groups and institutions too harshly and some others too gently.

CHAPTER

32

Newspapers exist to gather, assort and disperse information. Great papers do it with accuracy, determination, fairness and style. There are few great papers. *The Wall Street Journal* has a touch of greatness —it achieves the high but narrow goals it has set for itself. *The Washington Post* and *The New York Times* aspire to a broader excellence. By and large the *Times* succeeds and the *Post* does not. Both have highly skilled staffs and provide extraordinary ranges of coverage. The *Times* has its faults, some serious, but it seeks truth, disciplines itself, admits error though sometimes reluctantly, and maintains its own well-defined ideals. It is never silly.

The *Post*'s flaws are more glaring. They have been for most of this century but over the years they have changed and, in the long run, lessened.

Papers are shaped by goals, people and circumstances. Eugene Meyer had a goal when he bought it in 1933—he wanted the *Post* to be a political force. Since he was rich—at a time when few people were —and determined, he succeeded though not to the degree he had hoped.

Phil Graham's goals were similar but more ambitious. He wanted power, not greatness, though he confused the two. When his father-in-law bought the *Times-Herald* in 1954 he made the *Post* rich and invincible.

Katharine Graham inherited power and wealth and had an insight into their limitations. She wanted the paper to be readable, accurate and fair. She hired Ben Bradlee and he gave her what she wanted up to a point. He made it readable. He got rid of the old system of shaping the news. He made the *Post* exciting. It had long been aggressive but he made it victorious. He gave it, in his word, impact. He also built into it serious flaws. He valued stories for their immediate effect—he wanted readers to be astonished. They often were, but sometimes by the methods rather than the results. He made a dull, preachy newspaper into a lively one. In 1967 free-lancer Ben Bagdikian wrote in the *Columbia Journalism Review* that the *Post* was badly edited but that it was nevertheless within a lunge of greatness, and his vote of semi-confidence inspired Katharine Graham to acknowledge the paper's faults and enunciate her aspirations. She agreed that it was not competently edited but not that it was biased:

". . . The charge that we sometimes let opinion creep into the news columns I find painful because I think it a cardinal sin."

One of the two problems—the lack of quality editing—contributed to the other. Ben Bradlee and his top lieutenants did try to keep the opinions of reporters out of the paper. Once Ben wrote a note of explanation to a reporter who thought he'd been overedited.

"We are not trying to make this paper flatter. We are trying to make it fairer. What you interpret as an effort to remove flavor, individuality and allusion is in fact an effort to remove the tipped hand, the veiled stand, the editorial phrases that make your position clear while they cloud the news."

To some degree, particularly in respect to foreign and national coverage, they would succeed. William Greider, who came to work on the national side in the late sixties, remembers:

"It was a kind of random and eclectic paper in its coverage and we swung from the heels and did a lot of crazy stuff and I did some of it. Some of it was brilliant and some of it was embarrassing. We had David Broder, who was a kind of rock of stability, but a lot of the rest of us were doing off-the-wall stuff. Then we got steadier and steadier."

The *Post* felt best about itself in the early seventies. The publication of *The Pentagon Papers* was not the clear-cut triumph for the First Amendment over the forces of darkness that Ben would say it was but it was a stunning display of competitive newspapering.

Watergate was a landmark and a positive one. The *Post*'s role was key and possibly essential. Its effect on the *Post* was mixed. Greider believes it was also fundamental. "It changed the *Post,* mostly for the good, in the sense that from then on people regarded the *Post* in a way they hadn't before. Everything the *Post* did after Watergate was taken more seriously."

This meant that its attitudes would have greater weight in the halls of Congress and in the minds of its subscribers, and it established a new tolerance for permissive reporting. Woodward and Bernstein had for the most part used the traditional techniques of investigative reporting but in their first book they introduced the romantic tale of Deep Throat and its accompanying hocus-pocus and in their second mixed selected facts with disguised fiction.

The *Post* grew increasingly reckless and arrogant. It seemed to acquire a new set of guidelines that could have been enunciated by Sally Quinn: pick a proper victim, then gather, select and discard evidence to support your intended conclusion. Sally used them to exalt Castro and demolish the Arabs of London. In time she used them once too often.

She set the style and no one said no. She was Bradlee's girl friend and then his wife and to her Bradlee's old rules did not seem to apply.

It grew more difficult to apply them to others.

A squad of reporters tracked down Congressman Hays and accomplished the end of his Congressional career. By the time Janet Cooke arrived, the pattern had become routine.

Most of the paper was not affected. Foreign coverage grew more extensive and reliable, second only to the *Times'*. National coverage was better than the *Times'*, the best in the country. The editorial page under Meg Greenfield was also the best.

But the "Metro" section under Bob Woodward and the "Style" section showed an increasing lack of basic adherence to standards. Larry Stern and Sally Quinn tilted things to their purposes, Dorothy Gilliam, Richard Cohen and Tom Shales to theirs.

As the *Post* became the only major paper in town its credibility went down. More and more people began to doubt that it always tried to tell the truth.

As it made its way into the eighties it was still, in Bagdikian's phrase, a lunge from greatness but it also seemed a lunge from disgrace. There was a deliberate effort to tighten up the paper and to improve its credibility. Diana McLellan and "Ear" were allowed to move over to the Washington *Times,* and the *Post*'s other gossip column, Rudy Maxa's, which had printed the dubious story about

Hamilton Jordan dashing amaretto on a brassy young woman in a Georgetown pub, was closed down; and David Maraniss, who had congratulated Janet Cooke on her refusal to be pushed around by an insensitive management, was replaced as "Metro" editor by a hard-nosed man from New Jersey who announced that from then on, "Metro" would concentrate on real, hard news. Still the paper seemed curiously adrift, fifteen years after Bagdikian had said it was unedited, and tilted parts of it still conspicuously were. No one was clearly in charge. Ben Bradlee, over sixty and by precedent approaching retirement, had lost both prestige and the admiration of the troops. Even Katherine Graham seemed to have lost faith. She told a visitor that Ben hadn't had an original idea in twenty years. Donald remained a mysterious stranger, a self-controlled man who was always polite and never relaxed. He had been only eighteen when his father killed himself and some who knew him then said that was when his remoteness first became apparent.

The most perceptive descriptions of him may be those of two former colleagues at Harvard, where he was president of the *Crimson.* One, a young woman, said he was "like a good king, brought up to realize everything he did would have a moral resonance, and so he knew to be very careful in everything he did."

The other, a young man, said Donald had perfected the ability to seem "absolutely normal—not to escape notice but because he believes all these values to be absolutely right."

His style remains unobtrusive and friendly. He tours the *Post* regularly, greeting people by their correct names (a trick his mother never mastered) and asking about their families. He writes notes of praise to reporters whose work has caught his attention but some, such as those to Janet Cooke, suggest more a desire to please than a perceptive knowledge.

For better or worse the future of *The Washington Post* is now in his hands. He is the descendant of four driven people. He is driven too but in a less personal way: he is modest, patient and shuns the spotlight. The least successful of his forebears was perhaps his grandmother Agnes. She left her own Ozymandias-type monument—the Agnes Meyer collection of photographs in the Library of Congress, donated after her death. It includes thousands of pictures, plaques and awards, all bundled together in large gray boxes, still unclassified; studio portraits, home snapshots, intimate family scenes and autographed pictures of Agnes with the great, some still in silver or brass frames. Agnes wanted personal power and lasting glory. Her grandson seems to have a more reasonable goal. He wants to make the *Post* great and good. He has expressed a continuing interest in giving it a solid, reliable core that will appeal not only to movers and shakers but also to ordinary people in a workaday world. He can perhaps, in time, with luck and persistence, make it what it has always claimed to be— complete, accurate, well written, well edited and fair. It has been most of those things here and there, now and then, but never all of them at once. It would be good for the Grahams, the city, the country and the memory of Donald's predecessors if it became so.

BIBLIOGRAPHY

Apple, R. W., Jr., and *The New York Times* staff, eds. *The Watergate Hearings, Break-in and Cover-up.* New York: Viking Press, 1973.

Bernstein, Carl, and Bob Woodward. *All the President's Men.* New York: Simon & Schuster, 1974.

———. *The Final Days.* New York: Simon & Schuster, 1976.

Bradlee, Benjamin C. *Conversations with Kennedy.* New York: W. W. Norton, 1975.

Bray, Howard. *The Pillars of The Post: The Making of a News Empire in Washington.* New York: W. W. Norton, 1980.

Collier, Barney. *Hope and Fear in Washington (the Early Seventies): The Story of the Washington Press Corps.* New York: Dial Press, 1975.

Congressional Quarterly. *Chronology of a Crisis.* Washington, D.C.: Congressional Quarterly, 1973.

Cooney, John. *The Annenbergs: The Salvaging of a Tainted Dynasty.* New York: Simon & Schuster, 1982.

Daugherty, Harry M. *The Inside Story of the Harding Tragedy.* New York: Churchill, 1932.

Davis, Deborah. *Katharine the Great: Katharine Graham and The Washington Post.* New York: Harcourt Brace Jovanovich, 1979.

Drew, Elizabeth. *Washington Journal: The Events of 1973–1974.* New York: Random House, 1975.

Folliard, Edward T. Unpublished history of *The Washington Post.*

Friendly, Alfred, and Ronald L. Goldfarb. *Crime and Publicity: The Impact of News on the Administration of Justice.* New York: Twentieth Century Fund, 1967.

Halberstam, David. *The Powers That Be.* New York: Random House, 1979.

Hamlin, Charles Sumner. Unpublished diary of first governor of the Federal Reserve Board. Library of Congress, manuscript division, Washington, D.C.

Jaworski, Leon. *The Right and the Power.* New York: Pocket Books, 1977.

Lattimore, Owen. *Ordeal by Slander.* Boston: Atlantic-Little, Brown, 1950.

London *Sunday Times. Watergate: The Full Inside Story,* by the London *Times* Team. New York: Ballantine Books, 1973.

McLean, Evalyn Walsh, with Boyden Sparkes. *Father Struck It Rich.* Boston: Little, Brown, 1936.

Manchester, William. *The Glory and the Dream.* Boston: Little, Brown, 1973.

Marchetti, Victor, and John D. Marks. *The CIA and the Cult of Intelligence.* New York: Alfred A. Knopf, 1974.

Martin, Ralph G. *Cissy.* New York: Simon & Schuster, 1979.

Means, Gaston B. *The Strange Death of President Harding, from the diaries of Gaston B. Means as told to May Dixon Thacker.* New York: Guild Publishing Corporation, 1930.

Meyer, Agnes. *Chinese Painting as Reflected in the Thought and Art of Li Lung-Mein.* New York: Duffield, 1924.

———. *Out of These Roots: The Autobiography of an American Woman.* Boston: Little, Brown, 1953.

Noggle, Burl. *Teapot Dome, Oil and Politics in the 1920's.* New York: W. W. Norton, 1962.

Osborne, John. *The First Two Years of the Nixon Watch.* New York: Liveright, 1971.

Powers, Thomas. *The Man Who Kept the Secrets: Richard Helms and the CIA.* New York: Alfred A. Knopf, 1974.

Pusey, Merlo J. *Eugene Meyer.* New York: Alfred A. Knopf, 1974.

Quinn, Sally. *We're Going to Make You a Star.* New York: Simon & Schuster, 1975.

Roberts, Chalmers M. *The Washington Post: The First Hundred Years.* Boston: Houghton Mifflin, 1977.

Russell, Francis. *The Shadow of Blooming Grove: The One Hundred Years of Warren Gamaliel Harding.* New York: McGraw-Hill, 1968.

Schlesinger, Arthur M., Jr. *A Thousand Days: John F. Kennedy in the White House.* Boston: Houghton Mifflin, 1965.

U.S. Senate hearings. The nomination of Eugene Meyer to be a member of the Federal Reserve Board. Hearings before a subcommittee of the Committee on Banking and Currency. Washington, D.C.: Government Printing Office, 1931.

————. Investigation of Hon. Harry M. Daugherty. Hearings before the Select Committee on Investigation of the Attorney General. Washington, D.C.: Government Printing Office, 1931.

Weinstein, Allen. *Perjury: The Hiss-Chambers Case.* New York: Alfred A. Knopf, 1978.

Woodward, Bob, and Scott Armstrong. *The Brethren.* New York: Simon & Schuster, 1978.

MAGAZINE ARTICLES

Anonymous. "The Quality of an Appointee: A view of Russell Wiggins by a former top *Washington Post* reporter." *Washingtonian.*

Cameron, Julia. "Investigative Reporter as Star: Has Success Spoiled Bob Woodward and Carl Bernstein?" *Washingtonian* (May, 1974).

Fallows, James. "Big Ben." *Esquire* (April, 1976).

Howard, Jane. "Katharine Graham: The Power That Didn't Corrupt." *Ms.* (October, 1974).

Kelly, Tom. "Can Portfolio Save the Star-News?" *Washingtonian* (March, 1977).

———. "Sally Quinn: Still Breaking Butterflies." *Washington Dossier* (December, 1977).

Lee, Richard. "Sally Quinn's True Confession: Intimate Profile of the Merry Star of the *Post* Style Section." *Washingtonian* (November, 1972).

Noah, Timothy. "*The Washington Post*'s Ear Problem." *Washington Journalism Review* (December, 1981).

Sherman, Norman. " 'Who the Hell Was That?' 'He's the Editor of The Post.' 'Jesus, I Thought He Was Your Bookie.' " *Washingtonian* (September, 1974).

Viorst, Judith. "Katharine Graham." *Washingtonian* (September, 1967).

Since I began researching this book in the early 1970s, I have spoken with a great many people, some briefly and some several times at great length.

These include:

Robert Asher	Frank Getlein	Morton Mintz
Wes Barthelmes	Ben Gilbert	Laughlin Philips
Grace Basset	Sandy Golden	Sally Quinn
Carl Bernstein	Donald Graham	Joseph Rauh, Jr.
Herbert Block	Katharine Graham	Harry Rosenfeld
Ben Bradlee	William Greider	Howard Simons
Peter Braestrup	Richard Hollander	Laurence Stern
Elsie Carper	Paul Hume	Lon Tuck
Phil Casey	Catherine Jensen	Judith Viorst
Maxine Cheshire	Robert Jensen	Milton Viorst
Richard Coe	Tom Kendrick	John Waits
Clare Crawford-Mason	John H. Kauffman	Frank Waldrop
Ann Crutcher	Jack Lemon	David Waters
Nancy Dickerson	William Mackaye	Elizabeth Young
Tom Donnelly	Myra MacPherson	(Mary Hayworth)
Edward T. Folliard	Judith Martin	Marty Zad
Brian Flores	Colman McCarthy	

There are others who would prefer not to be named.

INDEX

Accuracy in Media (AIM), 214, 239–241, 286–287
Acosta, Teofilo, 241
Adams, Sherman, 140
Ade, Bob, 107
Adler, Renata, 219–220
advertising, 17, 35, 91–92, 94, 273
   repro and, 198
   in *Star* vs. *Post*, 112, 119, 123
AFL-CIO, 206
Agnew, Spiro, 168, 169, 185, 187, 188
Aimee, Mrs., 68
Albright, Robert C., 73, 94, 95, 123
Allbritton, Joseph, 272
Allen, Henry, 246
Allied Chemicals, 47
All the President's Men, 210–211, 218
Alsop, Joseph, 83, 116, 124, 142
Alsop, Stewart, 125
American Newspaper Guild, 64–65, 121, 200–201, 204, 205, 206, 213
American Security and Trust Company, 45, 58
Anaconda, Eugene Meyer's coup and, 28
Angleton, James, 139–140, 214, 237, 238
Annenberg, Walter, 286, 287
anti-Semitism, 12, 15, 16, 34, 44, 124, 126
Aplin-Brownlee, Vivian, 259, 260–261, 263, 268
Arena Stage, 108
Armstrong, Scott, 219–220, 247
Arnett, Peter, 155–156
ARTnews, 125, 157
Associated Press (AP), 42, 44, 60, 61–62, 73, 88, 265, 295

Astor, Mrs. Vincent, 125
Atlas Maritime Company, 294, 295–296
automobile industry, Eugene Meyer's investments in, 29–30

Bachinski, Eugene, 183
Bagdikian, Ben, 141, 156, 173–174, 175, 178–179, 300, 301, 302
Bagley, Smith and Vicky, 221
Baker, Bernard L., 186
Baluch, Ismail, 222
Bargeon, Carlisle, 62
Barnard, Francine, 220
Barney, Alice, 194
Barrett, Robert, 103–105
Barry, Marion, 262
Barth, Alan, 108, 109–111, 142
Barthelmes, Wes, 99, 107, 115, 121, 122
Bassett, Grace, 106–107
Beach, Beverly, 105
Beale, Betty, 100–101
Beard, Charles, 30
Beckers, William Gerard, 33
Beckett, Marion, 51
Beebe, Frederick (Fritz), 130, 131, 164, 174
Bellows, James, 272
Benjamin, Burton, 287
Bennett, Ira, 62
Bernstein, Carl, 155, 191, 201, 209, 211
   alienation of, 181, 182
   background of, 182
   post-Watergate career of, 217–219
   Watergate and, 182, 183–189, 217, 301
Berryman, Clifford, 74–83
Beverly (Mass.) *Evening Times,* 137–138

Black, Hugo, 86
blacks, 91
  Cooke's hoax and, 255–269
  election of 1920 and, 38–39
  hired by *Post,* 106, 107, 171, 176–179
  as newspaper readers, 158, 170, 171, 226
  see also integration, racial; violence, racial
Block, Herbert, *see* Herblock
Blum, Léon, 71
Blumenthal, George, 29
Boccardi, Louis D., 265
Booker, Simon, 106, 107
Borglum, Gutzon, 19
Bowater Mersey Paper Company, 125
Braden, Joan, 161
Braden, Tom, 239
Bradlee, Ben, 128, 132–154, 167, 181–182,
    188–189, 209–215, 218–219, 245–247,
    278, 294, 302
  background of, 137–138, 214
  boredom of, 137, 139, 141, 152
  CIA connection of, 139–140, 237, 238
  Cooke's hoax and, 256, 258–259, 260, 264–
    266, 267
  creative tension and, 154, 176
  critics and enemies of, 212–215
  on East Potomac Park riots, 105–106
  education of, 138, 141
  independence of, 151–152
  Katharine Graham's relationship with,
    132–133, 134, 151–152, 163–164, 202,
    245, 300
  labor problems of, 175–180, 201
  marriages of, 138, 139, 193, 224, 301
  Newsweek and, 124–125, 132
  Pentagon Papers and, 174, 175
  Post hierarchy shuffled by, 133, 134–135
  Quinn's relationship with, 159, 160, 161,
    191, 193, 212, 213, 215, 224, 253, 301
  "Style" launched by, 156–162
  Tavoulareas and, 293, 295–296, 297
Bradlee, Frederick (Beebo), 137
Bradley, Mary, 96
Brady, James, 29–30
Braestrup, Peter, 142
Brancusi, Constantin, 24–25
Brandeis, Louis D., 33
Bray, Howard, 175
Brethren, The (Woodward and Armstrong),
    219–220, 248
Brewster, William Tenny, 22–23
Bridges, Harry, 85
Broder, David, 154, 209, 300
Brooklyn Rapid Transit, 48

Broun, Heywood, 64
Browder, Earl, 110–111
Brown, George Rothwell, 39, 40, 45
Bryan, William Jennings, 17, 22
Brzezinski, Zbigniew, 249–253
Burden, Amanda, 161, 193
Burden, Carter, 161
Burton, Philip, 224

Califano, Joseph A., Jr., 182
Cambodia, *Post* coverage of, 239–241
Capote, Truman, 163
Carper, Elsie, 93, 101, 123, 135, 158, 263
Carter, Jimmy, 158, 221, 252, 278–281
Carter, Philip D., 155
Carter, Rosalynn, 278–281
cartoons, 43, 74–83, 95, 117, 126, 168, 169
Cassini, Margaret, 194
Castiglione, Baldassare, 212–213
Castro, Fidel, 222–224
Catholics, 44, 45, 50–51, 73, 95, 111–112
CBS News, 286–288
Central Intelligence Agency (CIA), 115–116,
    131, 139–140, 175, 183, 219, 223, 237–
    239
Chamberlain, Ann, 220
Chambers, Whittaker, 109, 168
Chapin, Dwight L., 186
Chavez, Cesar, 221
Cheshire, Maxine, 123, 158
Chestnut Lodge, 127
Chicago, University of, 85, 97–98
Chicago Seven, 157–158
Chicago *Tribune,* 60, 113, 117, 247
Chicago Tribune-New York News Syndi-
    cate, 60–61
Chile, CIA activities in, 238–239
Churchill, Winston, 86–87
Cincinnati Enquirer, 20, 37–38
Clark, Marion, 224–225
Claudel, Paul, 50–51, 111
Clawson, Ken W., 186
Cleveland, Robert, 271
Cloud, Joe, 93–94
Cockburn, Alexander, 241, 293
Coffey, Shelby, 252, 278
Cohen, Richard, 275–277, 301
Colby, William, 238
Coleman, Milton, 259–260, 261, 262–263,
    265–267
Collier, Barney, 214–215
Collins, Nancy, 277–278
Colson, Charles (Chuck), 183
Columbia Journalism Review, 156, 300

comic strips, 35, 60–61, 74, 83, 117, 118, 245–247
Committee to Re-elect The President (CREEP), 183, 184–185, 237
Communists, 23, 68–69, 105, 108–111, 168
  in Cambodia, 239–241
Comnas, John, 295, 296
computerization, printers and, 197–198, 199
Congress, U.S., 19, 49, 55, 63, 72, 301
  see also House of Representatives, U.S.; Senate, U.S.
Conversations with Kennedy (Bradlee), 212–213, 214
Cooke, Janet, 255–269, 301, 302
  background and education of, 256, 258–259, 264, 265
Coolidge, Calvin, 37, 42, 43–44, 48, 167
Cooper, Kent, 117–118
copper industry, 28, 29, 34
Corbett, James J. ("Gentleman Jim"), 12
Coughlin, Charles E., 54
Cox, Edward Finch, 172
Coy, Wayne, 95
Crawford-Mason, Clare, 251–252
"credibility gap," coining of, 141
crime rates, 104, 108
crimes, compensation for victims of, 235
Croker, Richard (Boss), 49
Cummins, Homer, 63

Dahlberg, Kenneth H., 184
Daly, James, 165
Daniel, Clifton, 193, 195
Dash, Leon, 178
Daugherty, Harry, 38, 39, 43
Davis, Charles, 206
Davis, Deborah, 237
Davis, John, 106
Dawes, Charles, 55
Dean, John, 188
Democratic convention (1960), 123–124
Democratic convention (1964), 131
Democratic National Committee (DNC), 182–183, 184, 186, 187, 238
Democrats, 12, 17, 49, 53–54, 224–225
  in election of 1920, 38–39
  in election of 1952, 117
  Post's support of, 12, 89–90, 123–124, 141–142
Denby, Edwin, 41
Dewey, John, 68–69
Dewey, Thomas E., 74, 83, 167
"Diana Hears," 281
Dickerson, Nancy, 288–289

Dingell, John D., 295, 296–297
Doheny, Edward L., 41–43
Dole, Robert, 187
Donero, George A., 110
Donnelly, Tom, 127, 272
Dreyfus, Alfred, 16
Dreyfus, Joel, 179
Duckstein, William, 41
Dudman, Helen, 156
Dugan, James, 199, 202–203
Dun, Angus, 9
Dure, Leon, 64
Dutkin, Howard, 93–94

"Ear" column, 277–281, 301
Ehrlichman, John, 169, 188
Eisenhower, Dwight D., 116–117, 120, 122, 123, 187
election of 1920, 38–39
election of 1952, 116–117
election of 1960, 123–124
election of 1964, 131
Elizabeth (N.J.) Journal, 182
Elkins, Davis, 37
Elliott, Osborn, 133
Elliston, Herbert, 90, 95, 99
Ellsberg, Daniel, 173–174, 175
"Empire And The Chic of Araby, The" (Quinn), 221–222
employment, in New Deal, 62, 67–68
"End Of The Jimmy Story," 257
Epstein, William A., 96
Equal Employment Opportunities Commission (EEOC), 178, 179
Ernst, Agnes Elizabeth, see Meyer, Agnes Elizabeth Ernst
Ernst, Bill, 21, 23
Ernst, Fred (son), 23
Ernst, Frederick (father), 21–22, 23, 24, 25, 26, 32, 68
Estabrook, Robert, 111, 123
Ethridge, Mark, 62, 64

Fall, Albert, 41–43
Fallows, James, 179
Farm Loan Board, 48
Fass, Horst, 155–156
Federal Bureau of Investigation (FBI), 173, 186, 187, 237
Federal Reserve Board, 48, 53–54, 55
Felker, Clay, 192–193
Fenton, Harold, 65
Final Hours, The (Woodward and Bernstein), 218

First Amendment, 174–175, 258, 300
Fisher Body Company, 30
Flores, Brian, 200, 204
Folliard, Ed, 45, 73, 94, 95, 116, 123
Fortas, Abe, 132
Fortune magazine, 54
France, 29, 139–140
  art scene in, 24–25, 28
  in 1930s, 70, 71
Francis, David R., 34
Frankfurter, Felix, 85, 111
Freer, Charles, 30, 33, 51
Freer Gallery of Art, 51–52
Frelinghuysen, Joe, 37
Friendly, Alfred, 99–101, 105, 106–107, 120,
    123, 126, 131, 153
  Bradlee's shuffling of hierarchy and, 133,
    134–135, 142
  Newsweek purchase and, 124–125
  Simons and, 133, 134
Friendship (McLean estate), 37, 38, 39
"FYI (For Your Information)," 278–281

Gasch, Oliver, 297, 298
General Chemical, 47
Germany, Nazi, 70, 71
Germany, in World War I, 33
Geyelin, Philip L., 125, 151, 167, 174, 238–
    239, 245
Gilbert, Ben, 94, 95, 99, 123, 133, 138
  Barrett and, 104, 105
  bumping of, 135
  hiring and firing by, 100, 101
  as manager, 103, 121
  "stream of news" coverage and, 105, 106
Gilliam, Dorothy, 226, 275, 301
Glass, Carter, 63–64
Gold, Bill, 95
Golden, Sandy, 294–295, 297
Goldfine, Bernard, 140
Goldwater, Barry, 159–160, 220–221
"Gossip Column," 277–278
Graham, Donald, 9, 89, 167, 203, 219, 247–
    248, 280, 298, 302
  Cooke and, 261–262, 267
  editorial interests of, 243, 245
  mother's relationship with, 243–244
Graham, Elizabeth (Lally), 9, 89, 116, 130
Graham, Katharine Meyer, 9, 58–59, 70, 73,
    118, 129–134, 219
  aloofness of, 131, 162, 163, 164, 174, 217
  in attempt to buy *Times-Herald,* 112–113
  as businesswoman, 129, 130, 162, 163,
    164–165, 197, 243

correspondence of, 123, 142–151, 156, 162,
    170–171, 239–241
Donald Graham's relationship with, 243–
    244
education of, 52, 85, 97–98
errors of judgment made by, 163, 164–165,
    244
on father, 95, 99
father compared to, 97, 130, 162–163
father's relationship with, 97–98, 129
on husband, 86, 89, 121, 123, 151
husband's illness and, 123, 126, 127, 130
as husband's inferior, 86, 88–89, 129
as journalist, 85, 89, 98
labor problems and, 198–207, 213, 235
as least competitive child, 52, 95–96
marriage of, 10, 86, 129
masquerade in honor of, 163
mentors of, 131–132, 162
as mother, 129–130
mother's relationship with, 52–53, 88–89,
    97–98, 129
personality of, 97, 129–130, 162–163
pregnancies and childbirths of, 89
rudeness of, 131–132, 162, 245
"Style" as viewed by, 158, 162, 169
travels of, 123, 130, 132
Watergate and, 185, 186, 187, 197, 209–
    210, 217, 237
Graham, Philip Leslie, 85–87, 110–128, 134,
    139, 157, 158
  anti-Semitism of, 124, 126
  appearance of, 85, 86, 119
  in attempts to buy *Times-Herald,* 112–113,
    118, 271, 299
  background of, 9–10, 85
  as benevolent elitist, 99, 103
  education of, 10, 85
  employee relations of, 121
  father-in-law's relationship with, 86, 89,
    98, 123, 124
  girl friend of, 126
  as manic depressive, 10, 113, 121–128, 130
  mother-in-law's relationship with, 86, 87,
    89, 111–112, 123
  politicians manipulated by, 10, 99, 115–
    117, 119–120, 123–124, 167
  suicide of, 9–10, 128, 302
  travels of, 123, 126
  wife's relationship with, *see* Graham, Kath-
    arine Meyer
  will of, 126
  in World War II, 87, 89, 99, 122
Graham, Stephen, 9

Graham, William (Philip's brother), 122
Graham, William (Philip's son), 9
Great Britain:
  Foreign Office of, 115
  in 1930s, 70, 71
  in World War II, 86–88, 89
Great Depression, 10, 45, 47, 64
Green, Bill, 258, 260–261, 267–268, 275
Greenfield, Meg, 174, 245, 301
Greider, William, 170, 199, 298, 300–301
Guellal, Cherif, 160
Guggenheim family, 28, 29
Gulialtec, Alyce, 261
Gurfein, Murray I., 173, 174

Haggard, William, 64
Haig, Alexander, 284–285
Haldeman, H. R., 187, 188
Hale, Frederick, 37
Hamilton, George E., 57–58
Hamlin, Charles Sumner, 53–55
Harding, Warren G., 35–41, 44, 48, 167
Harigan, Dr., 24
Harriman, Averell, 124–125, 239
Harriman, Edward, 18
Harrison, Floyd R., 54, 58, 62
Harrison, Selig, 142
Harvey, George, 44–45
Harwood, Richard, 153, 154, 169–170, 175, 178
Hatton, Frank, 14
Hauptmann, Bruno Richard, 61–62
Hawks, Richard, 276
Hayes, John, 131
Hayes, Rutherford B., 12
Hays, Wayne, 224–225, 301
Hearst, Millicent, 37
Hearst, William Randolph, 37, 45, 58, 60, 61, 66
Helms, Richard, 237, 238–239
Henry, John C., 83
Herblock, 95, 116, 117, 126, 168, 169
Herter, Christian, 138
Hiss, Alger, 109–110, 168
Hitchcock, Frank, 27
Hitler, Adolf, 70, 74, 87, 159
Hoffman, Abbie, 157
Hoffman, Dustin, 210, 218–219
Hoffman, Julian, 157–158
Hoge, Warren, 160, 193
Homolka, Oscar, 96
Hooker's Division, 11–12
Hoover, Herbert, 37, 48, 53–55

Hope and Fear in Washington (Collier), 214–215
Hopkins, Harry, 68
House of Representatives, U.S., 53–54, 94, 224–225, 295, 296
  UnAmerican Activities Committee of, 108–111
Houston, David F., 48
Hover, John, 203
"How to Woo Washington Men" (Quinn), 160
Hughes, Charles Evans, Jr., 59
Hughes, Emmett, 127
Humphrey, Hubert, 167–168
Hunt, Howard, 175, 183, 184, 185, 188

Ignatius, Paul R., 164–165
Inspiration Copper, 28, 29
integration, racial, 105–107, 122
International Exhibition of Arts and Techniques, French, 71
International Herald Tribune, 164
Irish Catholics, 73, 95
Irvine, Reed, 214, 239–241, 286–287, 288
Isaacs, Steve, 135

Japan, 87
  Meyers' visit to, 27–28
Jay, Peter, 154, 222
Jews, 11, 27, 53, 61
  Protestant views on, 12, 33
  as reporters, 95
  see also anti-Semitism
"Jimmy's World" (Cooke), 255–269
John Paul II, Pope, 224
Johnson, Haynes, 154, 209, 268–269
Johnson, Hugh, 63
Johnson, Lyndon B., 115, 120, 135, 141–151, 160, 168, 225, 289
  Katharine Graham's relationship with, 131–132, 142–151, 167
  Philip Graham's influence on, 122, 123–124
Jones, Alexander (Casey), 65, 90, 91–92, 94, 99, 100
Jones, Jesse H., 90
Jordan, Hamilton, 302
Just, Ward, 142, 168
Justice Department, U.S., 173, 238–239
J. Walter Thompson public-relations firm, 204

Kahn, Ernestine and Zadoc, 16
Kaiser, Robert, 154, 206

Karnow, Stanley, 155
Katharine the Great (Davis), 237
Kauffmann, John H. (Golden Boy), 272
Kauffmann, Samuel H., 57, 119, 271–272
Kefauver, Estes, 119–120
Kelly, Edward J., 103
Kendall, Lyman B., 19
Kendrick, Tom, 158
Kennedy, John F., 9, 123–124, 127, 151, 168, 225
  Bradlee's relationship with, 140–141, 212–214
  Mary Meyer's affair with, 139, 213–214
Kennedy, Joseph, 124
Kent State students, killing of, 169
Kerensky, Alexander, 34
Kilmer, Billy, 162
King, Mackenzie, 83
Kissinger, Henry, 169, 218, 239
Kohler, Edgar, 20
Krug, Julius (Cap), 106
Ku Klux Klan, 86

Labor Mediation Board, 90
labor unions, 16, 64–65, 74, 85, 121, 126, 164–165, 197–207
La Guardia, Fiorello, 54
Landon, Alf, 69, 167
Lansing, Robert, 34
Lash, Joe, 68
Latham, Aaron, 192–193
Laventhol, David, 157, 158
Lazard, Max, 16
Lazard Frères, 15, 16, 29
Lecky, William Edward Hartpole, 16
Lee, Richard, 247, 288–289
Lennon, John and Yoko, 161
lesbianism, Longworth on, 194
Lewis, Alfred E., 182, 183
Lewis, Anthony, 219, 280–281
libel suits, 278, 280, 296–298
Liddy, G. Gordon, 185
Life as Chance and Destiny (Agnes Meyer), 25
Lincoln, Abraham, 19, 86
Lindsay, Malvina, 74, 86
Lippmann, Walter, 72, 74, 118, 125, 133, 134, 138
Literary Digest, 64
Loeb, William, 138
London, Jack, 105
Longworth, Alice Roosevelt, 9, 37, 172, 193–195
Lorentz, Pare, 96

Los Angeles Times, 201, 247
Los Angeles Times-Washington Post News Service, 125, 260
Lubell, Sam, 65
Luce, Clare Boothe, 73
Luce, Henry, 54, 72
Lyon, Dick, 123

McAdoo, William Gibbs, 33, 48
McBride, Tom, 93–94
McCarthy, Colman, 226
McCarthy, Joseph, 110, 111, 117, 118, 120, 219
McCloskey, Robert J., 275, 284, 285
McCord, James, 183, 188
McCormick, Robert R. (Bertie), 60, 61, 113, 117–119
McGeachy, Craig, 87–88
MacGregor, Clark, 186–187
McGrory, Mary, 125
McKelway, Ben, 58
McKinley, William, 17
McLean, Edward B. (Ned), 20, 35–45, 58, 61, 62, 126, 167
  Harding's campaign and, 37–39
  Teapot Dome scandal and, 41–44
McLean, Evalyn Walsh, 37–41, 44, 45
  in attempt to keep *Post,* 45, 58
  marriage of, 20, 36
McLean, John R., 20, 36
McLellan, Diana, 277–278, 281, 301
McLeod, Freddie, 37, 39
McNamara, Robert S., 163, 164, 173, 239
MacPherson, Myra, 180, 264
Major, John, 41, 45
Mann, Thomas, 70, 87
Manning, Gordon, 191
Mansfield, Stephanie, 289–291
Map of Life, The (Lecky), 16
Maraniss, David, 261, 264, 266–267, 275, 302
Marder, Murrey, 141, 173, 174, 201
marijuana use, police and, 276–277
Marshall, George Preston, 60
Martin, Judith, 155, 180
Martindale, Steve, 161–162
"Mary Haworth's Mail," 73–74
Mason, Hatley, 246–247
Maxa, Rudy, 224–225, 301–302
Maxwell Motors, 30
Maynard, Robert, 177–178
Meagher, Mark, 203, 207, 244
Meany, George, 206
Meglia, Joe, 65
Mellet, Lowell, 60

Mellon, Andrew, 53, 66
"Message to America" (Sheil), 112
"Metro" section, 259–261, 302
  upside-down reporting in, 275–277, 301
  Woodward as editor of, 247, 248, 275, 293–294, 301
Meyer, Agnes Elizabeth Ernst, 10, 21–34, 48–53, 61, 67–70, 120–121
  appearance of, 20, 24, 51
  artistic interests of, 24–25, 27–28, 30, 51–52, 70
  beaux of, 24, 25, 31
  books by, 21–22, 25, 51, 87, 88
  brother's shooting of, 21
  Catholics as viewed by, 111–112
  Chinese studies of, 30, 34
  death of, 170
  debts of, 23, 24, 26
  destiny of, 21, 48, 51
  determination of, 22, 26, 27, 92
  drinking of, 69–70, 86
  education of, 22–23
  egotism of, 23–24, 30, 32–33
  family background of, 21–22
  father-figure attachments of, 24, 28, 32, 51
  father's relationship with, 21–22, 24, 25, 32, 68
  friendships of, 23, 24–25, 30, 87
  guilt of, 30, 32
  as hostess, 34, 50
  husband's relationship with, see Meyer, Eugene
  infatuations of, 25, 30, 31–32, 33, 50–51, 55, 67
  as journalist, 23, 68–69, 88, 91–92, 94
  Katharine Graham's relationship with, 52–53, 88–89, 97–98, 129
  mansion purchased by, 108
  as mother, 30, 31, 34, 49, 52–53, 98
  mother's relationship with, 21, 22, 24
  personality of, 22, 28, 33
  Philip Graham's relationship with, 86, 87, 89, 111–112, 123
  poor as viewed by, 23–24, 91
  pregnancies and childbirths of, 28, 30, 31, 34
  purchase of Post and, 58–59
  rebelliousness of, 23, 28, 31–33
  as Republican, 48–50, 67–68, 87, 167
  richness and power desired by, 26, 32, 48, 170
  travels of, 9, 24–26, 27–28, 31–33, 52, 70, 87, 130
  in war effort, 87–88, 91–92
  writing styles of, 22–23, 51, 69

Meyer, Cord, 139–140, 214
Meyer, Elizabeth, 31, 52, 96, 129
Meyer, Elsie, 13, 15
Meyer, Eugene, 10, 11–20, 26–34, 53–66, 85, 108, 112–113, 120–121, 167, 187
  as art patron, 19
  business partners of, 19, 27
  conservatism of, 17, 29, 96
  death of, 123
  determination of, 16–19, 24, 27, 66, 299
  early employment of, 15, 16
  education of, 12–14, 15–16
  family background of, 11, 12–14
  as father, 52, 96
  father's relationship with, 11, 12–13, 14, 17
  financial problems of, 29–30, 64–66, 72
  investments of, 16, 17–19, 28, 29–30, 33, 34
  as Jew, 12, 15, 16, 27, 34, 53, 61, 124
  life plan of, 16–17, 47–48, 57
  marriage and honeymoon of, 26–28
  Philip Graham compared to, 99
  Philip Graham's relationship with, 86, 89, 98, 123, 124
  power pursued by, 32, 59, 299
  public service of, 33–34, 47–48, 53–55, 90, 98
  in purchase of Times-Herald, 117–119
  seventieth birthday of, 95–96, 98
  shyness of, 95, 96
  travels of, 24, 25–26, 52, 70–71, 87
  wife as bore to, 95
  wife distrusted by, 123, 170–171
  wife's correspondence with, 25, 31, 32, 52
  wife's drinking and, 69, 70, 86
  wife's first meeting with, 20, 24
  wife's infatuations and, 31–32, 50, 51
Meyer, Eugene (Bill), III, 52, 87, 96
Meyer, Florence, 30, 31, 50, 52, 96, 129
Meyer, Harriet Newman, 11, 12, 13, 15
Meyer, Katharine, see Graham, Katharine Meyer
Meyer, Marc Eugene, 11, 12–13, 14, 15, 17, 18
Meyer, Mary Pinchot, 139, 213–214
Meyer, Rosalie, 12, 13, 15, 17–18
Meyer, Ruth, 69, 96, 129
Meyer family, competition as central to, 52, 95–96
Miami Herald, 122, 205
Miller, Harlan, 73
Milloy, Courtland, 262–263, 268

Mitchell, John, 169, 184, 186, 188
Mobil Oil, 293–296
Montgomery *Journal,* 294, 295
Morgan, John Pierpont, 18
Morgenthau, Henry, Sr., 18–19
Morley, Felix, 62, 70–72, 74
Morrill, Chester, 54
Moyers, Bill, 283–284
"Mr. Jones' Excuses" (Elliston), 90
Ms. magazine, 244
Mueller, Eugene, 199
Murphy, Pat, 132
Murrow, Edward R., 88
Muskie, Edmund, 186

National Aniline and Chemical Company,
    33, 47
National Capital Planning Commission, 108
National Credit Corporation, 54
National Enquirer, 213–214
National Guard, 169
National Youth Administration (NYA),
    68
Neumann, Jonathan, 248, 264, 268
New Deal, 62–64, 67–68, 72, 90
Newspaper Production and Research Cen-
    ter, 198
newspapers, stereotypes about, 210–211
Newsweek magazine, 131, 139–140, 193, 197,
    238
    Philip Graham's purchase of, 124–125
New York *Herald Tribune,* 72, 164
New York magazine, 192–193
New York *Morning Sun,* 23, 24
New York *News,* 60, 113
New York Post, 50
New York Printing Pressmen's strike, 126
New York Review of Books, 212–213, 219
New York Times, 26, 70, 72, 99, 164, 188,
    280–281, 283–284, 295
    Brethren reviewed in, 219–220
    Pentagon Papers published in, 173
    Post compared to, 10, 142, 154–155, 175,
        200, 209, 299, 301
    Quinn and, 193, 195
New York Times Bureau, 120, 193
Nichols, William H., 47
Nixon, Richard M., 109, 117, 124, 155, 167,
    168–169, 172, 218, 288
    Cooke compared to, 266, 267
    Katharine Graham's relationship with,
        168, 169
    Watergate and, 10, 175, 183–184, 186–188,
        237

Nixon, Tricia, 172, 194
Norris, James, 42
Northcliff, Lord, 72
Northern Pacific Railroad stock, 16, 17, 18
Nossiter, Bernard, 201

Ober, Richard, 237
Oberdorfer, Don, 174, 204
O'Connor, John J., 283–284
Okuma, Shigenobu, 27
Olson, Sid, 64
O'Neill, Frank (Buck), 83
Osborne, John, 218
Osnos, Peter, 154, 170, 240

Paderewski, Ignace, 55, 67
Padilla, Michael, 199, 202
Palmer, A. Mitchell, 41–42
Patterson, Cissy, 57, 58, 60–62, 66, 89
    death of, 112–113
Patterson, Eugene, 151, 153, 154, 174, 294
Patterson, Joe, 60, 61, 89
Pegler, Westbrook, 74
Pei, I. M., 164
Pentagon Papers, The, 173–175, 300
Penkovsky papers, 139
People Like Us, 283–284
Perkins, George W., 29
Phelps, William Lyon, 16
Pinchot, Antoinette, 139, 193, 214
Pincus, Walter and Ann, 192
Piro, Philip, 294, 296, 297
Platt, Edmund, 53–54
Points, Juliet, 23
police, 108
    in Washington, D.C., 103–105, 132, 183,
        276–277
Povich, Shirley, 74, 95
Powell, Jody, 252
Powell, Margaret, 31, 34, 49
Powers, Bertram A., 126
Prescott, John, 198–199, 201–202
pressmen, labor problems of, 126, 202–207,
    213, 235
Price, Ray, 218
printers, 206
    computerization feared by, 197–198, 199
    in negotiations with *Post,* 199–200, 201–
        202
Project X, 198, 204
Pulitzer, Joseph, Jr., 128
Pulitzer Prize, 135, 151, 154, 188–189, 213,
    237, 255, 256, 263–265
Pusey, Merlo, 25, 52, 105, 110, 142

Quinn, Sally, 159–162, 191–195, 211, 214, 218–219, 220–224, 264, 301
  Bradlee's relationship with, 159, 160, 161, 191, 193, 212, 213, 215, 224, 253, 301
  Brzezinski series by, 249–253
  Longworth interviewed by, 193–195
  TV career of, 162, 191–193, 220
Quinn, William (Buffalo Bill), 159–160

Rader, Dotson, 278
Raspberry, William, 170
Rauh, Joe, 98, 122, 123, 126, 127–128
Ray, Elizabeth, 225
Reagan, Nancy, 278–281, 289
Reagan, Ronald, 283–284, 286, 289
Reconstruction Finance Corporation (RFC), 54–55
Redevelopment Land Agency (RLA), 107
Redford, Robert, 210, 218–219, 247
Reed, Stanley, 85
Reedy, George, 201
repro, publishers vs. unions and, 198, 201
Republican Campaign Committee, 69
Republican convention (1924), 49
Republicans, 12, 17, 48
  Agnes Meyer and, 48–50, 67–68, 87, 167
  in election of 1920, 37–39
  in election of 1952, 116–117
  in Westchester County, 48–50, 57, 67
Reston, James, 133
Rhoades, Katherine, 51
Richmond *Times-Dispatch,* 64
Ripley, Dillon, 160
"Road Back to America, The" (Philip Graham), 111
Roberts, Chalmers, 121, 123, 125, 151, 157, 185
  Pentagon Papers and, 173, 174
Roberts, Roy, 69
Robinson, James Harvey, 30
Rockefeller, Nelson, 161, 162
Rodin, Auguste, 25
Rogers, William P., 169, 187
Rolling Stone, 219
Roosevelt, Eleanor, 68, 73
Roosevelt, Franklin Delano, 55, 72, 74, 83, 89–90
Roosevelt, Theodore, 19
Root, Elihu, 34
Rosenfeld, Harry, 176, 177, 182, 184, 209–211, 214
Rosenfeld, Stephen, 142, 169
Rovner, Sandy, 251
Royal Canadian Mounted Police, 108

Rudd, Hughes, 191, 193
Russia, 68–69
  Bill Meyer's visit to, 96
  Kerensky government in, 34
Ryan, John D., 28

Sadler, Christine, 94
Saltonstall, Jean, 138, 139
"Salty Comment on Washington Life," 73
San Francisco *Examiner,* 85
Sastri, Shrinvasi, 50
Sauer, Marie, 156
Sauter, Van Gordon, 287–288
Schacht, Hjalmar, 70
Schlesinger, Arthur, Jr., 128
Schmuch, Peter, 61
Schorr, Daniel, 159
Securities and Exchange Commission (SEC), 295, 296–297
Segretti, Donald H., 186
Senate, U.S., 94, 104–105, 116, 119–120, 238
  Daugherty investigated by, 43
  Teapot Dome investigated by, 41–44
Senger, Henry, 13
Shaffer, Sam, 140
Shales, Tom, 283–284, 285–288, 301
Sheil, Bernard J., 112
Sheridan, Dixie, 265
Simons, Howard, 155, 158, 163–164, 174, 176, 192, 195, 201, 214
  background of, 134
  as Bradlee's lieutenant, 133–134, 153, 154
  Cooke's hoax and, 260, 263, 265, 267
  Watergate and, 182, 183–184, 209, 210
Sirica, John, 188
Slemp, Bascom, 41–43
Sloan, Hugh W., 185
Smathers, George, 9
Smith, Jesse, 39
Sousa, John Philip, 14
Spargo, Mary, 94
sports news, 74, 83, 117, 118
Stackey, Norman, 83
Stalin, Joseph, 68, 69, 110
Stans, Maurice, 184–185
Stapleton, Ruth Carter, 278
State Department, U.S., 34, 109, 173, 284–285
Stein, Gertrude, 25
Stern, Larry, 142, 154, 158, 176, 201, 240–241, 245–247, 293, 301
  death of, 241, 246–247
Stern, Sigmund, 13
Stevenson, Adlai, 117, 168

stock market crash (1929), 45, 53
Stockton, Peter, 295
Stone, I. F., 155
strikes, 198, 200–201
  pressmen's, 126, 203–207, 235
Sturm, Joanna, 194
"Style" section, 156–162, 210–211, 275, 277–
  281, 283–291, 301
  counterculture tilt of, 157–158, 169–170
  fading of first stars of, 226–235
  Quinn's writing for, 160–162, 193–195,
  249–253
Sullivan, Mark, 72, 74
Sumner, William Graham, 16
Supreme Court, U.S., 17, 61, 174, 219, 248, 280
Sussman, Barry, 176, 178, 182, 184
Sweeterman, John W., 118, 122, 131, 164

Taft, Robert, 83, 116
Tankersley, Ruth McCormick Miller (Bazy),
  118
Tavoulareas, Peter, 293–297
Tavoulareas, William P., 293–298
taxes, 17, 91
Taylor, Elizabeth, 87–88
Teapot Dome scandals, 40–44
Thompson, "Big Bill," 27
Time, Inc., 272–273, 275
Time magazine, 85, 109, 119–120, 134, 140,
  157
  Brzezinski's photo in, 252, 253
  as devoted to Post, 72–73
  new comic strip announced in, 246–247
Times (London), 115, 198
Timmins, Bascom, 58
Tobriner, Commissioner, 132
Toledo Blade, 258–259, 265
Trescott, Jacqueline, 226
Truitt, James, 120, 157, 158, 213–214
Truman, Harry S, 95, 98, 104, 116
Turner, Maurice T., 276–277
TV Guide, 286–288
Tyler, Patrick, 261, 293–298

Ungar, Harold, 126
United Nations, 95, 151
United States Motor Company, 29–30
"Unvarnished Haig, The" (Woodward),
  284–285
urban renewal, 107–108

Veblen, Thorstein, 30–31
Vietnam War, 141–142, 155–156, 167
  Pentagon Papers and, 173–175

violence, racial, 36–37, 105–106
Viorst, Judith, 163
Viorst, Milton, 121
"Viva La Causa! Radical Chic Revisited"
  (Quinn), 221
von Heymel, Alfred, 24, 31
von Hoffman, Nicholas, 157–158, 162, 174,
  191, 206, 293
  identity crisis of, 226–235
Votaw, Helen, 38

Wadsworth, Mrs. Herbert, 27
Waits, John, 203
Wallace, Lawrence A., 202–203, 204
Walsh, Elsa, 261, 266
Walsh, Evalyn, see McLean, Evalyn Walsh
Walsh, John, 297
Walsh, Thomas F., 36
Walsh, Thomas J., 41–42
Walters, Barbara, 193
Ward, William L., 49–50, 57, 67
War Finance Commission, U.S., 48, 54
Washington, D.C.:
  police force in, 103–105, 132, 183, 276–277
  society life in, 27, 35, 39, 50, 100–101, 160–
  162, 226
  urban renewal in, 107–108
  World War I years in, 33–34
Washington, Walter, 135
Washington Daily News, 60, 105, 112, 118,
  119, 127, 200, 271, 272
Washington Evening Star, 14, 59, 119
Washington Evening Times, 60, 83
Washington Herald, 57, 58, 72, 83
  as Post's competitor, 60–62, 65–66
Washington Post:
  advertising in, 17, 35, 91–92, 94, 112, 119,
  123, 198, 255, 273
  Agnes Meyer's articles in, 68–69, 70, 88,
  94
  as anti-Roosevelt, 62–64
  in April, 1940, 73–74
  arrogance of, 10, 158, 168, 169, 281, 301
  bankruptcy of, 10, 57–58, 59, 61
  birth of, 11–12
  boycotts of, 111–112, 178–179
  Bradlee appointed editor of, 132–135, 300
  Bradlee's quitting of, 124, 138–139
  cartoons in, 43, 95, 117, 126, 168, 169
  CIA and, 131, 139–140, 237–239
  circulation of, 45, 60, 65, 72, 94, 112, 117,
  119, 123, 273
  comic strips in, 35, 60–61, 74, 118, 245–
  247

competition of, 60–62, 65–66, 72, 74–83, 110, 112, 117, 245, 271–273, 281
Cooke's hoax and, 255–269
copydesk of, 154–155
creative tension of, 154, 176, 181, 268
as Democratic journal, 12, 89–90, 123–124, 141–142
difficulties of working for, 106, 154, 180, 200, 201, 244
Donald Graham made publisher of, 243, 245, 302
"Ear" in, 277–281, 301
early years of, 14, 17
editorials in, 43, 44, 45, 62, 74, 85, 90, 94, 108–111, 116–117, 141–142, 151–152, 168, 169, 171, 185, 238–239, 257, 275, 278–280, 288, 301
effects of fame on, 224–235
erratic quality of, 10, 155–156, 169–170
errors of, 61–62, 249–253, 275–277
Eugene Meyer's anonymous reporting in, 63–64
Eugene Meyer's mistakes and, 62–65
Eugene Meyer's purchase of, 10, 57–59, 271, 299
February 20, 1921 edition of, 35
financial problems of (1930s), 64–66, 72
financial problems of (1940s), 112–113
financial problems of (1950s), 111
firings and hirings at, 62, 64, 99–101
foreign news in, 35, 70–71, 88, 90, 94, 108, 120, 141–142, 155–156, 239–241, 301
"Gossip Column" in, 277–278
growth in quality of, 10, 73, 85, 95, 153–155, 244, 299–302
Harding's death and, 40
Harvey as editor of, 44–45
as independent paper, 37, 58, 167
"Jehovah Complex" of, 100
John McLean's purchase of, 20
Katharine Graham as writer for, 85, 89
Katharine Graham's takeover of, 130–131, 299–302
labor problems of, 64–65, 164–165, 175–180, 197–207
magazine of, 160
"Metro" in, 247, 248, 259–261, 275–277, 293–294, 301, 302
Morley as editor of, 62, 70–72, 74
Ned McLean's inheritance of, 36
Ned McLean's strange brand of journalism in, 36–37
news omitted from, 36, 43, 106, 107

Pentagon Papers and, 173–175, 300
Philip Graham's takeover of, 10, 95, 97, 98–101, 299
political power of, 10, 35, 37–39, 59, 115–117, 167, 210, 224–225, 244, 299
profits of, 10, 94, 120–121, 197, 201, 207, 244
Pulitzer Prize awarded to, 188–189, 213, 237
racial issues and, 36–37, 38, 90–91, 105–107, 171, 176–179
religious issues and, 45, 111–112
as Republican paper, 37–39, 62, 116–117, 167
Roosevelt supported by, 89–90
Saigon bureau of, 142
September 7, 1969 edition of, 155–156
social crusades of, 103–108
sports pages of, 42, 74, 118
stock of, 120–121, 273
"stream of news" coverage in, 105–107
"Style" in, see "Style" section
"Sunday Outlook" in, 141, 155
Time's devotion to, 72–73
Tricia Nixon's wedding and, 172
wages paid by, 62, 64–65, 121, 165, 200, 202, 205
Watergate and, 10, 182–189, 197, 209–212, 217, 237–238, 300–301
women's page in, 73–74, 156, 226
in World War II, 88, 91–92, 93–95
Washington Post Company, 174, 188
"Washington Post March, The," 14
Washington Star, 48, 57, 58, 103, 105, 119, 200, 275, 295
Philip Graham's death and, 10, 130
as Post's competitor, 60, 74–83, 112, 245, 271–273
Washington Times, 281, 301
Washington Times-Herald, 83, 103, 110, 112–113
sale of, 117–119, 271, 299
Watergate, 10, 175, 182–189, 197, 209–212, 237–238, 300–301
Deep Throat and, 183, 186, 238, 301
Webb, Robin, 126
Weill, Alexandre, 16
Weinstein, Allen, 110
We're Going To Make You a Star (Quinn), 220
Westchester County, politics in, 48–50, 57, 67
Westmoreland, William C., 286–288
Wheeler, Burton K., 43

White, Stanford, 51
White, Stephen, 13
Whitney, John Hay (Jock), 163, 164
Wiggins, Russell, 99, 100, 116, 120, 126, 131, 135, 153, 167
    editorials of, 141–142
    Philip Graham's illness and, 122, 123
    retirement of, 133, 151
Wilkins, Beriah, 14
Wilkins, Roger, 179–180
Wilkinson, Tom, 265, 266–267
Williams, Edward Bennett, 126, 182, 187, 239
Wills, Gary, 212–213
Wilson, Woodrow, 33–34, 48
Wisner, Frank, 115–116
Witcover, Jules, 204
women:
    limited career aspirations of, 97, 98

Post's labor problems with, 176, 179, 180
    as voters, 49
Women's Wear Daily, 131
Woodward, Bob, 181–189, 191, 209, 213, 224
    post-Watergate career of, 217–220, 247–248, 259, 260, 262, 263, 264, 265–267, 275, 284–285, 293–294
    Watergate and, 182–189, 217, 301
Works Progress Administration (WPA), 67–68, 83
World Bank, 98
World War I, 33–34, 35, 54
World War II, 10, 47, 83, 86–95, 99

Yathay, Pin, 239
Young, Elizabeth, 66, 73–74, 89, 95
Young, Roy, 53–54
Younger, Irving, 298

Ziegler, Ron, 184, 187